OUT
LOUD

OUT LOUD

a memoir

MARK MORRIS

and **WESLEY STACE**

FABER & FABER

First published in the UK in 2019
by Faber & Faber Ltd
Bloomsbury House
74–77 Great Russell Street
London WC1B 3DA

First published in the USA in 2019
by Penguin Random House LLC
375 Hudson Street
New York, NY 10014

Printed and bound by CPI Group (UK) Ltd, Croydon CR0 4YY

Designed by Meighan Cavanaugh

Image credits, unless listed below, appear alongside the images:
Photograph on page ii, "Taking a Bow at Dance Theater Workshop, 1985"
by Tom Brazil, courtesy of the photographer
Photograph on page 362, "Watching from the Wings, Madrid, 2014"
by Nancy Umanoff, courtesy of the photographer

The right of Mark Morris and Wesley Stace to be identified as
authors of this work has been asserted in accordance with Section 77
of the Copyright, Designs and Patents Act 1988

A CIP record for this book
is available from the British Library

ISBN 978–0–571–35666–9

I dedicate this book with love and gratitude to Nancy
for every bit of success. My unusual vocation,
the company, our school, a Dance Center, and any
hint of humanity I may possess I owe to her.

Her limitless kindness, trust, and generosity benefit us all.

No bow I could take would be deep enough to honor her adequately.

CONTENTS

Prologue

There is an obsession with process that I don't share. I want the surprise: I don't need to know how the magic trick works. If the audience has already watched the magician *practice* sawing a woman in half, it's not going to be overly impressed when he does it again during the show, unless he's suddenly doing it lengthwise.

I am not interested in works in progress. Finish it, then I'll buy a ticket. Art isn't reality TV or a director's cut with three unexpurgated hours of bloopers. I don't want to catch people with their pants down. I don't want to know the awful secrets that happened backstage. I only want to see, in conjuring terms, the prestige.

THIS IS HOW IT WORKS. You decide what you want to do: play the piano or sing. You practice *alone*, learn how to do it well *alone*, get good at it. Then you play for an audience: "Here's something I prepared earlier." And you do it as well as you can.

And then it's over.

When the curtain goes up, the audience sees something it's never seen before and, particularly with dance, something it'll never see again. I don't show a piece until I'm ready to pinch it off, and sometimes that isn't until the very last minute.

I was once choreographing for a ballet company in a many-windowed studio. A window to the outside world is one thing, but a window through which people can observe is another. You feel like you're in some kind of a Louis Quatorze petting zoo, an attraction for the aristocracy—board members accustomed to the access, the kind of people who call the dancers "boys" and "girls." It's creepy. I'm notorious for covering these windows, because if someone's watching, it's automatically a performance it shouldn't have to be—the dancers need to feel safe to explore—and rehearsals can be boring, a dull process about which none of the participants, least of all me, should feel self-conscious. I may work on eight bars for a week or eighteen bars for five minutes. I might keep some of it or none of it. I might joke around, and somehow only that bit stays, purely because it was funny. These aren't interesting secrets.

My rehearsals are closed.

THIS IS A MEMOIR, not a cookbook—I can't tell you the recipe exactly—but here's what I can tell you about my process.

I always start with a piece of music that I love, or at least admire, and can bear to listen to hundreds of times. It's very rare that this is music that was specifically composed to be danced to—a lot of that isn't very interesting—and I gravitate toward music on a scale I can take on tour, because I won't use recorded music. I work with living musicians. I listen to the music and study the score in depth so that when rehearsals begin, I arrive with some ideas, perhaps a key movement (that I'll then develop as I make up the dance) or a rule or constraint that I'll impose upon my choreography, something to kick-start me. But I never work alone in the studio. I make up everything in the room with and on the dancers.

My dances are worked out in advance, practiced relentlessly. They aspire to the highest level of accomplishment and excellence. I believe that each piece should have a structure answerable only to itself; the language I create for a particular dance has to resolve itself in that dance. It's a complete thought. There will be no sequel.

A question I am often asked is "Do you choreograph every move or is everything entirely improvised?" as though those are the only two possibilities and mutually exclusive. Well, it's neither one nor the other—though more the former—but the point is that everybody is improvising all the time they're performing, no matter what they're playing, however fiendish the Bach toccata, and regardless of the fact that they know exactly what they're doing. In rehearsal, I might say, "I want this to look like the ocean: Go!" or "Something that reminds me of skeletons!" It's not only "right, left, right, kick," though there's plenty of that. It's not *only* dictatorial; it's participatory (and I'm the boss). Improvisation doesn't equal freedom; it usually equals chaos. If improvisation is so liberating, why does it always look exactly the same? As indistinct as the rinse water for an artist's brush.

And don't forget the contribution of the designers—décor, lighting, costumes. I give them the music I'm planning to confront; they listen to it and come up with their own ideas. The final say may be mine, but I'm no lighting designer. I work with people I trust.

The dancers contribute by dancing, not by improvising. Very few actors are playwrights; very few opera singers are composers. They're different jobs. Though dancing and choreography are related, relatively few dancers are interested in the composition of a dance. I found myself interested from the very beginning. And the dancers I choose for my company have to be interested too. Not just so they'll hear music the same way I do; they have to know everything that's going on, what everybody else is doing, so they grasp the architecture of the dance, in the same way that I wish each player in a string quartet had all four parts in front of him.

The management of emotion is an essential part of any performer's bag of tricks. I was once bumped from a plane in Tokyo and forced to spend the night in a hotel in a mall on the outskirts of the city, where an electronics shop had a display of a thousand TVs. On every one was the same image: a geisha crying into a handkerchief. I watched transfixed for a long while. I couldn't believe how touching it was. The camera pulled out from the close-up, and I realized that the crying geisha was in fact a puppet, a chunk of wood manipulated by a seventy-five-year-old man (and his two assistants). I have never forgotten it—Bunraku, a form of Japanese puppetry that dates back to the beginning of the seventeenth century. It was the expertise of that puppet master granting a soul to an inanimate object that had so profoundly moved me, not the fact that I had witnessed a human experiencing deep emotion. That is how art works.

When it comes to emotion, mastery—and not indulgence—is everything. I once said in an interview, "I'm not interested in self-expression but in expressiveness." Geoffrey Hill, the great English poet, later said that this "put perfectly what [he'd] been trying to say gropingly and inadequately for years. The idea that you write to express yourself seems to me revolting. The idea that you write to glorify or to make glorious the art of expressiveness seems to me spot on." I never want to see someone pour it all out. I want to see only what they let me see.

———

LIVE PERFORMANCE HAS FASCINATED me ever since, at the age of four, I stood amazed on the curb as a band marched by at the Seattle Seafair parade. The startling physical fact, the vibration, of the bass drum hitting me in the stomach was a revelation. Loud, but not *just* loud. It was present, inside me. I was the resonator. And it felt like I was being told something important, something essential that I didn't yet understand.

It was the same thing that Janet Baker told me years later at Carnegie Hall. As she stood in recital, in ravishing voice, singing song after song in languages I didn't understand, I knew her only essential message could be translated as "I love *you*, I love *you*, I love each one of you individually." All present felt she was speaking to, and making eye contact with, them only. That is the bravery and honesty of getting out in front of people and performing, the fact and mystery of live performance.

As a teenager I would go on Sundays to compline, the last evening service before bed, at St. Mark's Cathedral in Seattle, the "music church." This experience, still available, is one of the greatest Seattle has to offer. It was the first time I ever heard countertenors, the first time I heard plainchant. Sitting in the back in the dark, high on pot, bathing in the glorious music, alone—with others. That was the crucial thing: crowded, jammed up beside one another, and yet utterly private. Alone with my own thoughts and feelings, and the music we all shared.

And I recognized an inherent contradiction in that live performance: others felt alone too. There was a commonality in feeling alone; Bach felt alone. And I became more myself, and I felt less alone.

THE LIVE ASPECT OF PERFORMANCE is what appeals: the dancers, the musicians, the audience—all living beings in the same room. People might say they've watched a dance on YouTube, and they have. But they haven't. It isn't live. All the technological advances in the world—the 3-D glasses, the virtual reality, whatever comes next—aren't going to help that. We already live in 3-D.

When a performance is over, it's over. It can't be done that way again and it can't be preserved. And with regard to dance, no notation system can perfectly preserve the moves. It's the dancers who teach other dancers—the oral tradition. You'll never have that same meal again. "I cooked all day long to make the food I served you this evening, and you finished it in a second!" I love that feeling. Gone forever. Maybe the Etch A Sketch is the most appropriate device for recording dance. You write it down, shake it, and it's gone forever, a love letter in the sand.

I DON'T LIKE TO GIVE TALKS before a show. I don't need program notes to prove I did the homework, what I read, what it all means. William Forsythe, a master choreographer and a great guy, makes up a dance and writes ten pages of program notes about Schopenhauer, telos, and other Greek rhetorical terms. That works for him. Jiří Kylián, the director of Nederlands Dans Theater, is another example: page after page of program notes about the underpinning theory, how he came to that conclusion, and what it therefore all means. (Actually, he came to a rehearsal of mine at Les Grands Ballets Canadiens and commented, "You're so brave to do something that simple." I'd say that was an insult.) Of course, Maurice Béjart, the choreographer I replaced as the director of dance at the Théâtre Royal de la Monnaie in Brussels, wrote the longest program notes ever. The show would be a pastiche of recorded music—some Piaf songs, a Piazzola tango, and then one movement of Beethoven's Ninth—and he'd write about its relevance to dance history and contemporary society. My reaction to the verbiage is always *"And how was the dance?"*

The dance is all I want people to see. If it's not in the dance, it's not there. If the audience doesn't see it, it doesn't matter. No one wants to be told what he or she is meant to understand. Art shouldn't need translation. If the artist has to explain things, then he or she may be working in the wrong form. I'm happy to talk about everything, and I will, but I won't explain in advance.

The truth may be simpler than people want to hear, and sometimes I feel cornered, as though I have to defend myself and my work. For example, I don't ever want to say more about the music than the fact that I like it, that I am able to listen to it many times and have it remain interesting. I realize that's not very helpful, but the irony is that it's an unhelpful truth. People seriously ask, "What is it about the story of *Romeo and Juliet* that brought you to it?" A question like that isn't asked because anyone thinks it's terribly interesting; it's asked because it's acceptably bland. I'm a "difficult artist." People don't want to set me off. All that particular question really amounts to is "Will you start talking, please?" The question is really "Why did you choose this over that?" I made a judgment, the same as "I go to the restaurant where I like the food better."

"So many people have choreographed this. Why again?"

Because I like it.

"What do you want the audience to *get*?"

Home safely.

At a press conference when I took that job in Belgium, on being asked my philosophy of dance, I answered, "I make it up and you watch it." It was looked upon as a snub or a provocation, but it's how I feel. It's the truth, though it's perceived as an evasion. You try *not* to lie, but you *have* to lie: both. I'm not the President of Dance itself, or a dance

critic, or a musicologist; I'm me. I'm not making art to promote anything, to sell an idea, or to get something done. I'm not an accom-
plisher. I'm an artist. There aren't many of us. Every painter I know is
crazy, never leaves his house, and doesn't want anybody to see his
work; I know composers who can't leave their rooms or their computers, have regular nervous breakdowns, and are three years late with
every commission.

I do at least function.

I'm sixty-two, in case I haven't mentioned that yet, and I am done
dancing: my dancing days are gone. I make up dances, and I don't
really have to do anything except satisfy that need. Though I still work
constantly, I have time to look back, to see where I fit in, if I ever did.
I sleep more nowadays, I waste more time, but I don't panic about
learning the things that I have to do next, because I'm comfortable
doing what I do.

My place is now in the studio. There isn't even a lot for me to do
when I'm on tour with my company, unless I'm conducting. I teach
class; I watch rehearsals, fix things, and give notes—not my favorite
thing to do, because I don't like to get in the way or bother the dancers
with too many notes—but I'm there because it's good for publicity and
I love watching a good show.

I take a bow.

AND YOU'RE READING THIS: my memoir. I now find myself less reluctant to share secrets, happier to let people in on what goes into
making up a dance, the workings of my company, my choreographic
imagination, and the way these are all aspects of who I am.

Perhaps this relaxation is due to my age, perhaps simply to the urge
to set it down right. But if you're going to read about me, you might as
well read *me*.

Dressed for a Verla Flowers recital, aged ten, in a costume made by my mother. *(Courtesy of Verla Flowers)*

One

Verla Flowers Dance Arts

I asked for dancing lessons when I was nine.

My mother—I called her Maxine—used to take me to see various touring companies at the Seattle Opera House, a series called *Sol Hurok Presents*. On one of these outings, we saw the great flamenco dancer José Greco, a gorgeous New Yorker with a big nose and a big basket. Flamenco excited me—it was sexy, virtuosic, stylized, and very alone—and, perhaps inspired by my mother's love for all things Spanish, my immediate reaction was "I want to do that!" My sister Marianne, nine years older, may also have been influential. She'd had some ballet lessons, doing jazz numbers to boogie-woogie, and was just starting pointe classes (which was also when she stopped). But that technique caught my eye. After one of her classes, I crammed my feet into Tupperware juice glasses so I could imitate her by walking on pointe in the front room. My sister thought I was going to die.

So my mother, seeing I was serious, opened the phone book and found a teacher, Verla Flowers, who taught Spanish dancing.

DANCER WITH CORNISH'S REVUE

Verla Flowers, young Cornish dancer, who was chief assistant to Weiland Lathrop in the program which the Cornish Dancers presented last night at the Stilliguamish Valley fair.
—McBride & Anderson photo

Verla Flowers in her
vaudeville days.

Verla—always just Verla—was from the old school, the Depression era. She'd danced on the vaudeville circuit and studied with famous people, including Matteo, the American-born choreographer, a master of Spanish dance (who only recently died at ninety-two). There's a Verla Flowers in every single town in America, but her school wasn't just "Dolly Dinkle," the term embarrassed dancers use for their hometown dance school, a phrase I've never liked. Verla was well connected in Seattle, with friends who ran Cornish College of the Arts, the preeminent performing arts establishment.

Verla had an amazing beehive that was loopy and tall—it wasn't one big puff—bold, big, and auburn. Her hair was done fresh once a week, and you could tell what day of the week it was by how far it had collapsed. She wore comfortable muumuus—this was a long time ago—and had different shoes for every dance: black character shoes for Spanish class and big silver tap shoes with jingles. She'd taught herself a lot of the classic repertoire on the piano. Her daughter taught also, and there was a devoted husband, Ted, who did odd jobs and drove people around.

She seemed old to me because I was young (she was fifty-two when we met, older than my mother), and we were friendly in that inter-generational way. Though flamboyant, she was old-fashioned, big on manners like a strict mother who makes her children wear neckties to church. Above all else, however, she needed to keep her students, so she couldn't afford to be one of those vicious ninety-year-old classical ballet teachers from Russia, the kind you can't ever get rid of. There aren't a lot of the crazy ones left anyway, because you can't touch the students anymore, let alone hit them with your walking stick.

She taught all over Seattle in satellite studios, church halls, and so on, but her own studio—Verla Flowers Dance Arts, where she taught hula, tap, and "toe dancing" (as people used to call dancing on pointe)—was north of the zoo in the Greenwood area. At my very first lesson, a private lesson, we learned a well-known flamenco solo form called a *farruca*, traditionally performed only by men, a dance of intense foot-work and quick steps. I learned a couple of phrases a week. I still know most of them, and thirty-five years later, some of that very first dance made it into my own dance *Four Saints in Three Acts*, to music by Virgil Thomson.

Verla's Spanish dancing lessons, every Saturday for an hour and a half, were so exhilarating, so much fun, that I couldn't stop practicing on my own time. I'd do a move forever until I got it down. Immedi-ately, I was a full-on committed perfectionist, purely because I was doing something I really liked. Verla saw something in me right away and quickly picked me out. I was new, I was eager, and I was a boy. Basically it was pretty much free—and it often is if you're a young male, because there's a paucity of dancing boys, partly because you're required to wear tights and therefore everyone thinks you're a sissy. And I *was* a sissy, but I was bolder than everyone else. I was also gifted, a quick study, good rhythmically, and smart, and she soon tricked me into taking ballet classes to keep me interested and busy. There was also some kind of arrangement with my mother for making and sewing costumes, the barter system in action. And as soon as I was old enough to know more than the other students, Verla had me teaching. She didn't teach ballet herself; she had other young ballet dancers for that. And if there was a ballet number in the recital, I'd get the only boy's part.

The fact is, Verla saw in me a prodigy, someone worthy of her extra attention and time. While my mother was working, I spent all day at the studio; I'd help Verla teach, take classes myself, or simply wrangle the younger kids. At the end of the day she'd take me to the greasy spoon around the corner for a grilled cheese or a patty melt. Somebody told me there was always a secret bottle of vodka in her desk. I never saw her take so much as a sip.

THERE HAD BEEN earlier performances.

In kindergarten, we did a production of *The Three Billy Goats Gruff*—my first performing experience. I was a Billy Goat, but I did something naughty and found myself relegated to Troll under the Bridge (which I would now consider a better part). This was the first in a litany of humiliating theatrical demotions.

In another show, a journey quest, I played the part of a wise old owl. Someone asked me, "Are you my mommy?" My line was "No. Please go over there and ask them!" But instead I improvised a joke: "Scram, Scrambled Eggs!" I got in terrible trouble and ended up recast as a rock. Not until the third or fourth grade did I manage to keep a part: the unnamed narrator, the victim, in *The Pit and the Pendulum*.

So I started putting on entertainments of my own, improvising scenes and doing shows in the living room or the backyard. I cast all the neighbor kids and forced my parents to watch. I was very bossy: that was me.

My sisters remember a big hit when I was about ten, at Franklin High, the school down the street where my father taught and that I was later to attend, for some kind of international dinner—these were the days of pancake breakfasts and spaghetti feeds at which they'd fix different foods and present some examples of "international" entertainment. I was quite good at Russian dance by then, and I think Dad, who'd been with the family to see me dance and play balalaika at the local Russian center, suggested that his son represent Russia. Grandma and Maxine sewed me a costume with balloon pants, and I kicked my legs very high, to my parents' pride.

Dressed for a Russian number with the Seattle Russian Balalaika Orchestra, 1967. (Courtesy of Maureen Morris)

BY THE AGE OF TEN I must have had the requisite ballet chops, because Verla drove me down to Portland, Oregon, to audition for a bit part with the Bolshoi Ballet, the legendary Russian company that often visited America. During their tour, the Bolshoi would come to a town and audition local children, a good public relations idea to this day. The particular piece I was auditioning for, *Rehearsal*, starts at the barre in the studio with little kids, progresses through training, and, as if in time-lapse, ends with the adult professionals from the company. The real draw would have been *Swan Lake*; *Rehearsal* would have been part of a repertory show.

It was a big trip away from home, and I was in Verla's charge, which my mother wouldn't have worried about for a moment, even though it was my first time out of town without family. We shared a room— Verla was strict with lights-out and said her prayers, which I didn't like—and she took me to the audition. I got the gig; we rehearsed for a week and then performed.

I've since met dancers all over the world of every age who were in *Rehearsal*. Richard Colton, a great dancer with Twyla Tharp, did exactly the same part somewhere else in the world via precisely the same audition process. And it was a very big deal for me at that age—a professional performance, probably two or three shows—simultaneously thrilling and terrifying. Everyone was speaking Russian, giants wearing weird clothes, makeup, and perfume that couldn't mask the smell of sweat. Some of them must have been famous, but I don't remember their names. The performing was magic (one of my roles in *Rehearsal* was pretend sprinkling with a watering can, which is how they kept a wooden floor from being too slippery in the old days before rosin), but I don't remember much about it, and I don't remember the music at all. My family drove down.

A year or so later, Verla took me to another audition—the cutoff was fifteen and I was underage, by far the youngest—with the result that I was chosen by José Greco, *the* José Greco, my original inspiration, to go on his own two-week workshop in, of all places and names,

French Lick, Indiana, a strange derelict resort at a hot spring where they'd rented a scary old hotel for cheap. My mother and I flew: my first time on a plane.

French Lick, which didn't observe daylight savings, was hot and humid like I imagined the South to be, with mosquitoes and fascinating fireflies. I have no idea what José Greco was doing in French Lick, but it certainly wasn't for the money. He was simply trying to get people interested in his kind of dance on the basis that you don't know what you hate until you've tasted it. He wasn't performing a cliché of flamenco passed down to him. José was the original from which the cliché derives.

It was dancing all day—I studied flamenco, ballet, and jota with the older kids—and I was in heaven. Everyone around me spoke Spanish, though it wasn't required of me, and there was a wonderful ballet master who taught classical comportment. My mother probably watched some rehearsals and read *a lot*. My memory of the other kids is hazy, but I made one friend, a girl of fourteen. She played the accordion and wrote me letters afterward, always signing off with "Accordionly yours." I remember begging my mother to buy me finger cymbals on the pretense that I needed them for a particular kind of Morisco dance, a *zambra*. It was a lie; I just wanted the cymbals.

I left French Lick exhilarated. I'd been fully challenged. And I'd started to get crushes on boys there, so that was part of the exhilaration. And I went back home, and back to Verla's. I was eleven, and dancing was already all that mattered, at the expense of almost everything else, even my own well-being.

Nothing hurts when you're a teenager, and if it does, you recover fast. It doesn't matter whether you're dancing on a hard floor or outside. It's only later, when dancing starts to feel bone-shatteringly difficult, that you get the Princess and the Pea Syndrome. There was, however, a serious early problem, supposedly career ending, from which only chemical intervention saved me. When I was twelve, I was trying too hard without understanding quite how things work, and I developed incredible Achilles tendonitis from overuse and underarticulation, from abusing my body by dancing too much. In ballet training, and in fact in all dance training, the tendency, when learning something new, is toward endless repetition, and the accompanying mentality is "if it hurts, it's good for you."

The nurse told me straight: "You should do something other than dancing; you don't have the Achilles tendon for it." The doctor gave me cortisone shots directly into the tendon. The problem with cortisone is that though it cures whatever ails you immediately, you then have to use ever-greater quantities to get the same result (as with heroin), so it's very damaging. Nowadays a doctor probably wouldn't prescribe it for a twelve-year-old. Luckily for me, no one thought twice about it back then.

By the time I was fourteen, Verla was encouraging me to choreograph when I really had no right to. She wouldn't even ask what I was going to do; she'd just give me a place on the recital, and I'd make up whatever dance I wanted. These recitals happened annually—three hours long—with two hundred six-year-olds, a few of them peeing on the stage, older students (who were even worse), and then the better ones to finish the show. She'd allow me about fifteen minutes, for which she'd give me carte blanche, not to mention the time to rehearse with people I was taking class with.

Verla was my sponsor, and later she sweetly referred to me as the son she'd never had. I never lost touch with her, and she saw all my early dances. One of her daughters took over, and to this day whenever I perform in Seattle, Dance Arts alumni show up: "Remember us from Verla's?" They're sixty-plus now. Go figure.

My own school in Brooklyn, the School at the Mark Morris Dance Center, is meant to be like Verla Flowers Dance Arts, a dancing school rather than a conservatory. We teach you to dance from the ground up.

———

SEATTLE HAD VERY DISTINCT neighborhoods back then, but Mount Baker, where we lived—south of downtown, past the baseball stadium, before the airport—had a little bit of everything. This was before "multicultural," and our neighborhood was constantly changing, though slowly becoming predominantly African American. My best friend (from second grade) was Peter Tudor, whose parents were Barbadian, strict Episcopalians. His father, Winfield, with his beautiful lilting accent, was a countertenor in that glorious compline choir at St. Mark's.

In the seventies, there was a huge influx of Thai, Cambodians, and Lao, refugees from the Golden Triangle, and the signs in the grocery stores became much more exotic. I remember my mother standing at the bus stop, like the Queen Mother, the white lady with a purse, with five or six young Hmong women on the ground around her with their incredible needlepoint and their hats, babies tied to their backs, as though Mount Baker were a village in the Mekong delta. One particular apartment complex had been derelict for years—home only to junkie squatters—until these families moved in. They turned the blackberry patch into a terraced garden where they grew their own vegetables. We'd comment on the beautiful poppies. Then the news broke that they'd been busted for growing opium. The grandmothers sat outside with their long-stemmed pipes, smoking, right by my sweet mother's house.

There were Catholic kids (the girls had pierced ears; nobody else did at that time), a lot of Japanese GI war brides, and a more affluent Jewish community on Mercer Island. These little places had been trolley stops with their own identities; now they're all part of a larger homogenized Seattle. Columbia City—now slightly chic, with its own jazz club—was the location of the library, where I was taken for story time on Saturdays, and the funeral home, where I'd wait outside in the car with my next-door neighbor, Nona Weatherford, while her father, Jim, the undertaker, popped inside and did something with a cadaver. Mrs. Weatherford died horribly young of a burst aneurysm; I saw her carried out of the house screaming.

My grandma shopped at what is now the delightful bustling tourist-filled attraction of Pike Place Market. Back then it was a dangerous, intense no-man's-land, full of fishermen, drunk grifters, and scary hobos. Nonetheless, that's where my tiny grandmother Mabel took me to buy clams and oysters to fry. She knew everyone down there. Occasionally we'd go to the thriving Chinatown to a particular chicken butcher. Unlike a lot of kids nowadays, I knew quite early on that chicken was an animal.

MY PARENTS, BILL AND MAXINE, coincidentally both from Montana, had met in Denver; they both worked for the military. Dad was always a teacher, then of navigation, and he'd been in Europe for the war, noncombat, an eyewitness to history at the first General Assembly of the United Nations in London on January 10, 1946. Maxine had excellent clerical skills and was a secretary and court recorder.

They moved to Seattle, the destination of choice for every Montanan who wants to get away from their hick ranch town. It was either there, Minneapolis, or North Dakota, but Seattle was the big getaway, and they got away. Maxine moved with her parents via Spokane, where they ran a soda fountain. She used to talk about driving from Montana to Seattle, a round-trip we made every summer to see her brother, my fabulous uncle Jim, who lived in Great Falls, which could at least lay claim to being an actual city.

They moved into our family home in 1950—two years after the birth of my oldest sister, Marianne, and two years before Maureen. I wasn't to arrive for another seven years, born into a whole neighborhood of girls of my sisters' ages; I was such a local highlight that my own sisters had to get in line to hold me. Marianne, who always seemed of a previous generation, a beautiful Breck girl, wasn't a huge presence in my youth. She moved out as soon as she

With my sisters, 1958.
(Courtesy of Maureen Morris)

could, at eighteen, when I was nine, went to the University of Washington, got an apartment, married young, and then moved into the house where she lived for years. That left Maureen, five years my senior, and me living with my parents.

Marianne, Maureen, and Mark Morris. The alliteration must have appealed to my parents; perhaps it was my mother Maxine's idea; her mother, after all, was Mabel. And I was nearly called Meredith Morris, a very good man's name, particularly if you're Welsh, which was my father's heritage. (All Welshmen think they're good singers, as did he—but he wasn't. He was, however, a loud and enthusiastic singer, traits I inherited.)

In the early eighties, in one of my workshops before I had my own company, I met a woman, Rachel Murray, who later danced with me for a while. She said she'd just seen a psychic; at the time Seattle was nothing but lesbian psychics. The psychic had told her she was going to meet someone with the initials MM who would go on to become a great choreographer and dance artist, surpassing even LL (meaning, she assumed, the choreographer Lar Lubovitch, one of my first employers when I later moved to New York City). Very Nostradamus. Can NN be far behind?

I KNEW NO OTHER HOUSE growing up. Always wallpapered, a grayish-green lattice with big squares; always carpeted. The fireplace had built-in bookshelves, and the décor was true to the period: tall bottles filled with colored water. Maxine had a flair for something Spanishy, which is no doubt the reason she took me to the flamenco concert that changed my life. There was a dining and living room, with room dividers, and a large kitchen with a back door where an actual milkman left actual milk.

My first memory is sitting on the living room carpet, as only children can, feet on the outside and knees touching, and peeing my pants when I was old enough to know better. I felt myself warming; then I walked upstairs in that way that means you have to go, or just went, to the bathroom. Upstairs, there were three bedrooms: my parents' at the front, Marianne's, then the room I shared with Maureen, where we had bunk beds. She'd lift up the top mattress and pour water on my face when I least expected it. As soon as Marianne left, Maureen took her room and I had my own bedroom until I moved out.

Another early memory is watching my mother make the beds in my parents' bedroom—twin beds, of course. It was the first time I'd seen the exposed fattened mattress and beneath it the fake satin cover on the box spring, so beautiful and floral that I imagined it must have belonged to Marilyn Monroe. I didn't precisely know who Marilyn Monroe was, though I knew who shared the same initials, but I did know that she was both famous and beautiful. Given that the mattress was the most sophisticated thing in the world, it was only logical that Marilyn Monroe had lived in our house at some point.

Nothing much else about that house—a standard 1930s bungalow amid many others—was either beautiful or sophisticated, except the bathroom, a relatively large one for such a house, complete with bathtub, vanity (as we always called it), and a porcelain sink. A previous owner, perhaps Monroe herself, had customized it, exponentially increasing its glamour factor with the addition of a bidet. I had no idea what it was for, but that bidet was the fountainhead of my lifelong obsession with water features. I'd fill it, dye the water blue, make fountains, and decorate it all with floating camellias as though it were the set for that magnificent Busby Berkeley number "By a Waterfall" from *Footlight Parade*, waiting for cameras to bring it to life. At the time, I couldn't imagine any other use for it, though I did once discover feminine items, syringes and so forth, in the closet. The bidet had to be disconnected when it started leaking.

My favorite room, however, was next door, the smallest room, a toilet with a little window and nothing else. It was exotic (French poodle wallpaper in black, white, and pink), beautiful (naturally), and, above all, private. Once I graffitied on the wall in ink. I thought it was grown-up, cursive handwriting, but it was hieroglyphic nonsense. My mother left it there until the next change of wallpaper, either to torment me or because its mysterious beauty intrigued her.

When I was in trouble, I'd punish the cat—I was the youngest child, but Tom was even lower on the totem pole (and Maureen used to put me in my place by saying, "You're the part of the totem pole that's underground")—by locking him in that little room and turning off the lights. I thought it would be worse for him in darkness (as it would have been for me), not realizing he'd just go to sleep, thinking, "Thank God the kid has left me alone." Horrible.

———

THE BACKYARD HAD A RECTANGLE of cement we called a patio (it was rumored to have been a fishpond, of which there was now no sign) and a lattice arbor that sprouted enormous wisteria and out-of-control bamboo. In Seattle, everything grew over. If you didn't cut it back, it took over the world. Beyond the patio was an alley, impenetrably brambly with wild blackberries. Maxine's favorite book was Frances Hodgson Burnett's *The Secret Garden*, and she was always making secret gardens behind the house. She was a rock gardener and a rose gardener—there were always flowers, which was a big deal—and it was her obsession to have a little tea garden with a pond and pagoda. And mine too. I've always had an eye on the East, and it started early on. Japanese influence was everywhere in Seattle, particularly in the gardens. I fantasized about living in the beautiful Japanese tea garden at the Seattle arboretum in my very own pagoda among the mosses, ferns, and koi.

Maxine always had, from the time they were popular until the day she died, a pair of plastic pink flamingoes loitering in the front yard. Her love for them was sincere, though she later conceded they'd become kitsch. My grandma Mabel, on the other hand, favored a dramatic tableau of three little bunnies and a rabbit. She even stooped to trolls. Lawn ornaments are so thrilling to a child.

I spent a great deal of time with my mother's parents, my darling grandparents, Bill and Mabel Crittenden, who lived nearby. Though they weren't on the very outskirts of town, it was woodsy, something of a magic forest where they lived what seemed to me a rancher-style existence: squirrels and chipmunks, a potting shed, all rock-gardened in the old-fashioned way, wild with roses and raspberry bushes. They were old, and I'd help out cooking and gardening.

Bill was funny, a real card. He kept the lower plate of his dentures

My family dressed for my grandparents' fiftieth wedding
anniversary, our house, 1965. *(Courtesy of Maureen Morris)*

in his pocket and had us kids reach in and get them out, for the pleasure of hearing us scream. One of his other tricks was to disguise himself as a lady, pay a call on a friend, and try to fool them: those were
different times. Their house was an Aladdin's cave of old-fashioned
practical jokes and comedy props: a fake mangled swollen purple hand
stuck in the door, a cast-iron set of teeth that was actually a bottle
opener, an old trolley bell from one of the long gone Seattle streetcars.
He'd once been a bit of a song and dance man too, not to mention a
radio personality ("Chicken Bill") combining his natural goofiness
with his love for and knowledge of chickens, taking questions on air.
But that was in Montana in the 1930s; by the '60s, he was a little cranky
and worn out. Diabetic, he got an infection in his toe but was too embarrassed to admit it, and by the time he was taken to the hospital,
they had to amputate his leg just above the knee. That was the start of
his decline. He used to get me to water the knee joint of his replacement plastic leg through a funnel, which he thought was a total riot.

Mabel, who was everybody's favorite grandma (she had twelve

grandchildren), worked at Frederick & Nelson, a branch of Marshall Field's, in the factory dipping chocolates (Frango mints, a Marshall Field's classic), so she hated chocolate. She took the bus to work from the bottom of the hill. Bill would drive their Corvair down the hill once a day to drop her off and once again to pick her up.

When he died, she moved in with us. She was very shy, but we encouraged her to go to a senior center to socialize, and she ended up dating—I remember someone telling her that a particular gentleman was "gay," a word she'd never heard before—and she started wearing pants and a chic wig. When she died, she didn't want her age in the obituary, because she was dating a sixty-five-year-old. She was eighty-five.

She'd been long dead when I found out her story. I was in the bathtub at home, my mother was coming and going, and Maureen was at the vanity (not uncommon) when she told me. Mabel had accidentally shot and killed her brother, Friendly, the golden boy of the family. They were on a picnic, shooting bottles off a fence, because that's what you did if you lived on a ranch and there was nobody around, and she fired at a bottle just as Friendly was setting it up. She killed him. She lay in bed in silence for two weeks, more or less comatose, and hardly talked or left her room for a couple of years—what we'd now refer to as PTSD. Finally, her family sent her to Spokane to become an au pair, primarily to get her out of the house, but also because local people were mean to her. And that's where Bill and Mabel met and married, and, after running the soda fountain, they moved to Seattle.

Nobody ever spoke of the shooting. Maureen had found out only after my grandfather had a stroke. She was sitting with him in the hospital as he chatted with my great-uncle Earl, who was visiting from Packwood, Washington. "Mabel was never the same after that," Bill said casually, and it all came out.

———

MY FATHER WAS VERY SWEET and kind: a doll. He occasionally wanted to play devil's advocate, and Maureen remembers him yelling at me once, but though he blew up occasionally, he wasn't abusive in any way. In his youth, he'd been on the debate team, and as he got older that spirit manifested itself as he became a little more argumentative, but he never struck or hit anything; in fact, there was no real discipline or punishment at all. When I was driving my mother crazy, on the other hand, she'd put her arms on my shoulders and rattle me and I'd laugh. He'd always been hard of hearing—his hearing aids whistled—so he couldn't tell how loud he was talking, which was particularly embarrassing at the movies. We'd go late, miss the start, then stay the whole way through the credits, as you did, until you'd seen it all. In the rapt silence of the theater, he'd lean over to me and shout, "WHAT DID HE SAY?"

Dad was also a musician; he'd had a dance band in high school and marched in the Rose Parade playing the trumpet. In college, he'd go around with his sister-in-law Eunice armed only with ukuleles. He was quite gregarious and a little nervous—he jiggled in church—and always lovingly supportive, even of things he didn't fully understand (though he did understand my dancing: we were a family of performers). My mother was glamorous—with her dark wavy hair, she reminded Maureen of Loretta Young—and even though she was quieter, she was very funny; my father was more bewildered. He wasn't particularly good with money and never made much either.

Dad was the youngest of six brothers and a sister, and he seemed from another age. He never left the house without a hat, a tie, and either what he called a "topcoat" or the much more casual wool Pendleton jacket (appropriate attire for a picnic). His shirts were pressed on cardboard at the cleaners in the old style. He was rather conservative, and felt guilty about not being sufficiently religious, which would periodically lead him to drag us to the Presbyterian church. His family wasn't much fun, his brothers were bossy, and he'd been the tender blossom. I even had thoughts about my father perhaps being gay on the basis that he was sensitive, smart, and musical (all those euphemisms) and that he had a bowling buddy I never liked called Bruce, who lived alone nearby.

My father's ambitions on my behalf were that I learn to type, play the piano, and fix a car, but most of all that I go to college; having "something to fall back on" was extremely important to his generation. Of course I give that same advice to my dancers; it makes perfect sense. The irony is that I never had anything to fall back on, and never even went to college (though I can read). Yet I now have twelve honorary doctorates of which I am very proud—and I don't think I'd have a single one of those if I'd actually gone to college. In fact, I was very fortunate not to have something to fall back on, because there were times when a more prudent man might have fallen back on it. But it's still what I tell my dancers, as though I were my father.

He worked at a piano store during the summer but, as far as I could tell, never sold anything to anyone. They'd loan him an organ—a feature of our living room—so he could master it at home in order then to demonstrate it to customers at the store. He played from charts, and though by no means a great technician, he could fake his way through the Great American Songbook. He later taught me to sight-read, though I could only ever do it well enough to accompany Maureen, who had a beautiful soprano. My father and I played together, but I didn't like his repertoire—"Always," "Autumn Leaves," or (for my grandparents' fiftieth wedding anniversary) "I Love You Truly," vamped on the Wurlitzer with lots of vibrato. His relaxation was to play the organ, complete with sound effects: he pulled out all the stops.

He wasn't one of those dads who had his own chair. Home from work, he'd read the paper (he didn't read for pleasure) and fall asleep on the sofa in his shirtsleeves and slacks, and we'd have dinner at six. My mother was a standard postwar cook, frozen and canned food. We ate as a family every night, then watched TV. My mother read all the time. She stopped reading later, when she was a widow, because she couldn't put books down: she'd never get anything done, even though there wasn't that much to do. There were books everywhere: *On the Beach* by Nevil Shute, *Hawaii* by James A. Michener. My father had a free teacher's subscription to *Reader's Digest,* and we had a shelf full of the *Encyclopaedia Britannica* like you had to. There was always a copy of a West Coast lifestyle magazine called *Sunset* lying around with beautiful photography and recipes for chili.

Dad taught—English and typing—at Franklin High, though his job changed to managing what were then called "potential dropouts" (juvenile delinquents or what we'd now call at-risk students). He'd employ them as handymen outside of school. There was always some cute older teenage guy mowing the lawn without his shirt on . . . very sexy, of course.

Later there was an incident—I never knew the full story—some sort of altercation during a demonstration in which a bunch of kids ran riot and locked the principal up. One kid slapped my dad's face in front of the class, as I know it, broke his glasses, and knocked out his hearing aid. He was profoundly demoralized by the incident, and found himself taken out of the firing line and moved downtown to an office job, responsible for special needs kids.

He never had an alcoholic drink ever, a complete teetotaler. I remember a whispering fight between him and my mother after Marianne's wedding, for which I lit and extinguished the candles at the gloomy Presbyterian church a few blocks away. There was champagne at the reception—and I heard my father bristling with anger, referring to the bride herself: "Did you see her guzzling that crap?" That was his exact line, hissed through gritted teeth.

My mom didn't drink either. She'd occasionally, later in life and only at our urging, have a little glass of rosé, the tiniest sip, and say, "My knees are getting weak!"

TWO THINGS I BELIEVED as a little kid: First, that the car automatically turned into any donut shop by the side of the road. "Oh no!" my father would say. "I can't stop it! We have to have a donie!" Second, that my mother risked her life for me once a week. When we went to church, the reward was McDonald's on the way home. "Let me taste your french fries," she'd say, "to see if they're poisoned." I'd watch, thinking, "Dear God, what has she done? What if they are? My mother would give her life to save mine!"

Only after her life-or-death taste test was I allowed a fry.

Jr. High performance poster, Seattle, 1982.

Two

Jr. High

S chool, as opposed to dancing school, was a story of diminishing enjoyment.

One of the tests to see if you were ready for first grade was whether you could walk to school by yourself. Nowadays that would only be evidence of parental neglect, yet we happily walked those several blocks unmurdered every day, then home for lunch, then back again to John Muir Elementary, a big old brick schoolhouse that smelled of chalk and furniture polish.

Mrs. Graves, my third-grade teacher, was tiny, strict, and Chinese American and wore sensible witchy shoes. You had to stay after school for five minutes if you dropped your pencil, and of course the desk was on an incline, and the pencil rolled. She once forbade the use of the colors pink and red together. On another occasion, she announced, "Jupiter is the largest planet in the world." I pointed out the flaw in this remark. That was my downfall.

I mostly liked grade school, but I don't know how much attention I was paying, given all the extracurricular dancing. I had one particular friend, a girl called Donna Miller, with an absent GI father and a very reserved traditional Japanese mother who took me to the Bon Odori Festival, just a short bus ride away at the Seattle Buddhist temple, where we'd gone in advance to learn the dances. Every dancer had a fan, and we ate shaved ice with bean paste: fully Japanese. I was dancing everywhere I could.

Donna loved origami, and her mother was an expert in *bankei*—related to *ikebana* (flower arranging) and bonsai (miniature plants)—a hobby in which I was briefly very interested. It's a crazy subset of Japanese culture in which you make miniature scenes with living things, involving a tray with a canvas frame above it and water underneath, and a kind of mud-peat soil in which you sculpt miniature islands and mountains. You can't actually grow things, but the soil is just damp enough that moss, placed upon it, stays alive. Then you might decorate your scene with little bridges, boats, or figures (all on sale at your local Japanese emporium), and design, say, a coastline with blue sand for the seas and white sand where it breaks. I loved these beautiful tableaux, but it was clear you had to devote your life to *bankei*, and this was a commitment I couldn't make. Donna and I fell out for some petty reason, and she started the I Hate Mark Morris Club. She actually bribed people with candy to join, to sign the petition.

I certainly wasn't much into sports either. I fenced for a few years, solely because there was a woman who exchanged her daughter's dancing lessons at Verla's for fencing lessons. I fenced foil only, pre-buzzer, but I stopped because, though I loved it, I didn't want to develop one giant lobster arm. (The choreography I did for Prokofiev's *Romeo and Juliet, on Motifs of Shakespeare* many years later is full of those moves.) My father used to take me to see his students play basketball. I didn't like the sport, though I did like the boys, the noise, and the bleachers. Once a year we went to see the Harlem Globetrotters at the arena. That was my sports experience—comedy basketball. Mind you, now that I think of it, the Harlem Globetrotters weren't too dissimilar to Sol Hurok bringing vernacular dance around America. That's it for sports, though I will say that I was exceptional at hopscotch, which, although it isn't yet an Olympic sport, isn't thought as sissy now as it was then.

Fencing class at Verla Flowers's studio, Seattle, 1968. *(Courtesy of Maureen Morris)*

We had Spanish language lessons on TV for fifteen minutes a week—"¡Buenos días, Señor Ybarra!" We were all supposed to respond together, but I wasn't talking fucking Spanish to a TV! And there were a couple of hours of music for everybody. We were taught the Autoharp—"Roll On, Columbia" by Woody Guthrie—and we sang rounds and harmonies. There was always a talent show, and there is nothing better than a talent show. When I opened our dance center in Brooklyn, I wanted a monthly talent show: seven-year-olds telling knock-knock jokes. What beats that?

There was culture galore, and the school took it upon itself to educate us in that way. The first opera I ever saw, on a school trip, was *La Périchole* by Offenbach at the Seattle Opera. The star Edie Adams, a popular singer in the 1960s, famous for Muriel cigar ads, wasn't even a legit opera singer. I loved it. And it wasn't only José Greco I saw with my mother. She also took me to see the whole world of dance—a kathakali company from India, Moiseyev Russian Folk Dance Company, and Bayanihan, the Philippine National Folk Dance Company. My father used to take me to the musical events, including recitals of the great Vladimir Horowitz (who, as a scary, shriveled-up old man, came on to me many years later in a Manhattan restaurant).

OUR ANNUAL VACATION was to visit our incredible uncle Jim Crittenden, my mother's brother, in Great Falls, Montana. He was flamboyant, married, and fabulous. It was where I learned how to put on a show.

My father, being a teacher, had three months off every summer; my mother worked sporadically, depending; and every year we made the road trip. Both sides of the family had relatives in Montana, mostly in Helena (where we'd see my father's many brothers, one of whom was a Bircher John). One uncle lived in nearby Tacoma, another (Chuck, a crazy born-again Christian who used Hawaiian Punch concentrate as salad dressing on his iceberg lettuce) lived in Seattle, but everyone else was in Montana—all the Morrises and the Munzenriders (Maxine's sister, Eva, a Crittenden like her and Uncle Jim, had married a Munzenrider). The Morris cousins were more my parents' age, but the Catholic Munzenriders (who were fun, particularly compared to the Presbyterian Morrises) were our contemporaries.

In the olden days, it was a two-day drive to Montana with a stop somewhere in eastern Washington at one of those motels with matching cabins. As cars improved, we did it in one long day over Snoqualmie Pass, five of us. I'd sit in either the middle or the back of the station wagon, and we'd sing the whole way: "The Church in the Wildwood," "Don't Fence Me In," and "The Merry-Go-Round Broke Down," during which my father would misbehave on the horn at the relevant moments, not to mention "K-K-K-Katy," a stammering novelty song that would today be regarded as a hate crime against the disfluent. I always wanted us to stop and loiter at every point of interest and roadside attraction along the way, but we never did. Just as you get into Montana, there's the Continental Divide, and I imagined that a drop of water would split in two at that exact place and go to either the Pacific or the Atlantic, a fifty-fifty chance. Another roadside attraction usually

denied me was Frontier Town, supposedly a full ghost town with boardwalk. Years later, when my company was on tour one January, in ten feet of snow, I got to walk around the buildings, automated trains, and wagon wheels. At that time of year, it really was a terrifying ghost town.

Uncle Jim, who had been an ambulance driver in the war in Europe, where he'd met up with my dad, was corpulent, not to say fat. He was married to an English lady, a

Uncle Jim and my father (right) on the banks of the Blue Danube, 1944.
(Courtesy of Mark Morris)

beautiful ginger war bride from Sheffield. Audrey, or Old Aud, as he called her, had terrible back problems and was always frail, having endured numerous surgeries after a fall from a horse years before. She was normally found reclining on a divan in their split-level ranch house, her English accent (of which my mother used to make fun, "I'm going to take a *bahth* in a minute and a *hahlf*") exaggerated from years in America. I don't know whether they managed sex, but they did have one child, my lovely cousin Caroline, who looked a lot like the beautiful Doris Day and was close friends with Marianne. Audrey was messed up, poor thing, a semi-invalid constantly in pain, yet she died only recently, outliving her husband by decades.

Jim was the Western states distributor for Miller High Life, "the Champagne of Bottle Beer," and a very dreamy entrepreneur. A lot of his ventures failed, and he and Audrey pretended they had money when they didn't, but he somehow always had enough for the latest model of Cadillac, in which he'd drive with his little dogs on his shoulder. He and his wife always had a pair of little white toy poodles that Audrey would dye to match her hair (say, champagne). And they had the exact same Margaret Keane prints that I have in my front room in Manhattan today, not to mention a fiberglass dish fountain with a plastic lotus in it and other waterworks, rekindling my love affair with water features, post-bidet. Being effectively housebound, Aunt Audrey would reupholster the furniture every few months. You'd arrive and everything would be leopard, then the next visit, green corduroy, and the next year totally gold and white. And we'd go for other holidays: Christmas was a thrilling winter wonderland of a million blue and red lights.

Jim was a complete showman, but it wasn't only the poodles, the upholstery, and the car. He was flamboyant even in his choice of cigarette—Nat Sherman Fantasias, the brightly colored ones with the gold tips. He had a great sense of humor and was, most memorably, a cinematic pioneer, an auteur of elaborate homemade movies starring all the cousins. These were full-costume dramas, with titles rather than dialogue, like old silent movies but in color, with special effects, musical numbers, and a voice-over, sometimes primitive stop-motion animation. We lip-synched to songs.

One movie, *Safari to Irafas* (it may not have escaped your attention that Irafas is "safari" backward), began with sand blowing off a piece of paper to reveal the title credit: very *Desert Song.* My sister Marianne was the beautiful Arabian princess and my sexy cousin Pinky her dashing lover. There was the Riff clan and the Raff clan, and at age seven I was one or the other. In one scene, we, boys in Arab outfits (and I still have mine), tortured my cousin Caroline, a French Foreign Legionnaire in pith helmet and safari shorts, tied by her arms to stakes in the "desert." There I was, slicing her wrists with a wooden scimitar as the director applied fake blood. There were love songs and a big fight on the beach. It was deadly serious.

Being one of the youngest, I wasn't in all of them. There was a great western (one of many), supposedly set in the town of Skunk's Misery, for which they went on location somewhere far away in Montana. Maureen was shot in the forehead, and one of my cousins, aged twelve or thirteen, was hanged in the movie; my mother hated the shot of the swinging feet. That movie was called, brilliantly, *The Day Skunk's Misery Smelled.* Another title was *El Toro Guano:* only the adults got that one. There was a jungle-themed movie (actually shot outside Seattle in the forest, where we tied bananas to rhododendron bushes) for which Audrey rallied to play the beautiful (white) queen with a snake coiled around her and a big diamond ring; we cut off her finger to steal it. Maureen played an ape (for which she wore a fur coat backward, a gorilla mask, and her ponytail down to her ass). You can only imagine how good these movies were. On the video versions I have, the sound is slightly out of sync, which makes them even better. You see a gunshot and a second or two later . . . *bang!*

We, the kids, were more or less feral for the summers, and this extended beyond the movies. I was gay but we didn't talk about it; we just acted on it. Even before that, back in Seattle, Steve Munzenrider and I, cousins, had shared a bed. He'd seen *Rosemary's Baby*, I hadn't, and, late at night, he told me how you could see the profile of Satan with a gigantic erection (which you can't). Well, you know where that led. In Montana, we slept in the same room, he'd tell a scary story, and we'd jerk off. He tutored me in fellatio. I was thirteen, and he was fifteen, and I remember having gay semi-sex and then going outside and looking at the *Apollo 11* spacecraft. You could actually see it, and we were looking for it, because they knew the stars in Big Sky Country. I've always associated the exploration of space with sex. A small step for me, a giant leap for mankind.

Steve, handsome, dark-skinned, and usually mustachioed, became a musician, teacher, and puppeteer, and went to live for a while in Alexandria, Egypt, where he ran an international school for children's early education. He died of AIDS, from which he first went blind, about twenty years ago.

Once he drove with Uncle Jim to Canada in the big Cadillac only to be stopped at immigration. Of course they were! Not only did Steve have a bong with him, because he was a hippie, but my uncle smoked the gayest gold-tipped cigarettes. Jim had every symptom of being a fabulous queer, and maybe he was; we don't know. He was lonely and his wife was impossible. Where did the talent and urge to make those movies come from?

JUNIOR HIGH—A BUS RIDE AWAY—was a 1960s modern school called Asa Mercer, after the man who founded the University of Washington. (His big idea was the Mercer Girls, the mail-order brides imported to boost the female population of Seattle.) I hated everything about that school, and I used to leave the grounds. I was a pain in the ass and I got into a lot of trouble. In eighth grade, a bunch of us stood as one and walked out of a class to go to a demonstration against the Vietnam War. It started to be thrilling to be a revolutionary.

The cartoonist Lynda Barry and I were very close friends. She remembers one day in the corridor when a couple of guys were calling me a fag: "Hey, are you a guy or a girl?" As she tells it, she was nervous, but I didn't even break stride. "Follow me to the bathroom," I said over my shoulder, "and see which door I go into!" Lynda also came to a Bastille Day party I threw with a French theme; I'd just started taking over the home cuisine, and I successfully made crepes with chicken cream sauce for thirty people, almost dying in the attempt. She's quoted as saying someone came as Chef Boyardee, but he's Italian, not French. I do remember someone coming as the Eiffel Tower, and someone else as Marie Antoinette, a bloody stump; we were fun and hip, pretend bohemians. I wore old men's overcoats and a different rhinestone brooch, shoplifted from the Goodwill store, every day. Later in our respective high schools, we were both coincidentally voted the "weirdest" (that on top of our earlier joint win in ninth grade for "loudest laugh").

I summed up my feelings about Mercer in a very autobiographical dance called *Jr. High*, which we premiered in 1982 in the early days of the Mark Morris Dance Group at On the Boards, the Seattle dance and performance arts venue. It was set to music by the underappreciated genius Conlon Nancarrow from *Studies for Player Piano*. Nancarrow, who composed exclusively on modified player pianos, had only relatively recently been rediscovered (and died soon after that rediscovery), but he'd been writing a long time, counting composers Lou Harrison and John Cage among his friends. He volunteered to fight against Franco during the Spanish Civil War, and lived in Mexico City half his life, a citizen since 1956. He stayed there until he died, and if you wanted to hear his music, you basically had to go to Mexico City and have him play it for you. Many of his pieces are Spanish inflected.

We costumed the dance in the humiliating gym uniform we were required to wear at Mercer—white T-shirt, shorts, and shoes. At school, we had to write our names legibly on our white T-shirts with a felt pen, so for *Jr. High*, I insisted that our costumes were marked "M. Morris" and "C. Henry" (my friend Chad, who was in the show), our actual names. I hated gym class more than anything else in the world and skipped it, with dancing as my excuse, as often as I could. I hated the entire scene: I hated running; I hated climbing ropes. There was a creepy, handsome young gym teacher who took pleasure in humiliating us. He'd take roll call, for which we sat on the floor with our arms around our knees. When we said, "Here!" we were supposed to snap our jockstraps to prove that we were wearing them. *Snap! Snap! Snap!* down the line. He'd taunt us, "You're wearing jockstraps, though some of you could get away with a Band-Aid!" Nightmarish, degrading, and kind of funny. My dance *Jr. High* even smelled of the gym: the only time I've ever used Odorama. In the blackout before that piece, I sprayed the stage with Right Guard deodorant, so it had the vile smell of the locker room, a smell I detest. I don't know whether the audience could precisely identify it, but they certainly smelled it.

There was also a "sissy test" in *Jr. High*. I've heard there are regional variations, but here's how I remember it from Mercer: First, the boy taking the test—in this case, me—was told to look at one of his heels, the idea being that straight boys look at their heel to the front, as if they're looking to see if they stepped in dog shit, and sissies look over their shoulder to the back; next it was "carry your books"— straight boys carry them under their arms to the side like an ape, whereas sissies clutch them to their breast; then, look at your nails—

butch boys make a soft fist, fingernails facing up and toward them, whereas sissies do it with their hand straight out, wrist flexed, fingers up, like a lovely lady. One movement of the dance included me taking that test.

I was subjected to that sissy test many times, not to mention other old favorites like "Why are you hitting yourself?" Of course I sympathize with and support the contemporary anti-bully movement, but in my own case, if there hadn't been bullies, how would I have known I was a sissy? Thank you! I'd been wondering what I was going to do with my life! Another humiliating memory in *Jr. High* had me examining my chest to see whether I was growing breasts. It was tragic, at least to me, but I wasn't surprised when people laughed.

There was more Nancarrow in *Etudes Modernes*, a dance for four women, which I did a year after *Jr. High* to some of the composer's Spanish pieces, weird, swanny flamenco. Nancarrow's music, far from being merely mathematical (although some of his best pieces are), also contains a great deal of ragtime and early twentieth-century influence, blues and frenzied honky-tonk; it's just strange and disguised. I was very influenced by *The Lawrence Welk Show*, which I watched with my family. We all loved it (except during that brief compulsory period as an older teen when I found it corny and embarrassing). In order to force my family to watch me dance, I'd improvise between them and the TV set, so my parents had to peer around me just to get a glimpse of the dancers, Bobby Burgess and Cissy King. I worshipped the honky-tonk pianist on that show, Jo Ann Castle, who played straight to the camera. Those Nancarrow pieces sounded like her on amphetamines.

We finally did those two Nancarrow dances together, interleaving *Jr. High* and *Etudes Modernes*, male and female. I added a final part, the *Zombie Dance*, that could be done with any number of people in rhythmic unison. It's a thankless, uncomfortable, robotic dance, a canon at the ratio of one to one, done in a straight line to funny and horrible machine music. You can't copy anybody because you can't see anybody, except in your peripheral vision; you simply have to know it.

Those pieces together were my autobiography of queer humiliation, martyrdom, and triumph at Mercer. I was never ashamed of being a sissy, and I wore the bullying as a badge of honor. It may have hurt my little feelings, but I was defiant. I knew what was going on and I knew who I was, so I took care of myself by being funny. Nevertheless, every solo I made up in the first part of my career was a humiliation dance in one way or another.

As far as Mercer was concerned, I was simply too much.

I'D BEEN GIVEN A BOOK called *A Doctor Talks to 9-to-12-Year-Olds* ("you will see changes in your body"). Ironically, by the time I read it, I'd already been having sex for a while: hand jobs on a sleepover with a cousin, of course, but also blow jobs in the park with strangers. I wasn't trolling, but I was cute, open, and into it. In fact, once I started having sex, I started having sex all the time with whomever I ran into, and by fourteen, I was having sex regularly. I wasn't exactly hanging around bus stations, but I sought it out. My attitude was quite casual. By today's standards, almost everyone I had sex with should be in prison, because I was underage and they were mostly adults. But I loved it. It was my idea.

The first time I ever had anal sex was with a full adult who probably shouldn't have. It hurt, I didn't like it, and I had to go to the doctor a few days later. He asked if anything traumatic had happened, and I said no, which was the truth. The doctor thought it might be colitis, but it was gonorrhea. He didn't tell my parents; I have no idea why. But thank God he didn't.

My father's best and only sex advice to me ever was "Keep it in your pants." That was it. He once said to me, as I was on my way out with friends, "You're not going out dressed like that—you look like a homo." He was right, and I guess he knew, but I certainly wouldn't tell him. At that precise moment, I happened to be wearing a gospel choir robe, bell-bottoms, and platform shoes. I had long hair and I was high. My mother would never have said anything like that to me. Besides, she already knew, and therefore it wasn't something worth saying.

My sister Maureen is gay too. She was never as obviously lesbian as I was gay, and I don't know if she's ever used the word "lesbian," but she was a full-on radical lesbian feminist. I was careful not to use the word "lady" in front of her, let alone "bitch." She had boyfriends (though the last nominal boyfriend, this beautiful young Thai guy, may have been transitional in more ways than one) until finally she brought home a girlfriend, Ruth, who then became a boyfriend, Rudy. When Ruth transitioned into Rudy, our grandmother was living with us, right through the reassignment period, and called him Ruth throughout, even when he had a beard and a baritone. Grandma would call out, "Would you like another Coke, Ruth dear?" And "Ruth" would answer in this deep, gravelly voice, "Sure, Grandma!"

AT HOME, we had a modest, semiportable record player with attached speakers in the dining room, along with an interesting collection of LPs, including Al Hirt, the trumpeter, and Spanish-flavored stuff that Uncle Jim used to send—the 101 Strings Orchestra's album *The Soul of Spain*, for example, which he'd use as the exotic soundtrack for his home movies.

I had to use a nickel to increase the weight on the needle so the worn-out copy of *Stars for a Summer Night*, a record that was very influential on my burgeoning musical tastes, wouldn't skip. It was dressed up as a pops concert with a mix of orchestral and vocal music—"22 brilliant performers in a sparkling program designed for summer listening"—featuring everyone from Leonard Bernstein to Ray Conniff, whose version of "Summertime" I didn't like at all. But certain tracks have stayed with me forever. For example, the Columbia Symphony Orchestra's March from *The Love for Three Oranges* by Prokofiev. That, to me, was classical music, and perhaps even my first taste of it. And the famous "Russian Sailors' Dance" from *The Red Poppy*—it's a late nineteenth-century Russian opera by Glière, but I wouldn't have known that, because the cover didn't care to name the composers, just the performers. That collection had everything: "Greensleeves," "Clair de lune," "Londonderry Air," "Liebestraum"—not to mention the New York Philharmonic, conducted by Bernstein, playing "Hoe-Down" from *Rodeo* by Copland. *Stars for a Summer Night* is the reason why I like the music I like. It was the foundation of my interest in classical music, a sampler of everything that formed me. And on eBay right now, there are sixteen of those from ninety-seven cents.

A few years later, I heard *Switched-On Bach*, Wendy (then known as Walter) Carlos's groundbreaking 1968 debut, Bach reimagined for Moog synthesizer. So I bought the follow-up, *The Well-Tempered Synthesizer*. The jacket alone is wonderful, an actual group photo of Bach, Monteverdi, Scarlatti, and Handel themselves! I can precisely date my interest in baroque opera to this version of Monteverdi's *L'Orfeo*, here called *Orfeo Suite*. I knew a little opera by then, but I'd never even heard of Monteverdi. It was scintillating, even in this synthesized interpretation.

But an even bigger surprise than the LP itself—and a surprise that changed my musical outlook—was the accompanying bonus single, *The Wild Sounds of New Music*, disguised as a 45 but meant to be played at 33⅓. It was simply the record company cross-promoting its modern catalog, but to me it was the whole point, a priceless object. Columbia had selected the most radical avant-garde music of the time, not synthesized Carlos versions but the real thing, excerpted so they fit on a single: Terry Riley's *A Rainbow in Curved Air*, Harry Partch's *Castor and Pollux*, Luciano Berio, Steve Reich, and Conlon Nancarrow (and also Lasry-Baschet, the Baschet brothers, whose music was awful then and remains awful to this day, despite the fact that they invented an inflatable guitar). Even the liner notes to the single is priceless: "Are you getting bored . . . with Jimi Hendrix, maybe a little put off by Jim Morrison? Jaws tired of 'bubble gum music'? Want to broaden your horizons without getting trapped in that square symphony and opera stuff?" Columbia Masterworks wasn't pulling any punches, and I'd never heard anything like it. In me, they hit their mark, because I then bought every single one of the actual LPs excerpted. It wasn't only that I'd never heard anything like it. It was *thrilling* music, and I couldn't believe my ears.

The Steve Reich piece, *Violin Phase*, freaked me out; you might even call it irritating if you weren't listening properly. I liked the Terry Riley piece, but at the time *A Rainbow in Curved Air* was perhaps a little too pop for me, the sound of psychedelic rock; it seemed a little too easy, which is precisely what I didn't like about pop music. (I soon discovered that Riley's *In C*, written a few years earlier and perhaps the greatest piece of the twentieth century, was much more appealing.) The Harry Partch, however, made the deepest impression, and this was certainly the first time I had heard him. The sound of his music, played on homemade instruments—gongs and plucked strings—made perfect sense to me. It wasn't just because it was exotic; it was also because the modes sounded so attractive. Within a year or two of hearing *The Wild Sounds of New Music*, I'd be choreographing Partch's *Barstow* at dance camp, the Summer Dance Laboratory in Port Townsend, Washington.

Officially, however, the first dance I ever made up was *Boxcar Boogie (piece by piece)*—a terrible title; I was young—in 1971, the music for which were those exact edits of those exact tracks, the dance a pastiche of the little dances I made up to them. It was for a Verla Flowers recital, which took place at the Playhouse, the Seattle Repertory Theatre's home base. I used not just *Castor and Pollux*, but *Violin Phase*, some of the Conlon Nancarrow, and even the Lasry-Baschet.

This music was all extremely complicated, and there were no scores available, so in order to choreograph it, I just listened to it over and over again. That's what I did with all music anyway; still do, with the same yellow legal pad and precisely the same kind of pencil at the ready. (I'm a little crazy that way.) I'd listen, break it down myself, and notate it. Here's how: I'd put on the record and, first, record phrase changes, then sub-beats within them, and then exactly how many counts per section until it modulated or repeated, at least until something happened that I might actually recognize. After it was finally broken down, I could decode it much more easily. I was already involved with some unusual music through my dancing and could identify compound rhythms pretty readily. It was a crazy amount of effort, but it worked.

We weren't a tutored musical family, but we were a family that made a lot of music. I might not have shared my father's taste in repertoire, but left to my own devices when my parents were elsewhere, I'd head straight for the organ and improvise for endless hours. I used to use a cassette player to record myself, overdubbing to multiple tracks. I'd try to layer stuff—make a part and play along with it and rerecord it—but the original decayed and the quality got worse and worse and worse.

I got so I could fake my way through some of the two-part inventions of Bach on the piano, reading it slowly, then memorizing it. There was a songbook for solo voice and piano through the ages given to us by an old uncle, from which I learned "Come, and trip it as ye go / On the light fantastic toe" from *L'Allegro, il penseroso ed il moderato* (music by Handel, words by Milton), certainly my first exposure to that masterpiece, which I played in time-stopping slow motion with Maureen singing. (It's the origin of the lovely phrase "trip the light fantastic," which was in a Christmas dance of Verla's that the little kids did, called *Mister Dancing Santa Claus*: "He trips the light fantastic as he makes his merry rounds / He started taking dancing just to see if he could lose a few pounds!")

I was singing a lot too. (Maxine had taken all three of us in to be "tested," in the way people did in those days, to discover that we all had perfect pitch, about which she was very proud. It may not have been true, but she was happy to be told.) I was first a soprano, then an alto, in the choir at church when we were occasionally forced to go. I was also singing a lot of folk music outside school. By fifteen, I'd been singing with the chorus of a dance group called Koleda, which sang mostly Croatian, Serbian, and Appalachian music, full out, and also their all-male Macedonian choir. I loved madrigals, though the madrigal group at school, active when Maureen was there, was by then defunct.

I proudly bought myself a seventy-five-dollar piano from someone desperate to get rid of one. I had it forever. My friend Page Smith was (and is) a great cellist, and I was a very bad pianist, so I accompanied her on both very simple music and things that were way over my head, like Fauré and Hindemith. I didn't have her musical education, and I learned a lot about music from her. To this day, she and I can still whistle those two-part inventions of Bach.

The entire crew back then, gathering variously to sing and practice drinking wine, was my next-door neighbor Nona, Maureen, Page, Chad, and me. Chad was actually close to ten years older—a big deal when you're fourteen—and a very beautiful gay hippie with waist-length hair. I thought he was a genius: a very good guitarist and songwriter on the coffeehouse circuit, and a multi-instrumentalist who played the dulcimer and various stringed Balkan instruments, the long-necked tamboura and tamburica. Chad and I were never more than very good friends—he had a boyfriend/roommate whom he called Large Richard, a joke I only got later—but he knew what I liked. When I was fifteen, he handed me *Snow White* by Donald Barthelme.

The scene might be in the university district, late at night, in one of Chad's many houses, a glass jug of white or pink wine on the table, terrible pre-box Cribari "premium altar wine," and a pizza box on the floor. He'd be playing the dulcimer, perhaps the guitar, or an out-of-tune piano; Maureen, Page, Nona, and I singing shape note hymns, simple madrigals, or the Carter Family, or sight-singing from a hymnal.

Years later, Chad had a hit with a musical that played in Seattle for years, a hit in Tokyo, called *Angry Housewives*, about mothers forming a punk rock band, to their children's embarrassment. The big song was "Eat Your F*&king Cornflakes." I didn't even know he had served in Vietnam until many years later, when we went to a Vietnamese restaurant and he spoke to the waitress in Vietnamese. He'd been a translator; he'd never once mentioned it, and we were close. (The draft disappeared right when I would have been eligible.) He's now a visual artist, composer, and playwright with the Denver Children's Theatre, still ten years older than I am.

BY NOW I'D STARTED WRITING my own music because why not? I knew just enough to start. I wrote a piece for two flutes and two clarinets, and when we went to play it, I found that the clarinets were a step and a half down, because I didn't understand the concept of a B-flat clarinet. It was a very pretty canon for those four voices, despite the fact that two of them were a tone and a half off—it was a total accident, but it sounded better that way.

I strung up pots and pans for percussion, and I prepared a piano Cage-style (a necessity, really, because the piano had some really bad notes) with screws and paper and erasers to make it as exotic and weird as possible. I suppose I was a kind of by-mistake experimentalist, an avant-gardiste as a composer without fully understanding that any of it was avant-garde (beyond the fact that I'd heard that single). For example, I'd simultaneously play multiple piano rolls at the store where my father worked. I made that up. I had no idea that Charles Ives had done precisely the same thing years before. The only thing I ever choreographed that I wrote myself was *Mourning without Clouds*, another bad title, for seven-piece chamber orchestra, keyboard music instrumentalized. It was very primitive, and not on purpose.

I didn't take any piano lessons until later. Even then, it took an act of church charity: they gave me a little scholarship. But by then my bad self-taught technique was ingrained and I couldn't relearn it.

Besides, I was dancing full-time. It was too late.

Dad's Charts, Dance Theater Workshop, 1983. *(Tom Brazil)*

Three

Dad's Charts

My father was no longer teaching at Franklin High by the time I attended. I didn't apply myself to much academic work—I was smart enough to get by but not smart enough to study—and only bothered with the things that interested me: reading and music.

Penny Hutchinson, my friend from Verla's since I was fourteen (she was a couple of years older), was slightly rebellious, a little more chic, and got to go to what was then called an "alternative" high school, where they mostly smoked pot, ignored grades, sat on a couch, and had sex with their teachers in the time-honored tradition. I couldn't get in—they were *very* particular—and I was jealous. I wanted to be studying Advanced Lesbianism with her, as opposed to where I was, which I hated. We were so sophisticated by then, the teacher would leave and we'd work. The school offered Swahili, which only the students from Hong Kong studied. I took French. There was an African drumming group: full dashikis, Afros, black power.

I was a tenor in the honors choir, which sang jazzy pop, an unholy blend of hand jive and terrible cravats ("apache ties"), maybe a dozen of us singing mediocre arrangements (that I mostly loved). I was also in the big choir with thirty people (which is where I learned the Vivaldi Gloria, later to be music for my first large-scale dance). I had a big fight with the born-again Christian choirmaster. The class was at eight in the morning—I was habitually late by half an hour (and we lived a half block away)—and he assigned me the gesture choreography for a medley from *Jesus Christ Superstar*. I refused. I wasn't a Christian, and I didn't want to involve myself in bad religious music in that way, so he took me out of the concert; I didn't perform or even attend, and he failed me because I refused to allow him to exploit my skills as a choreographer for music in which I couldn't find myself believing. And *he* was the Christian. I knew I was leaving school anyway, which perhaps accounted for my attitude.

I was done with high school before I even began. I was there only two years.

IN POST–WORLD'S FAIR SEATTLE (the Century 21 Exposition had taken place throughout 1962), there was folk dance. People actually did that then. Interest in other lands and other cultures was high, all part of the general hippie culture and perhaps a result of postwar détente. People picked up the panpipes; *everybody* played the guitar. And I began going with Jewish friends once a week to do barefoot Israeli folk dancing. I was too young to be a real hippie, but I loved dancing and there was a touch of hippiedom about the whole scene, with a folk dance festival outside on the lawn every weekend. The dances themselves were athletic, totally exhausting and communitarian (not to mention many fake—manufactured primarily to get the kibbutzim revved up so they can work longer hours in the prison that is a kibbutz). We did every single dance every single Saturday until just after sundown; it was the most fun I'd ever had.

And there I met people who danced with Koleda, who rightly considered themselves superior to the Israeli folk dancers. Koleda had a much higher authenticity rating, with someone from Macedonia teaching his or her national dance one weekend, someone from Croatia the next. Their focus was on Balkan folk dancing, from all the then states of Yugoslavia: Serbia, Croatia, Macedonia, etc. In fact, my first exposure to Koleda had been a few years earlier in the sixth grade. Representatives of the group, newly returned from a tour in the Balkans, had come to do a show in the lunchroom at my grade school. They danced, demonstrating how they wrapped this twenty-foot-long wool sash around themselves. Their beautiful embroidered woolen costumes had made such an impression on me. It was as though they were in the mountains of Thrace, which, in their minds, they were.

They invited me to join them at international folk dance sessions, open to all, at the University of Washington. It appealed, not only because it was all ages and there was occasional live music but also because of the dances themselves. Some were straightforward, but others very difficult, particularly the extremely fast Bulgarian dances with variations called by the leader. They could be quite ornate yet also very spontaneously improvised to the specific theme of that particular dance and its compound rhythms and polyrhythms.

It was so much fun—the people, the vibe, the crazy Bulgarian dancing—that I started to go twice a week. The dance might be a long line circling a big ballroom. You'd study the dance until you got it, and finally you'd drum up enough courage to insinuate yourself. Then you'd follow along the back of the line as they were changing directions, very fast, very butchy, and then grab someone's belt (which by the way was not unsexy) and insert yourself into the line. Locked in, you'd dare not do anything wrong. First of all, everyone would hate you, and second, it would be dangerous. If you couldn't keep up, you were rejected; and if you couldn't cope with those rhythms, if you hadn't watched carefully enough and learned, you were out too. So it was very strict and challenging, the survival of the fittest. And those high stakes are extremely attractive to someone who can get it right.

There was a little bit of square dancing, Morris dancing too (the dance that would provide clever writers with so many headlines about me). I loved learning these figures. Often you were singing while you were dancing, and the dances went on for a long time, so you could talk and flirt and have a fabulous time. That, to this day, is what my work aspires to be, entirely.

Koleda was a collective, sometimes thirty or one hundred people, started by a man called Dennis Boxell, who died in 2010. It was a semi-professional company, which means that they put on professional shows and charged money for tickets but the dancers didn't actually get paid. All the money went, at least theoretically, back into the running of the company. Boxell himself was an expert in Bulgarian dance, and apparently a pederast who groomed boys of about my age—an "inspirational sleazebag" I once heard him called. He never bothered with me, though some of my friends were having sex with him. I tried but, thankfully, he wasn't interested. Perhaps I was repellent to him. There weren't a lot of actual gays in Koleda, but it was perfectly acceptable. I was basically out to them from the beginning, and I found myself accepted, not primarily as gay, just as someone with the chops for the dances. The Koleda family—and it was very familial—treated me well. I was the youngest of the performers, and whether they considered me a prodigy or not (though this was less important, given the group ethos), I occasionally got to lead the line or do an exciting little solo.

These were my hippie, musician, pothead, conscientious objector friends, some of whom were dropping acid daily. At fourteen, I felt very young among the sexy college students and kooky adults. There

Bulgarian Doll Dance, Koleda, Seattle, 1970.
(Courtesy of Maureen Morris)

were a lot of married couples in their thirties with kids nearly my age, and college students sleeping with each other in different combinations. All the women dated Serbian men, and to this day, I have American friends with Serbian last names. It was quite utopian. My friend Penny danced there with me too.

And it was a big social scene. There was a Koleda camp at a state park, which was full commune action, group cooking, dancing, and lots of drinking, particularly slivovitz, which I advise you to avoid. And for a while there was a "Koleda House" somewhere in Seattle, where three or four Koleda friends lived through college. My mother, for whatever reason, bless her, thought it was fine for me to spend the weekend there when I was sixteen or so. Heaven knows what she thought was going on, though I know from Maureen that she was worried that the scene was a little too grown-up for me. She was right. It was on one of these dancing and singing weekends that I first smoked pot, when a lid went for ten dollars. My friend Nona took her first hit, then projectile vomited against the wall. And the pot back then was mild.

I don't go a day without thinking of some aspect of Koleda culture. Every dance I make contains the germs of that experience, and those days were the first inklings of the life I have now. They provided me with so many life-changing ideas and experiences: queer power, pot smoking, independence, dancing and singing simultaneously, holding hands or belts, communality, adult friends, social fluency, rhythm, sex for fun, slivovitz, cooking for a mob, sight-singing, excellence, pride of accomplishment, enduring friendships, and a never-ending interest in the musics, dances, languages, and cultures of the terrifying, friendly, funny, incomprehensible world.

Every kind of dance is a variety of "folk dance," and my work is no exception. The kindness and inclusiveness of the greater Koleda family have been among the most moving and influential elements of my life.

Hail Koleda! Hail Terpsichore!

WHEN I WAS FOURTEEN, our house burned down.

I was on the bus at the top of the block coming home from school, and I looked out the window, and as a joke—I was a funny kid—I said, "Oh, I hope that isn't my house on fire!" I got off at my stop to find out that it was.

No one was inside, and though I wasn't the first one on the scene—the firemen were already there—it was close. The next-door neighbors' teenage ne'er-do-well son, whom I was always afraid of, had somehow saved the cats, but they were more or less all that survived. I calmly called my grandmother from next door. "Hey, Grandma, our house is burning down, so we're all coming over there to stay with you for a while."

"Okay, honey," she replied and hung up. (She normally ended phone calls with a cheerful "Better let you go!")

When we arrived, suitcases (and whatever wasn't burned or singed) in hand, she opened the door and said with a sigh, "Oh, Mark, I thought you were kidding."

The culprit was one of those high-intensity desk lamps that had just come on the market; very little, very strong, and very hot. (They don't sell them anymore. Why? Because they're very dangerous and could burn your house down.) The place was a wreck and we lost nearly everything. The bottom floor was completely burned out, while the upstairs was badly smoke damaged. We were out of the house for several months. The fact is we were badly underinsured, because my uncle Dave, the agent, hadn't kept the policy current. It was a financial tragedy. We couldn't sue and there wasn't nearly enough money to rebuild and refurbish the house, so all the woodwork was replaced with substandard material, crappy hollow doors, badly and cheaply done. We never seemed to get rid of that smoky smell.

I was teaching by then, and I remember giving private flamenco lessons to a high school kid (who drove me wild with desire) in the dining room of our burned-out house while it was under reconstruction. There was at least a usable wooden floor to dance on.

At the time my mother was working as the secretary in a local church we didn't attend. She ran the office, taking care of the scheduling. (I'd go there after school, get the keys to the organ, and play for hours, alone in this little church, improvising. This king of instruments fascinated me, and I played it as loud as possible, reducing myself to ecstatic tears in the process.) The church offered us temporary accommodation just around the corner from the smoldering embers. Christian charity! This cute house was newly empty because the old lady who had lived there had just been institutionalized, so in we moved while the builders did their shoddy work. That was when we started finding money. Literally. She had hidden money all over the house. You'd open a book and there'd be a twenty-dollar bill as a bookmark. My mother of course collected it and donated it to the church as a thank-you for their generosity (everything except what I found).

As if the fire wasn't bad enough, worse was to happen soon after, which added insult to injury. With the little insurance money we received, we went on a well-deserved family vacation to the Olympic Peninsula with brand-new clothes, brand-new suitcases, and the same old car.

We took the ferry over and found ourselves driving on a two-lane highway in an area around Belfair, behind an old couple slowing down to make a left turn. It was raining as usual, Maureen was at the wheel, I was next to her, and in the back were my mother and my father, who'd just had cataract surgery and had to wear contact lenses and glasses simultaneously. Maureen looked in the rearview mirror and, as time froze, exclaimed, "Oh God!" as a huge truck, which hadn't seen our brake lights, rear-ended us. We shot down the road. Maxine turned around at the moment of impact and got bad whiplash, as did Maureen. When we finally came to a stop, Maxine was just able to get out of the car, but we had to help my father. I was fine; Maureen's foot was cut; my father was fucked up.

We stood stunned at the side of the road. There was a small trickle of gasoline all the way from our car back to the truck and, as we watched, fire slowly burned down this trail, just like in a movie. The car burst into flames—it wasn't a huge explosion, but it exploded. Everything went, including our new clothes in our new suitcases in the trunk. We watched it burn. We hardly got any money for that insurance either, though Maureen fondly remembers a beautiful new gold velvet couch.

It was an annus horribilis, the year of fires, and the end of my youth. These two catastrophes occurred within months of each other. I honestly thought that an airplane would crash into me and kill me at any second—why wouldn't it?

MY FATHER DIED IN 1973 when he was fifty-nine. He wasn't in great shape. Though he wasn't obese, he'd always had a stomach—he was gluttonous in a different way from me—and had flatulence and burped a lot (which he has passed on to me). He was taking pep pills (speed) for weight loss, as many people did back then (and still do), and an appetite-suppressant candy, now discontinued, called Ayds. He'd have coffee with saccharine in it, then three donuts. He died at his desk at work, a heart attack.

On the particular day, I'd just driven home from a job teaching a weekly flamenco class at a community center, my first solo job after dancing school. Oddly, nobody was home, but I found a note telling me to call my grandma, who told me that my sister and mother were at the hospital. He'd been DOA.

My friend Page and I had put on a little concert for him at home a few nights before he died, Fauré's "Après un rêve" and Satie's *Trois Gymnopédies* on piano and cello; he fell asleep as we were playing. We were going to play the same music at his funeral, but I couldn't handle it. Someone else played my part for me.

All told, it was a pretty miserable last year of his life.

WHEN I WAS TWENTY-FOUR, I wanted to pay tribute to my father, though I don't know what suddenly brought that on.

The result was a solo called *Dad's Charts*, a distillation of my father in six and a half minutes: a jazz-structured improvisation—by which I mean that there were themes, then variations thereon, just as he used to improvise on the organ from his fake book, which provided only the melody, chord chart, and words of a given song: you made up the rest yourself. I set it to a cover of the standard "Robbins' Nest": direct, very listenable jazz by Milt Buckner, inventor of the "locked hands" style of organ playing. My father would have loved it.

The piece made reference to various scenes from my father's life, danced: keyboard playing (with its own appropriate gesture), typing (including a carriage return), bowling (which we used to do with that creepy friend, Bruce), taking a sauna (the three of us would go to the local Finnish saunas, so part of the dance was him naked in the sauna, though the audience couldn't necessarily tell, because I was clothed), falling asleep in front of the TV, and finally the tragedy of his being slapped across the face by that kid at his school. I slapped myself across the face many times.

And then at the end I died, because that's what he did. It was very personal and people laughed, which was fine. I wasn't blind to the fact that it was also funny.

We brought *Dad's Charts* back for our twenty-fifth anniversary in 2006, in a program called *Solos, Duets and Trios*. By then I was no longer dancing, so I had to teach it to someone else, in this case Maile Okamura. You can't just watch and learn a dance like that, so I explained every rule of the improvisation and imagery to her, all the background material. After that, I left her to figure it out on her own. She did it beautifully.

I FIRST HAD SEX with a woman when I was fifteen on a trip to Vancouver. She's now a midwife in Arizona, probably still recovering from the experience.

Some of my folk dance friends, three girls, and I naughtily sneaked off to Vancouver, British Columbia, to see Pennsylvania Ballet. We shared a hotel room, went to the ballet two or three times at the Queen Elizabeth Theatre, smoked Craven A cigarettes, and enjoyed our—my—first ever cocktail, a sloe gin fizz. I remember feeling drunk and grown-up.

There I also saw my first ever Balanchine dance, the genius *Concerto Barocco* to Bach's Concerto in D Minor for Two Violins. I found myself laughing out loud because I'd previously seen only knock-off Balanchine, choreography in his style that wasn't anywhere near as good. (I had much the same reaction the first time I saw real Martha Graham, because I'd seen so much overwrought ersatz Martha Graham.) *Concerto Barocco* has a section in the last movement where half of the dancers are doing four threes and the other half do three fours. If you see that without an understanding of music or dancing, it looks like they're not quite together, but if you have the ability to watch those two rhythms, it's mind-blowing. And that was what I experienced that night. It's what I loved about Balanchine and what inspired me. Though his choreography was structurally fascinating, direct, and show-offy, I couldn't believe how similar it was to the Busby Berkeley movies I'd been watching: *Footlight Parade, Dames, Gold Diggers of 1933.* Balanchine was the most American of choreographers, and the first person to choreograph instrumental music that wasn't written specifically to be danced to.

Later I went back to Vancouver to see my erstwhile employers the Bolshoi Ballet, three times, in fact. The lure on that occasion was the mature, somewhat scary Maya Plisetskaya dancing the *Dying Swan,* a famous encore number to Saint-Saëns choreographed by Michel Fokine (for Anna Pavlova)—the corniest, greatest solo in the world, Plisetskaya's signature. It's the *Reader's Digest* version of classical ballet for people who've never seen ballet, a sample of the nineteenth century done by one woman. Plisetskaya did it *twice* each night, once in the show and once as an encore, but one of those evenings she felt there wasn't quite enough applause to merit the encore. So I saw her swan die only five times.

Alexandra Danilova, the prima ballerina, referred to Plisetskaya once in a speech, in her heavy Russian accent, as the "best *Fokine* ballerina ever." I've heard that exact quote from multiple people, including Mr. Mikhail Baryshnikov, who also has an excellent Russian accent.

I BEGAN STUDYING with the First Chamber Dance Company, which with great fanfare had relocated from NYC to Seattle (around the same time that Pacific Northwest Ballet started), the idea being chamber dance as opposed to a big ballet company. There had always been a strong connection between the Seattle and New York ballet scenes, partly because the highly influential choreographer Robert Joffrey was a Seattleite. (It's crazy how many choreographers are from the Pacific Northwest.) The Joffrey Ballet did a Seattle summer residency every year, but I was always too young to go. Older friends had taken these workshops and then gotten into the Joffrey itself. That became my goal.

First Chamber Dance was run by a creep called Charles Bennett. The first move, on arrival, was to buy a derelict building—a nameless mess the entire time I lived there—in the Belltown district of downtown. We, as indentured servants, did the entire renovation: stripping paint, repairing, building, and cleaning mirrors and toilets. The company had a team of fifteen-to-eighteen-year-old full-on slaves. Incredible, looking back.

The First Chamber dancers themselves, all in their thirties, were glamorous in a way that hasn't been possible since the seventies. The artistic director and the costume designer, for example, who were lovers, dressed in identical one-piece bell-bottom jumpsuits with matching chain belts—impossibly gay. Sara de Luis was a wonderful teacher, a great flamenca, and Marjorie Mussman, with whom I was to have a long association, taught Limón, a technique based on the earlier movement style developed by Doris Humphrey and Charles Weidman in opposition to the strict rules of classical ballet. It was a full-time program with ballet class, men's class, partnering class, Spanish dance, modern, and jazz. Though it was basically free of charge, we had to commit to the whole thing, the building (of the building), the outreach. I have no *idea* how the company survived.

First Chamber also imported a tyrannical, notorious, excellent yet somewhat insane ballet master called Perry Brunson, who'd been with the Joffrey for many years, as had his wife (and he was the gayest thing in the world). He was revered as a teacher, hugely musical, inspiring in that way, and he arrived with a pianist, Harriet Cavalli, who moved wherever he moved and became my very closest friend. She was the best pianist I'd ever heard, the author of a rather scolding book, *Dance and Music*, that I still force on all of my accompanists. It's very good about precisely how to play for ballet class, now something of a lost art. She could reproduce any of the ballet scores and sound like a full orchestra, just by extrapolating on the piano score. She played barefoot, chain-smoking, though many years later she became diabetic and stopped playing. As a teenager, I spent a lot of time at her house drinking jugs of rosé, eating popcorn (which she taught me how to make perfectly), and talking endlessly. I learned a great deal from Harriet, a wonderful friend and inspiration to this day.

Perry Brunson, on the other hand, was a mess, bitter and cruel, though he and Harriet were close until he died. At class, if he was fucked up or hungover, he'd sit in the front in dark glasses, smoking a cigarette, and give a combination with his hands. You couldn't mark it (which I don't allow either, and by which I mean doing the moves minimally with your hands as you prerehearse them in your head, trying to learn it as you're being taught—the equivalent for singing would be humming along the first time you hear something); you couldn't lean against the barre and rest; you just had to watch it. Harriet would play a four-bar intro, and if you fucked up, he'd throw you out. His men's class was even crueler, jumping for half an hour, huge ballet jumps, dancing hard for far too long. If you did something wrong, out you went. For one class I was at the front of the barre, where you can't fake it or follow anyone else. A particular combination ended in plié, and though I ended correctly, all the other boys straightened their legs. He curtly dismissed them with "thank you, gentlemen, that'll be all" and gave me a private lesson for the endless rest of the hour. It was vengeful in the worst possible way. And he tortured the boys he had crushes on—he was in his forties and they were in their late teens— and that exploitation of the teacher-student relationship is the creepiest kind of predation. The straight boys were his prey; I was out as a queer, and glad of it, so he didn't bother me. Besides, I was busy elsewhere. I developed a huge crush on another dancer, an apprentice like me, despite the fact that he had a girlfriend, whom he later married and with whom he had kids (whom I knew). I was terribly in love, and when we were apart, I wrote him heartbroken letters, about which he was so sweet and affectionate. He later called me and said he was coming out, aged forty: who knew? It turned out he'd been gay while in the army.

Others who were in the same program remember it more fondly than I, my memories colored by the fact that, even as a teenager, I came to realize that a lot of the training was suspect. It was grueling, the pressure was horrible, and Perry worked us too hard, with the result that everybody's leg had a giant thigh, a giant calf, and a foot that couldn't point very well. Injuries were common. I'd already had that Achilles tendonitis, but when studying with Perry (after jumping up and down on one leg for an hour, doing precisely as he instructed), my knee bent backward and swelled up to the size of a gourd. I couldn't walk, and it was squishy to the touch, so I had to have it aspirated, a needle inserted to draw out the fluid. A second nurse advised me to stop dancing, if not forever then at least until the swelling had subsided, to which my reaction was of course to go back almost immediately.

That injury aside, it took me five or six years to change my anatomy after Perry's training. People come to me now at MMDG with that freakish shape. After a year or two in my company, they find themselves with a beautiful long line of balanced leg musculature. That's why my dancers look the way they do. It's what I teach.

Dancing hard is one thing; First Chamber was too hard. As a teacher, I can be demanding, even mean, but the health of my dancers comes first. I'd never do anything injurious; dancing itself is injurious enough. However, despite all the punishment, both physical and emotional—and I don't remember him fondly—I learned as much from Perry Brunson as from anyone else.

He famously said he didn't want to live past fifty. He died at forty-nine.

FIRST CHAMBER DANCE COMPANY ran a three-week summer camp in Port Townsend, which I attended three years running. Everybody in the company taught, and their boyfriends would come from New York, which meant, for example, that for one or two summers, my mime teacher, who was dating one of the dancers, was Patrick Duffy, both the *Man from Atlantis* and the man from *Dallas*.

Port Townsend was an old military base, farther west toward the Pacific, deserted except for beautiful early twentieth-century officers' houses with dormitories surrounding a parade ground, gun emplacements in case of a Japanese attack, and bunkers by the beach. It was freezing cold, perpetually pouring rain, and extremely windy. We danced all day long, stayed in dorms, watched whatever movies they screened for us (*The Passion of Joan of Arc*, *Battleship Potemkin*, and *A Dancer's World*, the great film about Martha Graham), fucked, drank, saw the aurora borealis for the first time, and then woke up and worked really hard.

In addition to the First Chamber teachers, there were guests, including the jazz teacher Jay Norman, who had danced and sung in the original Broadway cast of *West Side Story*, and a great Limón teacher, Danny Lewis, whose lover was twenty-year-old Teri Weksler. Danny was thirty. I was sixteen. He was my teacher, and Teri did the dancing for him, because he was usually too high to demonstrate. This led to a lifelong friendship. She became my teacher, then one of the founding women in the Mark Morris Dance Group. She was rational, reasonable, fascinating, and tiny—the only small being (apart from a couple of men) I ever had in the group. (Big women and small men seem to do my work better; I like them to be around the same fighting weight for partnering.) By the time I got the group together, she was already a professional dancer of renown.

Best of all, we got to make up dances. After my first exposure to Harry Partch via *The Wild Sounds of New Music*, I had found another LP, *The World of Harry Partch*, on which there was a track called "Barstow," and, aged probably sixteen, I made up a dance for some friends at the workshop, including Penny Hutchinson and this big guy Leo, not a very good dancer but a fabulous, kooky, Krishna Consciousness hippie. The dance was in eight short movements, each introducing a character, as the music does. Partch himself was on the road a lot, a hobo, and he found hitchhiker graffiti on a railing at the side of the road near Barstow, California: "Here she comes, a truck, not a fuck, but a truck. Just a truck. Hoping to get the hell out, here's my name—Johnnie Reinwald, 915 South Westlake Avenue, Los Angeles." They're beautiful texts, recited by Partch himself on the recording in what he called his "intoning voice": "I too am on the lookout for a suitable mate," "Car just passed by, make that two more, three more." He set these boring, touching, lonely inscriptions to his astonishing music. We danced to the recording.

Each of the dances starts the same, as does the music. Partch introduces them "Number One," "Number Two," and so forth. The structure is formal. The first dancer does a solo, then becomes the chorus for the next person's solo, and so on, accumulating until there are six people in total.

The choreography included citations from Chinese ballet. When Nixon visited China, PBS aired *The Red Detachment of Women*, the great ballet from the Cultural Revolution. Being a product of the People's Republic, it's simultaneously terrifying, funny, and beautiful, featuring rifles and pointe shoes. This combination of movement and music was highly inspirational to me and seemed just right for Partch's music, in which I recognized a Chinese element. Like Lou Harrison and John Cage, Partch had explored San Francisco's Chinatown in the early part of the century, when only the Chinese knew the incredible sounds of Peking opera. *Barstow*, the dance, therefore contains very distinctly stylized Chinese walks and rhythms, or what I remembered from what I'd once seen on TV. There was no video back then, but I'd memorized it and I knew it. *Barstow* also had complex rhythms like those of the Bulgarian and Macedonian dances I knew from Koleda. Partch's was difficult music, but I wasn't picking it to be modern or clever. I chose it because it was thrilling—what people called its "primitivism"—and it spoke to me (corny but true). I'd already heard a lot of world music (by which I mean simply "music"), but Partch was like the jungle: garbage, pots and pans, coconut shells.

Though I'd been studying the techniques, my exposure to actual

Modern Dance choreography had been pretty close to zero, so I was more or less making it up, but *Barstow* was my first real dance, because it was the first one that I structured formally in a way that satisfied me. Everything leading up to it was preparation.

FOR MY FINAL ENGLISH CLASS project in high school, I made up a dance. Page played the cello, and I got credit to graduate a full year early. I got credit for everything, for dancing, even I think for masturbating, simply because of the sympathy they had for my father dying. By then, I wasn't interested in school, and my father was no longer around to push me to go to college.

I had been planning for a long time to have a gap year abroad. Dance would be my passport around the world. The original concept, inspired by a Romanian woman whose class I loved at Koleda, had been to go to Bucharest for a year precollege (not that I was ever going to go to college) to study Romanian music and dancing. This was thwarted by the Ceaușescu coup. I then applied to work on an archaeological dig in Switzerland—further slave labor, the kind of thing young people are still suckered into—but on closer inspection, I decided against it. My new secret plan was to visit the smallest countries in Europe (Liechtenstein, Luxembourg, San Marino, Andorra, which no one had ever heard of at the time), to spend time in the Balkans, and, most important, to go to Spain. Being a flamenco, it was the obvious choice. The plan was to go from September through July, then move to NYC to join the Joffrey, with no thought of going back to school.

Despite the fact that my father died during the planning, my mother insisted I go. Whatever city I was in, I'd get a Social Security check from his death for $150 every month at an American Express office. The itinerary was planned out beforehand in minute detail, insanely so. We hardly did any of it, but I'd never traveled before. My companions were Linda Metzner, who danced in Koleda and had been a student at Verla's, and Nona Weatherford, the undertaker's daughter. The plan was to go on a Eurailpass with our backpacks for a couple of months, staying in hostels, ending up in Yugoslavia; then after Christmas, they'd go home while I continued on to Spain. It was also arranged that I would meet Maureen and Maxine (who, newly widowed, deserved a vacation) in Paris.

It was a fabulous European culture tour, everything you dreamed of: the sardana (a folk dance) in Barcelona, Tangier for a day by boat, Oktoberfest, Checkpoint Charlie when it was a perilous place rather than a theme park ride (though you could visit East Berlin for only a day). It was the first time I tried to get to Pompeii. (I've tried five times, it never happens, and I wonder whether it's there at all.) And we did get to go to the smallest countries and principalities: Monaco, Vatican City, Gibraltar—a rock from which you can see Africa. We couldn't afford to go to many performances, but we went to all the free *sons et lumières*, the cathedrals and museums. We did go to see some Balanchine (*Le Palais de cristal*) at the Wiener Staatsballett, where I had a fight with an elegant older lady who had reserved herself a standing room spot with a glove I ignored. I excused myself as she yelled at me in German.

In Macedonia, we traveled to Skopje and stayed with Atanas Kolarovski, choreographer of Tanec, the state dance company, at whose house I was introduced, for the first time, to the chicken we were going to eat for dinner. From there, we took an illegal day trip by bus to Petrič, Bulgaria, hidden among the regular Macedonians. The reason for this imprudence was a festival featuring dance from all the various regions of Bulgaria, and though we didn't have visas, the lure was too strong. The border patrol stopped the bus both ways, looking for people trying to illegally enter or exit. Scared to death, we tried to look as Macedonian as we could, but there was no trouble. We were seventeen.

Why would they suspect us of anything? From there we went to Athens, to all the ruins, and then by boat to a nearby whitewashed, goated island. These were dances we already knew, so we were able to walk into tavernas and join in. The reaction, initially one of surprise, became an immediate welcome. It was so satisfying.

There weren't any major disasters, except the odd missed train, though we bought too many records in East Berlin, where the state-sponsored recordings of the great orchestras were irresistible, if cumbersome. Periodically we ran out of money and slept a couple of nights in a bitterly cold train station, to be roused and moved on by the cops—nothing out of the ordinary. I was in Cape Sounion, at the very bottom of Greece, when I realized that I had inadvertently left my airplane ticket at some previous hostel. I kept this from my companions, had a quiet panic attack, and hoped that it was somewhere we might be returning to, perhaps Vienna. It was almost impossible to make an international phone call in Europe in those days, but somehow I called, got through to a concierge, and they found my ticket. A miniature miracle.

I ENDED UP IN MADRID, where I was planning to study flamenco. I had basic skills, and I was in the belly of the beast to find out more.

Flamenco's appeal had been immediate, and my passion raged for a long time. The clichés of flamenco are all true. It's arrogant, fiery, and supermasculine (even the women's dancing, which means that the women therefore have equal power to the men, unlike, for example, in classical ballet, where the women do the dancing and the men do all the portage). There is a posture of pride about flamenco, a self-possession that looks cocky. The first thing you learn is flamenco's archetypical expression (and ballet's, come to think of it), the "I smell shit" face. Then you learn the different techniques. Rhythmically, what those dancers do, second nature to them, is almost impossible, so infinitesimally subtle, yet completely over-the-top show-off. "Take that!" they seem to say as they dance. "I spit on you!"

Flamenco is originally "gypsy," from the Roma peoples of Spain and North Africa (and wherever the Roma people were, which includes the Middle East and South Asia). There's a direct relationship between flamenco, which is always solo and includes the music—the guitar playing, the singing, and the clapping—and a North Indian classical dance form, kathak, which is also always solo, all foot rhythms, turns, and arm gestures. The music itself is fascinating: Moorish, North African in origin, back when Spain was Muslim. The relevant term is *duende*, "soul," the thing inside you that makes the dance take off: the passion, the expressivity, the quick-firing capacity to improvise in a situation—the thing that Spanish people say you can't learn. But you *can*, and I felt inspired to do so.

There's a 1963 movie called *Los Tarantos*, inspired by *Romeo and Juliet*, about a *gitano* family in Barcelona (weird in itself because flamenco isn't Catalan), starring Carmen Amaya, the greatest ever flamenca, in the role of the matriarch, her last movie. She memorably dances in the dirt on a piece of wood. Her son, the Romeo character, played by the great Antonio Gades, does a number in which he dances down Las Ramblas, the pedestrian street in the middle of Barcelona, as they're hosing it down at night. Imagine *Singin' in the Rain*, only great. It's the absolute essence of flamenco, a wonder of a movie.

That's why I was in Spain.

But Spain was complicated. Generalissimo Franco was in charge, which was bad for everything. Flamenco was more or less dead, definitely old hat, and it wasn't national—Franco didn't like regional culture. No one was allowed to speak Catalan, Andalusian, Gallician, or, most pointedly, Basque.

I found a room in a pensione near the Prado belonging to an Andalusian woman and her daughter. No one spoke English, which is how I unavoidably learned Spanish. After a little while I could understand the daughter's *castellano*, but *andaluz* remained incomprehensible. This was a full cultural immersion. I went to the Prado on weekends and also to the bullfight, sitting in the cheap sun-drenched seats, where I systematically developed a huge crush on each and every matador.

I started taking classes at Amor de Dios, a bustling dance school recommended by friends in Seattle, with a teacher called Maria Magdalena in an old studio with splintery wooden floors and the smells of the perspiration of many years. I'd take two or three classes a day. This was her teaching method: Monday, hands, *just hands*; Tuesday, feet; Wednesday, turns *only*—and that's all you did, an hour of turning as this tiny Spanish woman screamed at you, and then hit you; Thursday, castanets; and Friday, finally, dance routines. She was very strict, very funny, and great. I was seventeen and made for this kind of class. And I was the only pale white boy among the Spanish, so very pale and thin that I was nicknamed Blancanieves, Snow White. I had very little money, and I ate a lot of Chinese food.

I also began studying jota, a regional dance from many different areas, the most beautiful being from Aragon. My teacher was the *jotero* Pedro Azorín, the star of *Nobleza baturra*, a famous movie set in Aragon. Jota is a real workout, very stylized. With flamenco, there's dance flamenco and sung flamenco, and it's the same with jota, though it isn't the same type of music at all and it's always for couples; the castanets are worn on your middle finger, and you shake your hands like a chimp.

I had been weighing whether I'd like Spain enough to move there and have a career, but there didn't seem to be a career to be had. The technique was great, as were the teachers and the guitarists (many of whom were Japanese), but what little flamenco work there might have been—cruise ships and tourist shows—wasn't appealing. Not that there was a career as a *jotero* available either, but it was livelier and more fun, and I ended up doing more of it.

For several months, I danced with a fly-by-night ballet company with the grand name of the Royal Chamber Ballet of Madrid, which had seen me in class and needed men to tour. The touring was mostly regional, little theaters in little towns, though we did go as far as the Canary Islands, closer to Africa than Spain. It kept me in money and therefore food.

I was on my own, making some kind of a living, and this felt like independence. I'd started making friends, gay dancers, and I even had an encounter with an older gentleman (he was in his twenties!) whom I met at a bar and on whom I developed a big crush. I'd even go so far as to say I stalked him a little. We had a couple of dates, some sex, and that's when I realized that I was unequivocally queer, that it was a one-way street. I wrote my mother an aerogram—"I am gay!"—and she replied, "We love you." She knew, of course she knew; I also knew she knew. Her only worry, she told me, was that she didn't want my life to be any more difficult.

It was certainly more difficult at that moment for one very specific reason. In Franco's Spain, homosexuality was illegal, and that law was enforced. The nightlife was fabulous in Madrid, where some of the bars closed at one a.m., then clandestinely reopened as gay bars. I didn't have a lot of sex, frankly, but I did have a lot of gay life. There was one very delicate guy we called Swanson, hair bleached blond like Gloria, who was arrested for public effeminacy. I wasn't there that night, but I saw others herded away. It was very dangerous—a repressive society and an oppressive atmosphere—and I couldn't take it. The timing of my coming-out wasn't coincidental.

Now, people think, "Hey, I am gay!" But it used to be that you *couldn't* be gay. Not only in Spain. In America too. It was against the law. I tell my younger gay dancers, "I worked hard so you don't even have to pay attention to the fact that you're gay. I was supergay on your behalf for the future." Now things are turning back again.

I WAS A FOLK DANCER, so everyone rightly sees folk dancing in my work, but it's rarely an actual quote. Mostly it's a paraphrase or an homage. Holding hands and going in a circle isn't a dance that belongs to anybody in particular. It's *everybody's* dance. I've occasionally made very specific citations of a dance, and I've done that very rarely with Spanish dance. *Four Saints in Three Acts*, however, has a jota, a sevillana, and a sardana, the national dance of Catalunya, and these are direct quotes.

Another dance of mine—*From Old Seville*—a novelty number, features a sevillana, an old folk dance for couples. If you go to a fiesta in Seville, the music starts and everybody in the room—male, female, young and old, drunk and sober—does the sevillana; mine was an exact copy. It's a beautiful form, always in four verses, short phrases that get more complicated as they go on.

The rule of my dance—for a man (me), a woman (Lauren Grant), and a bartender—was that we had to drink an entire bottle of Rioja in the dance's six-minute duration; that was the assignment, my dancing version of a drinking game, performed to a 1970s recording of a sevillana, "A esa mujer" by Manuel Requiebros. John Heginbotham, the original bartender, poured three glasses of wine at a high-top. I drank one, he drank one, and then Lauren did too. We danced the first verse, stopped, and, during the intro to verse two, went back to the bar, where we each took another glass of wine. Four verses, twelve drinks, three slightly drunk dancers. John smoked a cigar throughout, which was vile. We once shared a dressing room with Meredith Monk, and she was doing her vocal exercises while I was trying to teach John how to smoke a cigar. Bad idea.

From Old Seville was a pièce d'occasion that we've repurposed for other occasions, and is one of the few dances that I still perform, most recently during a program of *Solos, Duets and Trios*. Lauren performs a textbook sevillana four times, whereas my part—flamenco clichés, including the jacket flashing that has become a trademark of contemporary flamenco—is purely improvised, variations that become wackier as I try to disrupt and mess with her as the dance progresses. Between the verses at the high-top, we drink and I get increasingly carried away with Lauren, and the sexy bartender, and myself. She's the control and I'm the variable. It's an ideal dance for me.

IN MY EUROPEAN ABSENCE, Uncle Jim had died. Grandpa Bill died just after I returned, which was when Mabel moved in with us. That made one major death a year from 1973 to 1975: Dad, Jim, then Bill. Devastating. Maxine lived thirty-five years after Dad's death but never had a boyfriend.

There were now three generations of Morris women in the same house, and me again. (In fact, a Morris has lived there to this day, and it's now the home of Maureen and her partner of thirty years, V'kee.) Dad's death had left Maxine cash-strapped. None of us can now remember whether it was because he was fifty-nine when he died, one year short of the required sixty, or because he'd worked only twenty-four years rather than the required twenty-five, but the school district had provided no pension on what was basically a technicality. On top of that, he'd just been getting ready to pay the mortgage insurance, but he hadn't quite got around to it—the bill was sitting right there on the desk when he died—so there was still a mortgage to pay. There was a little life insurance, but it was hard for Maxine. She couldn't even get a credit card. Resourceful and pragmatic as ever, she went to work for the city engineering office for the next ten years.

I filled my time as I could, resuming my studies with First Chamber and teaching Spanish dance at Verla's, but a lot of my friends had moved on, some to New York City, and I felt I was done with Seattle. I occasionally went to Anacortes to teach Croatian dance to the people who started the Vela Luka Dance Ensemble, and did a little bit of art school modeling with Penny. Chad got us into it. The money wasn't bad, but it was excruciatingly hard work. I'm quite comfortable with being naked—that aspect was kind of sexy—but I had no idea how grueling it would be. You couldn't suffer any more than twenty minutes at a stretch, and twenty minutes was unbearably long. It was the opposite of dancing. But it's some consolation to think there may be some amateur nude portraits of me lingering in the thrift stores of the Pacific Northwest.

My dance *Ženska*, which translates to "Women's" in Bulgarian, is about all I have to show for this interim year in Seattle, a five-minute solo I made for Penny, set to the fourth movement of Bartók's Fourth String Quartet. The dance was based on Macedonian and Bulgarian dances, and a direct result of my European travels. I did it myself a few times as a solo. I revised it for our first company show in New York, adding a little bit of the Bulgarian women's choral music, the Voix Mystères, and made it a duet for two women, Penny Hutchinson and Hannah Kahn.

Weary of Seattle, I knew it was time to move to New York as planned. Maureen and Maxine drove me to the airport to see me off at the gate. Maureen cried. As far as she was concerned, I was leaving forever.

IT WASN'T THE FIRST TIME I'd been to New York City.

When I was fifteen, Verla sent me to a weeklong dance conference. Such conferences still exist. The registrant learns jazz from this person, tap from that person, all day, then takes those routines back to the studio and teaches them—a lot of my company dancers went through that machinery.

I was teaching already and somewhat responsible (for a fifteen-year-old), so Verla sent me to a conference at the old Biltmore Hotel. She paid for the whole thing and gave me some spending money. I flew by myself and was treated to lunch by older ladies entrusted with my welfare. The conference itself wasn't much, but that wasn't the point. Verla was testing me to see whether I was mature and trustworthy enough to be a representative of her school. I brought back a couple of routines, but I didn't teach the dumbest dances anyway.

On the second morning, I was wandering around being a tourist on Forty-Second Street. When I returned to my room at the hotel, the door didn't have a chance to close behind me before a man pushed his way in. He yanked the phone cord out of the wall and said, "Give me your money, don't tell anybody, and wait ten minutes before you do anything." He'd followed me up from the street. I must have just looked like an average victim tourist mark. I did as he said, gave him all Verla's cash, waited ten minutes, went down to the desk, told them, and phoned home weeping. It was arranged that I receive more money to live on, and I stayed the week, finished the conference, and then went home.

And now I was going back.

In rehearsal for *Brummagem* with Laura Bail, Pacific
Northwest Ballet, 1978. *(Chris Bennion)*

Four

Brummagem

I moved in with Ray Wolf, a friend from First Chamber, who was already in the city. We split the rent of his apartment in Washington Heights—at the very top of Manhattan, where the George Washington Bridge crosses over the Hudson from Jersey—and I started taking classes with Marjorie Mussman, who'd also moved back to NYC. I went to many classes—David Howard was the choice of the serious ballet types; Maggie Black, so popular she had to turn people away, though I couldn't stand her; and later on, Jocelyn Lorenz, a very fine ballet teacher—but Marjorie's were the best, an immediate benefit of my move. The Seattle diaspora congregated at Marjorie's—Penny took class there too—and it's where I met my dear friend Tina Fehlandt, not to mention Ruth Davidson, both of whom were to become founding members of the Mark Morris Dance Group.

Tina was one of those women who had wanted to be a great ballet dancer but was dissuaded by ballet's systematic body stereotyping, even though she was a fabulous dancer. She was big and she was strong—can you imagine such qualities in a ballet dancer?—but she remembers herself as "chubby little Tina" trying to get her life going, on the point of giving up dancing. She was wild too. On the occasion of her thirtieth birthday, she invited all of her ex-boyfriends to her party and went around slapping each of them across the face in turn. By the time the party was in full swing, she was out cold, facedown on her bed in her leather miniskirt.

Ruth, who had been to SUNY Purchase (where you went if you didn't get into Juilliard), was a big, fearless, long-limbed dancer—the finest imaginable—who went about it with such abandon that at every show, predictably, she'd fall down. I never minded. It was very exciting. (In fact, it turned out she couldn't see—after she got glasses, she never fell again.) She was fabulous, enthusiastic, quite vain, and very gullible. She never stopped talking and regularly screamed with laughter. I could never quite figure out how she thought.

I was nineteen, turning twenty; it was our nation's bicentennial, and my nephew Tyler was born (to my sister Marianne). I wasn't teaching or making any money—my entire income consisted solely of the Social Security from my father's death, money left specifically to me—so after a couple of months, I went to my first ever New York City audition. I had been hoping to get into the Joffrey, but it was the Eliot Feld Ballet that was looking for men.

I got the job.

ELIOT FELD WAS A GOOD DANCER, a precocious choreographer—he made his first piece for American Ballet Theatre when he was eighteen—and then a famously demanding and impatient boss, traits I may have learned from him. Through him I met some wonderful people with whom I later ended up working, for example James Maddalena, the great baritone, and Gladys Celeste, Eliot's marvelous pianist. One of my first gigs with Eliot, when I was too new to be cast, was turning Gladys's pages at the outdoor Filene Center at Wolf Trap in Virginia, for Prokofiev's fiendishly complicated Fifth Piano Concerto. I found myself in the pit with this giant orchestra, and though I could read the music, I couldn't read it quite fast enough . . . I will never ever forget the quicksand feeling as I tried to keep up. Terrifying, like a dream.

I'd commute to company rehearsal—a full hour each way, from the 181st Street subway station all the way down to Fiftieth Street on the 1 train, then across on the E, then up to Seventy-Fifth on the 6—at the Harkness House on the Upper East Side, owned by the madcap heiress Rebekah Harkness, who'd run the Harkness Ballet for years and then started the Harkness Foundation. This fancy Gilded Age mansion had been converted into studios where many choreographers worked, including Eliot, who based himself there until he moved downtown to take up residence at the Public Theater. It was a wacky fantasy palace— fireplaced, chandeliered, and tapestried—and a huge pain in the ass to get to. In the lobby, there was a rotating display with a jeweled cremation urn, the *Chalice of Life*, designed by Dalí, commissioned by Mrs. Harkness, which eventually held her ashes, though apparently they didn't all fit. You then entered a minuscule gated elevator that ascended three or four flights past bejeweled walls decorated with mosaics— glued-on shit—and murals.

After a scant two weeks' rehearsal, we embarked on an eleven-week State Department tour of Latin America. Back then, the State Department was a goodwill international propaganda arm of diplomacy, which brought over American art to show the people. These wonderful trips were part of the itineraries of many dance companies; then it all ground to a halt (and seems unlikely to be revived anytime soon). Everywhere we went seemed to be in the middle of a coup d'état, a junta singing the new national anthem composed the night before, with machine guns, militias, and gangs everywhere. It would have been scary, were we not endlessly performing. The United States had no trade with China, but in Venezuela I saw actual objects and artifacts from the People's Republic of China, including a program from the original production of my beloved *Red Detachment of Women*. It was an adventure. We sometimes shared three to a room—three young men to a hotel room—imagine!—as we toured Eliot's version of, appropriately enough, Stravinsky's *L'Histoire du soldat*, in which I played a soldier. Being the new boy, I still wasn't in much, and found myself most valued as a Spanish interpreter, though I did get to gamble away my per diem at the hotel casino. What I did most of all, as I recall, was dance a lot around the periphery of rehearsal. I'd happily assassinate anyone who does that at one of my rehearsals, but Eliot intuited that I was a choreographer in the making. I even fondly imagined that a couple of my steps showed up in his works, but then I did have such a high opinion of myself. Though I was by no means a draw for his company, Eliot trusted me with a few of his parts (including a promotion to the role of the pimp in the Stravinsky).

I stayed with Eliot for a year and a half, and left because I no longer liked it. It was too heteronormative, too "blokey," veering toward Jerome Robbins, and I was already tired of that. I don't remember whether he officially fired me, but I no longer wanted to be in a ballet company. I didn't want to wear tights and shoes.

But Eliot was a very good music man, and I even ended up choreographing some of the very same music. In 1977, I was in the original cast of his dance *A Footstep of Air*, set to Beethoven's arrangements of British folk songs. When I started working on my own dance to some of those same songs in 2009, I remember thinking, "I *know* this." I did the same with another piece of music he used beautifully, Samuel Barber's *Excursions for Piano*. In 2008, I thought I'd discovered it myself. I'd completely forgotten. The memory simply gets too full to hang on to everything, but it goes to show how deep Eliot's influence was, particularly musically, even thirty years later.

Right at the end of my tenure, his company moved to 890 Broadway, where Eliot invested in the top two floors. This incredible building was real old Broadway, a factory for Broadway productions and a home for its artisans and tradespeople. Theoni V. Aldredge, the most famous costumer in New York City, had her shop there, as did Woody Shelp, the ancient milliner, considered the greatest in Broadway history; there was even a cobbler. American Ballet Theatre then moved into three floors in the same building.

To this day, anytime you visit 890 Broadway, it's either Joel Grey or Bebe Neuwirth in the still manually operated elevator. And if you want to run into a sexy ballet dancer, you only have to stand outside.

A FEW MONTHS after I arrived, I moved into an apartment with Penny down in the East Village opposite the New York City Marble Cemetery on Second and Second. It was a fifth-floor walk-up (doable when you're twenty) with a bathtub in the kitchen, at the outlandish rent of $150 a month. My commute was greatly improved. We brought up a mattress we'd found on the street (because we were new in town and didn't know any better), around which we sprinkled a ring of boric acid as a moat to keep cockroaches from making love on it. Penny and I didn't make love in it either, though we did occasionally co-sleep.

Penny was a pixie without being small, a Limón dancer, erect with a very long waist. She'd moved to NYC a year or so previously, and in fact I'd choreographed her solo audition for Juilliard, set to the overture of *The Fantasticks*, the best Broadway show ever written. She went through many different looks, and our apartment share happened to coincide with her becoming a lesbian feminist, by which I mean an actual radical separatist. Unfairly cast in a new role as the male oppressor,

I'd walk in on one of her meetings in our apartment to general horror. She found herself temporarily banished. Then she became a radical lipstick lesbian. She's always been a mystic spiritualist, a fairies-at-the-bottom-of-my-garden type who's devoted herself to various gurus, and she did a lot of drugs when I didn't, but now she's totally straight edge, a Hindu-inspired meditator, and a professor of dance. But she's still quirky. She once fixed her radiator with Reiki. I suggested that perhaps they'd turned it on downstairs, but that's not the way she thinks.

Penny was a great dancer, very soulful, and I admire her more than almost anyone. When the dance group got going, people saw Ruth Davidson as the biggest star, but Penny was deeper.

IT'S SUPPOSEDLY ALWAYS boom or bust with dance, and if those are the only descriptive options, then at the precise moment I arrived in New York City in the late seventies, it was BOOM! Certainly, interest in dance was unusually high, much higher than it is today—the ballet film *Turning Point*, featuring Baryshnikov, was a huge hit the following year—and various foundations were pouring money into experimental downtown (as it was called) choreography. There were so many Modern Dance companies (many of which existed solely to justify the glorified hobbies of their choreographers), a few of which I danced for, and all of which would be financially unviable these days; and there were so many little one-hundred-seat theaters in which to dance, hardly any of which exist anymore. Put simply, there was work. And where there's work, there's a boom. In hindsight, however, it was really just a lot of stuff. And whenever there's a lot of stuff, much of it is very good, but not all of it is great. I saw *everything*.

I particularly loved Twyla Tharp's work. She had the best Modern Dance company in New York; there was unbelievable virtuosity and intelligence in her dancers and in her own dancing. Penny and I had seen a very good piece of hers in Seattle, *Deuce Coupe* (the first "crossover" ballet), which featured her company *plus* the Joffrey *plus* the music of the Beach Boys *plus*—radically for the time—a graffitist spray-painting live. We loved it so much. There was one part where a dancer went through the lexicon of ballet alphabetically: assemblé, battement, changement, developpé, échappé, failli, grand jeté . . . (I'm getting stuck at *h*. I'm making those up, but what can they have done for *h*?) The point is that it was an entire glossary of ballet terms, as if reading through the dictionary, a genuinely funny idea. At that time there was free dancing at the Seattle Center—swing was just coming back for one of its many revivals. You'd buy a milkshake and dance in a crowd that was a mix of old people and complete crazies. There's nothing more embarrassing than dancers out dancing, doing lifts and so forth—you never want to coincide with a dance company on a layover at an airport, all that public stretching—but ignoring that, Penny and I would improvise in the style of Twyla Tharp (or what we thought it to be), because hers was by far the grooviest and most interesting. I didn't see her actual company until I went to New York. In 1976, she was premiering her signature ballet *Push Comes to Shove* at American Ballet Theatre, featuring the young Mr. Baryshnikov.

At the time, I didn't like Merce Cunningham's work very much, but I went because I felt it was my job to see all the dance I could. I didn't know Merce personally, though I knew a lot of his dancers from Marjorie's class, along with dancers from Paul Taylor's company. I found his work as pleasurable as cod-liver oil; I could tell the dancers were great, but the shows themselves were lost on me. I got nothing from the music, and the choreography seemed random. It was rigorous but not very engaging, and at the time it just completely passed me by. It wasn't until much later, 1984, that I saw the dance that converted me: *Quartet*, for five dancers, including the sixty-five-year-old Merce, which automatically made it somewhat about the end of his dancing career. Previously all his work had seemed more or less the same, but this piece transformed me. I was fully im*merce*d. I realized that he'd been basically making up the same dance his entire life, because he couldn't get enough of one concept: the body in space and time. That's it. An entire life of curiosity, spent asking that question, and coming up with beautiful solutions. After this blinding insight, my friend and dancer Guillermo Resto and I would go to Merce shows and, as everyone was leaving, scream "BRAVO!" until we were totally hoarse.

With Merce Cunningham, 2007.

I also saw the work of Lucinda Childs, a piece her company does to this day called *Dance* (a fittingly bold title, as far as I was concerned, since I thought it the greatest dance I'd ever seen). A seemingly simple combination of upright moves, it was a collaboration between three similarly minded geniuses—Lucinda, the composer Philip Glass, and the painter Sol LeWitt. Lucinda's dance was the equivalent of LeWitt's conceptual art: a vertical line, a horizontal line, and both diagonals in every possible combination, then *done*. That was the finished object. End. Everything was beautiful, in both design and concept.

Lucinda herself seemed glacial (in temperament rather than speed) and scared the life out of me; she was so erect and glamorous, all sculpted cheekbones and hair pulled tightly back. I always felt like I was saying the wrong thing around her (and still do), but I later plucked up the courage to ask her out to lunch at the Noho Star, during which I admitted I'd stolen from her—moves and conceptual ideas—right from the beginning. Of course, she didn't mind at all. I borrowed many devices I thought were great, be they from Lucinda, Gerald Arpino, Busby Berkeley, or Paul Taylor. I also worshipped Meredith Monk, whose "mixed-media theater piece"—though she calls it an opera and so should I—*Quarry* (1976) was a life-changing experience. In those days, her performances started with a blackout that lasted for exactly one minute, just long enough for people to freak out.

Meredith, Lucinda, Trisha Brown, not to mention Yvonne Rainer— these powerful genius women—had all been part of Judson Dance Theater, a collective of dancers who performed at the Judson Memorial Church in the Village in the early 1960s, which was a reaction against not only ballet but Modern Dance itself in its heroics and theatrical artifice, its relationship to music. It started as happenings, anti-performances that spawned Yvonne Rainer's NO! manifesto delineating everything the movement rejected, including spectacle, virtuosity, style, camp, "moving or being moved." It was egalitarian, in that there wasn't a hierarchy of beauty or of skill; sometimes improvised, sometimes formless, it blurred distinctions between participant and viewer. The emphasis therefore turned to improvisational music and improvisational dancing that then became conceptual—"postmodern" is a word that can be accurately used—including Lucinda Childs's *Carnation* (1964), during which she puts rollers in her hair, and if you stretch the definition, Paul Taylor's piece, one from *Seven New Dances* (actually from 1957), where he stood still as the time was given over the phone (for which Louis Horst's famous review in *Dance Observer* was four inches of blank space).

Another important arts collective, an offshoot of Judson Memorial Church, that came out of Yvonne Rainer and Dancers was Grand Union—David Gordon, Trisha, Yvonne, and Deborah Hay—a post-hippie moment that left its mark. It was feminist, queer (but not quite queer enough), and chaotic, inspired by Fluxus and Dada. Very few people saw it (and I wasn't one of them), but everyone who was there, if they didn't walk out, found their lives changed. Some elements appealed to me a lot—the emphasis on the humanity of the body.

In a recent article, Joan Acocella wrote in *The New Yorker* that whenever someone just stops dancing and walks offstage, it's because of Judson Church. I prefer to dance people on and off. There's a modicum of improvisation in my work, but it's disguised; likewise there's minimalism, repetition, and systems but always in the service of something else. The art movements of that period were fully influential on me, yet, in terms of performance, I was never worried by the same things that worried these choreographers. Nor did I have to be, because they had been, so they freed me to be something else.

That's incidentally why people were so happy with early musical minimalism. It was no longer aleatoric, dependent on the throw of dice. Beauty had made a welcome return. It was no longer John Cage or Morton Feldman, those pioneers of indeterminate music; it wasn't the uncompromising serial music of the Darmstadt school of Stockhausen; it wasn't only experimental computer music. Even though there was often no more than a single major triad in minimalism, the tune was back, and the appeal was that music was consonant once more. It was no longer purely about theory, dissonance, harshness, and musique concrète. When Philip Glass added a third chord, it was like the sun rising again. People were relieved to return to consonance, suspension, and resolution, and that's what appealed to me too.

My spirit, despite being drawn to occasional ugliness, was more aligned with Western hymn harmony, which is why I loved Virgil Thomson, Henry Cowell, hula, baroque music, gospel music, and country music. Charles Ives's music appealed immediately, but Boulez's didn't, though I appreciated his music intellectually. The interwar modernism of the music elite writing for each other is certainly fascinating per se, but not to listen to. I don't particularly like listening to John Cage either. (Though I reject the idea that he was more of a philosopher than a musician. He was fully a musician.)

One reason I'm drawn to Indian classical music is the skill of the improvisation. The chaos of free jazz comes nowhere near it. Indian music is so sophisticated that I can't even keep the beat after a while. At a concert, I'll look around to find myself the only one on a different beat. It's a different galaxy of intelligence that I was never able to find in jazz, let alone the Grateful Dead, whose music I've always detested. I still don't find myself drawn to free jazz or late bebop. In fact, I wasn't really into jazz at all—much of John Coltrane and Miles Davis is incomprehensible to me—until I realized that ragtime was jazz, the blues was jazz, and big band (which I hated when my father played it but I now like) was jazz too. And then I fell in love with certain things: Erroll Garner (far and away my favorite pianist), Art Tatum, and of course the blues singer Bessie Smith, with whom my sister was obsessed and I am to this day.

Everything you wanted was in New York City. It was *the* boom time for both ballet and dance. I saw one of Martha Graham's greatest pieces, *Clytemnestra*, to music by Halim El-Dabh. Balanchine had his final hit, *Vienna Waltzes*, in 1977. And it wasn't just dance but all the arts. Shakespeare in the Park was in its infancy. I saw the director Andrei Serban's work *The Cherry Orchard* at Lincoln Center with Meryl

Streep and Irene Worth, and his incredible *Agamemnon*. *A Chorus Line* had just moved to Broadway from the Public Theater. With friends from Eliot Feld, I saw one of Dolly Parton's first appearances at the Bottom Line—plank tables, bottles of beer, and Dolly and her band—not long after she left Porter Waggoner. At the Felt Forum (now the Theater at Madison Square Garden) that same year, we saw the Texas Playboys. Bob Wills had died three years earlier, but it was his band of old farts in string ties, fronted by the young genius Merle Haggard. This was music that, to the bemusement of some, I'd revisit for my own dances for the dance group within a few years.

I WENT DIRECTLY from Eliot's company to Lar Lubovitch's. It was momentous. I'd read about Lar (who by the way isn't Swedish; Lar is short for Larry) in *Dance Magazine*. His work looked like sexy, beautiful hippie dancing. Dancers want to do it because it looks like it feels great. And it does.

So I went to Broadway, the Uris Theatre (now the Gershwin) on Fifty-First Street, to see Maurice Béjart's company, the Ballet du XXe Siècle, on tour from Brussels. (If only I'd known what the future held.) It was an expensive night out. I was used to "second acting" shows—I'd arrive late, mingle with the intermission audience enjoying their cigarettes outside, then sneak in off the street for the second half. But Lar's piece *Marimba* was in the first half, so this was a ticket I actually had to pay for. *Marimba* was the most beautiful thing I'd ever seen, set to the music of Steve Reich (whom I had heard previously only on that little bonus single), an exquisite piece to this day, *Music for Mallet Instruments, Voices, and Organ*. The dancing was trancey and I was transported. I lost my shit. When I joined Lar's company, *Marimba*, as luck would have it, was the very first thing I learned. It was challenging but immediately comfortable: flowing, traily, and deeply satisfying. You really felt like you were doing something. For the first time, and at last, I was dancing the way I felt like I should.

The company was only eight people, including Lar, who was himself a great dancer, Rob Besserer (his muse and boyfriend, my friend ever since, the original Drosselmeier in *The Hard Nut*, and also the first person to whom I taught my dance *The Vacant Chair*), and Susan Weber (who has also remained a dear friend and twenty years later was assisting me at San Francisco Ballet). Lar was "difficult," stormy (he threw the odd chair in rehearsal, which was allowed back then), and really smart, not exactly a hermit but a shy man who avoided crowds. He was gay, of course, and male choreographers weren't gay back then, by which I mean that every single one *was*, but officially they weren't.

Rehearsals took place far from the palatial splendor of Harkness House or 890 Broadway in a loft on Eighteenth Street that Lar shared with Rob. Lar probably built the interior himself because he'd been a carpenter, and in fact had a steel plate in his head because, while working with a crowbar, he hit himself and was hospitalized, out cold for hours. He'd intended to be a painter but became a fabulous choreographer. You can picture that loft quite clearly, because it served as Bill Murray's character Jeff's apartment in *Tootsie*. Lar and Rob moved out for a couple of months during the shooting, for which they were handsomely reimbursed, and moved back in to find it had been completely destroyed by the camera crew. That's my memory anyway. Rob claims the apartment was a wreck to begin with, and that the film crew actually left a lot of good things around, painted it, and put up new venetian blinds! One of us is right.

Lar was also a big pothead; he'd stop rehearsals, go to the partially walled-off portion where he lived (though the loft walls didn't go up to the ceiling), and return anywhere from ten to ninety minutes later. While he was gone, we'd hang out, rehearse a little bit, or sit around the table and talk as the smoke wafted out. They gave classes up there too; Rob's bedroom served as the women's dressing room. Madonna, then a student, would sit at the elevator to take the money and names so she could get a free class.

When I was with the company, Lar did a wonderful piece, *North Star*, to the music of Philip Glass at his earliest and most exciting. The dance was semi-improvisatory, a precise technique I use occasionally, in which the dancers, under close direction and with specific instructions, make it up until it's fixed. Lar's fabulous imaginative leap for the rippling, swoony dance of *North Star* was that the dancers were all parts of the same human body, with a quartet for the arms, a quartet for the legs, and one each for the torso and head. The dance was based on moves done by Rob, which we the dancers would then perform in a larger-scale version—he'd kick, for example, and the two people who were that particular leg would run out and run back in. When I was in the original cast, this beautiful dance had yet to be fixed, but now people would learn it from a video, not necessarily knowing the idea behind it (or the work that went into it).

Despite my love for Lar's work, I grew tired of it and left after about a year and a half (which is roughly how long I stayed with every company). He was hard to work for, as I am, but as far as I was concerned, he wasn't choreographing enough; I wanted more new material. However, despite my departure, our professional association wasn't over. After slamming the phone down on each other a few times ("I'll never work with you again!" "Fuck you!"), he called me up out of the blue. "I never thought I'd call you again," he said, "but I have a favor to ask." His dancer, my friend Harry Laird, was injured, and Lar needed someone immediately to cover his parts on a nine-week State Department tour of Asia: would I do it as a favor, *tomorrow*? To which my response was "Let-me-think-about-it-okay-fine." From that moment on, Lar and I were friends.

In fact, I hardly even had to perform on that tour—Rob and other good friends reunited to go to Korea, Japan, Thailand, Malaysia—which culminated in my first trip to Indonesia. It had been such a grueling itinerary (for those actually dancing) that the State Department finally gave us two days off in Bali, which was the beginning of a lifetime obsession.

On State Department–sponsored tours, the relevant ambassador threw a party at his house, and in Jakarta we were lucky enough to meet a couple from the United Nations who took us to a dance club where I witnessed a kind of social interaction the likes of which I'd never seen before. It was a dime-a-dance kind of place, and if it wasn't a whorehouse, that's only because sex wasn't the principal feature. The central idea, like in a hostess bar in Tokyo, was that the male customer felt fabulous on the way home from work with someone who wasn't necessarily his wife.

Inside that beautiful dimly lit ballroom, the men, in their short-sleeved batik shirts, sandals, and slacks, sat in twos and threes drinking Bintang beer, while the ladies—beautifully dressed in outfits similar to the ones they wore for temple: high heels, lace bodices, and ankle-length sarongs beneath big round black-lacquered Imelda Marcos hairdos—sat apart, waiting for someone to buy them a drink or ask for a dance.

The music, to which I became quite devoted, was jaipongan, a hybrid East/West popular dance music style in Indonesia, always sung in the local language—highly amplified with electric bass, saxophone, some gamelan instruments, a drum kit. When the band started up, the men and women, all of whom were familiar with the dances, would line up separately, facing each other down the hall. The music was full of surprising stops and starts, and the men did a full martial arts dance routine, while the women (conversing throughout) did their beautiful classical Javanese hand dancing. Given that the lines faced each other, it was as if the men were endlessly attacking and the women deflecting.

They knew precisely when the song ended, I had no idea, and the overall effect as it built to a climax was thrilling. I actually dared to dance once or twice. In these instances, I only try not to stick out.

On that first trip, we were housed in the most glamorous hotel I'd ever set foot in, a five-star beachfront property with beautiful gardens, wonderful room service, and AC. (When I went back there more recently, knowing Bali as I now do, I hated it.) Although we weren't performing, the people from the embassy entrusted with our care welcomed us. The expats were happy to inform us that we'd missed the boat, that Bali's glory was thirty years past. That had been the renaissance of Balinese art—the Indonesian National Awakening—when Walter Spies, the primitivist painter, was resident, along with Colin McPhee, the Canadian composer, who transcribed Balinese music for piano, which he then recorded with his friend Benjamin Britten. They lived in a benevolent but basically colonial way, helping to revive the lost arts—dance and music, the old style of painting. This revival, particularly of dance music, was astonishingly successful. The purity of some of it is in doubt, but it's legit simply because it *happened*. The renaissance worked.

Before the war, under Dutch rule, Bali had become a tourist spot for Europeans and Australians; Charlie Chaplin holidayed in the big Western hotel on Sanur Beach. Those were the glory days, when this incredible paradise was a Hollywood destination, before the Japanese took over and the Dutch were thrown out. Indonesia was in terrible shape during World War II.

And, to this day, no matter how we try to ruin it, Bali remains great. You might walk into the fanciest hotel with musicians playing in the lobby and imagine it's for the tourists, but they would be doing precisely the same thing at their village temple. The dancers might be teachers or computer programmers, or they might work at the car rental place, but they're all involved.

My Indian friend Lakshmi Viswanathan, who visits Bali often from Chennai, says it's like going back in time to prehistoric early Hinduism. They're worshipping deities unknown for the last five hundred years. Bali is the only Hindu animist island in Indonesia—everywhere else is Muslim—and everyone is either deeply religious and superstitious or not at all (but honor the fact that their parents are). They believe in magic, evil spirits, and good karma, but the sanctity of religious culture is a given. Everyone has a little temple in their yard where they pray and make offerings four or five times a day. It's not a big deal: "I just have to go and pray, you wait right here." It's how I imagine it was when poetry and singing were the same thing in the ancient world. It's the perfect blend for me, the way I imagine that religious culture used to be.

I've seen very great art and had—if you'll allow me—deep spiritual experiences in Bali. Though the concierge can't tell you where that day's ceremonies are, the housekeepers can, and anywhere you drive you might come upon a spontaneous festival of some kind. You'll follow the sound of a gamelan and find yourself welcomed—everyone is welcome—to, say, the Nyabutan, the hundred-day naming ceremony, where they touch a baby's feet to the ground for the first time since its birth—the idea being that they've decided this baby is viable (since it's managed to survive one hundred days) and they're therefore ready to grant it a name. At the temple, the baby's feet are ceremonially placed on the ground, and the baby is accepted on earth. Then there's a party.

When we were there with Lar that first time, we found out about the forthcoming dedication of a temple's gamelan. It took place in a temple hall, just columns and a roof, and we, in appropriate sarongs, were the guests of honor. The guests of honor found themselves in a particularly receptive state because we'd all just eaten banana omelets with magic mushrooms. You could get that in any restaurant then; it was part of their religious ritual, like peyote in Mexico. Now it's harder to find and there's a lot of fake psilocybin, but you can still get a cup of tea in the mountains. Sometimes you were ripped off—sandy mushrooms—but in this instance we were high on tea and omelets.

Rob and I, and a few others, the only white people, sat and watched as the elders of the village filed in. Outside, people crowded around to watch. Then the ceremony began, speeches and singing, and finally the musicians who prayed, thanked everyone, thanked the instruments. Then there was silence as everyone freaked out (though it's possible that was just us), during which eternity I was chain-smoking clove cigarettes. The only way I could tell that time was passing was when they burned my fingers. Then came the moment of dedication. They hit a loud BONG on the gong, and, as the sound breathed life into the sacred gamelan, everyone screamed. The ridiculous giant white people were in heaven, out of our trees, hypnotized by this crazy spectacle.

They then did a dance in which an old ugly fisherman, all eyebrows and conical hat, came upon a mermaid with a sarong tail. He looked at her, realizing she was a mermaid, and expressed in mime, "How am I supposed to fuck her if she doesn't have a pussy?" That was the moment I finally understood about mermaids—the irony of the sirens in the *Odyssey*—though the five-year-olds, who were in on the joke, were also screaming with laughter. It was the dirtiest dance I ever saw in my life, and we were truly shocked and delighted.

I've visited Bali many times over the intervening years, and I've had the same driver for my last three or four trips. He knows what I like. Once he accompanied me to a particular funeral as my guide and interpreter. We fell in with the men following the gamelan that ended up at the cremation grounds, where they were burning three different bodies. (A cremation is as great a financial commitment as a wedding: you might put someone in cold storage in a morgue for years, until it's the right day and you have enough money.) On this particular day, there was a poor person's cremation, with no more than a couple of instruments and some potato chips; then a middle-sized one; then a rich person's cremation, with hundreds of guests in attendance, a full banquet, a big gamelan, and a fancy pyre with flaming gas jets. (Sometimes the various gamelans all play whatever they are playing, regardless of the others: no one seems to notice or mind.)

"Come," this guy said to me as he tapped the ground beside him, "sit with me." As we sat in the little shade afforded by my umbrella, he said, "So that's my mother they're burning. She died two years ago!"

Then we ate ice cream.

I WAS NEVER without a job long enough for it to be scary, and my next stop post-Lar was with Hannah Kahn. Through classes, I'd again met up with Teri Weksler (now "Winkie," as I've called her ever since), who'd taught me Limón in Washington at the summer workshop and was now a year or two ahead of Penny at Juilliard. Hannah, a Juilliard-graduated choreographer (she'd been tormented there for being "big-boned"), was taking classes at Marjorie's too and asked me to be in her next concert.

Hannah was very intellectual, smarter than I, and we spent a lot of time at her loft, drinking and talking philosophy—for me, this was high-level intellectualism. She was a very sociable, warmhearted Marxist (though I don't know if she'd describe herself that way), always questioning and challenging. She choreographed music I loved, very meticulously, in puzzles. Hers was a completely different paradigm from any other dancing that had previously been asked of me. For the first time the choreography was simultaneously intellectually appealing *and* physically satisfying. Some of it was task based, almost like a theater game. For example, she might have you imagine an invisible ring of a particular dimension in a particular position through which, without its moving, you had to thread your body. Her work was non-intuitive, intellectually rigorous, and conceptual. The actual dancing, however, was friendly, full-throated, Limón-derived rather than Cunningham-rigid. It was very hard to execute, but not hard to remember.

Hannah was very musically motivated, and I learned a great deal from her, particularly in regard to how to flatten and clarify gesture, to perform without projecting in the classical sense, to dance the moves purely and well. The pieces were beautifully structured with a statement, its development, a recapitulation—classical structure, sonata form, everything analyzed. She was also a great teacher, and I've used a lot of her devices, the most important perhaps being her use of the barre in teaching, not normally used in Modern Dance. It's from her that I learned to make up such complicated and difficult solos for myself. Why? Because it's just me dancing. Who necessarily wants to watch that? It needs the extra element of complication and objectivity.

Eliot Feld always worked really hard and single-mindedly on one piece at a time; Hannah, on the other hand, always did new work because she didn't have much money, rarely enjoyed a steady gig, and the same dancers were not always available. Like Lar, she lived and rehearsed in her loft, in this case by Cinema Village on Twelfth Street and University, right across the street from Baryshnikov's apartment, where I later lived. Also like Lar, Hannah was a great dancer who was still performing with the company. Learning directly from the source of the esthetic as she or he is dancing is fascinating.

An archetypically great Hannah Kahn piece was the duet with the previously mentioned ring constraint choreographed for Winkie and me, to Debussy's "La Cathédrale engloutie" for piano. It seemed like a very long dance, mostly because we could barely do it due to the challenges of realizing the "task," in this case manipulating that invisible ring, the irony being that viewers wouldn't necessarily know that there was any task involved at all. It wasn't like doing a job where everybody realizes the difficulties and applauds their execution.

Hannah was very prolific, got enough work around New York, in addition to a little bit of touring, and her company, only seven or eight strong, was full of exquisite dancers: Winkie, Ruth, Keith Sabado, Peter Wing Healey, Kate Johnson, Ken Delap, who ended up marrying Winkie, and Dianne McPherson, who became a great Sufi belly dancer. It's no surprise I wound up working with so many of them in my own group.

I danced with her for a year and a half (as usual), but the work wasn't steady and I was working elsewhere as well. When I put on the first Mark Morris Dance Group show, I was still dancing with her, so of course she was in my show too. I owe a tremendous amount to her.

AROUND THIS TIME, Penny introduced me to Steve Yadeskie, a guilty Polish Catholic boy from Tacoma (my neck of the woods, coincidentally) who'd moved to New York to go to the School of Visual Arts. She'd had an affair with him, since he was bisexualish. He was handsome, troubled, rejected by his parents, ashamed of being queer, and as gay people say, "straight acting and appearing," beautiful and well dressed, with blondish-brown hair and an aquiline nose. He was an artist, a painter, and a carpenter, a hard worker paying the rent waiting tables at a Cajun restaurant in Kips Bay.

Stevie and I got together, and he found half a loft for us, divided by its occupant, on Tenth and something in Hoboken, where we moved in: $175 a week for two thousand square feet. He built everything himself, the bathroom, the shower, all of it. We couldn't afford to heat it in the winter, so we stapled up a plastic sheet around the window like people did, and collected tiles from the dump for the shower and kitchen. Hoboken didn't even exist then. There was nothing, just old abandoned warehouses; in the bodegas, they only spoke Spanish. I loved taking the PATH train from work every day, a fifteen-minute walk back to my house, then another long flight of stairs. The artist who'd divided the loft in half, our new neighbor and landlord, was Robert Bordo, now a painter of great renown and head of drawing at the Cooper Union, but then an unknown Quebecois Jew, whose teacher was Philip Guston. We became friends right away. At our first big Easter party—I was a vegetarian, but I'd make a big ham (thank you!)—Bobby met his boyfriend Donald Mouton, who went on to dance with my company for years. So it was we two queer couples, and Stevie's lovely dog Daisy, in barely divided apartments.

Stevie was absolutely the first real boyfriend I lived with as a mate or a spouse, a domestic move into boyfrienddom that turned almost immediately into a husband-and-wife scenario. He worked in the restaurant, and I baked, danced, and ironed his shirts. It was a little weird. I remember thinking, "Wait a minute! Noooo!" after which nightmare realization it continued for a couple of years. He was embarrassed to be gay, especially with me, the way I am. He tried to hide me. Once we went to see Laura Dean's choreography at the theater on Second Avenue, across from where *Stomp!* is now. It was so gorgeous that I cried. Stevie got mad, told me to shut up and control myself. Asshole!

And he drank. He wasn't drunk all the time, but when he binged, it was bad. Ours was a sex relationship, and there was a lot of guilt, at least on his part, which he took out on me. He ended up hitting me in the face, punched me while he was holding a glass. Nobody had ever hit me. I immediately knocked on the dividing door, asked Bobby if I could stay with him, and moved next door for a while. Stevie was mad at me. He was fucking some other friends of mine, even though he was barely gay. It was one-way monogamy, my role too wifely for me. He later punched me again, in the stomach, angry that I was staying the week with Hannah while he was alone in Hoboken. It was his way of trying to discourage me from doing EST—Werner Erhard's supposedly transformational (self-help) sixty hours of seminars that stretch over two weekends—perhaps intuiting that the sole reason I was doing EST was to have the strength to get rid of him. It was a psychologically abusive relationship, if only rarely physically abusive, and this was the second time I'd ever been hit by anybody, twice by the same man. Afterward, to make up for it, he said, "Let's have sex, and you can do whatever you want to me. Hit me as hard as you like wherever you like." I didn't want to either hit him or have sex.

His paintings metamorphosed from weird beautiful Sheetrock-stained fantasias to razor blades, chains, and spikes, scary nihilistic S-M imagery. At one point, because he wasn't making it as an artist, he decided to abandon personality and selfishness, and informed me that I too should work in the post office or join the Peace Corps because my art was doing nothing for humanity. Another time, he announced we were moving to Santa Fe. I said I'd stay in Hoboken for another couple of months, so he packed all of his shit, and Daisy, and drove across the country to get a house and a job in Santa Fe. We had sad, longing phone calls from New Mexico, but I was never intending to join him. Then he came back, we had a big fight, and he threw *me* out. I came back to find my possessions in a huge pile in the middle of our loft, like a bonfire waiting to be lit, and then we had an argument and he left. There wasn't a lot of logic involved. It was terrible.

Before he left, I lay in my own bed and took some mescaline. (We slept together or not. I don't like to sleep with people that much. I like sex, but I'm not a great cuddler in the aftermath. I also like sleep.) I placed speakers on either side of my head, lay back, and listened over and over to the same two records, alternating between the Vivaldi Gloria in D (I'd sung the tenor part in high school) and some old Tahitian chants. It was an insufferably hot summer, and I was lying in my underpants, tripping, looking at the peeling paint, and listening, for the whole day, only to those two records. Both of them became dances—*Gloria* and *Not Goodbye*, a set of three of those chants.

Stevie ended up dying of AIDS. I don't even remember when I found out or who told me, but I hadn't seen him in years by then.

I WAS PERIODICALLY going to Seattle to teach, and I applied to choreograph for a Pacific Northwest Ballet workshop. This is the hopeful handwritten application letter I sent:

Hoboken, NJ, March 12, 1978

Dear Mr. Stowell and Ms. Russell,

I understand you are commissioning works from young choreographers this summer. I'm a young choreographer who would like to apply.

My name is Mark Morris. I was born, raised and trained in Seattle. I now work in New York with the Lar Lubovitch Dance Co. I'll be out of work for most of this summer and would very much like to choreograph for your company and for Seattle. I could be there from around May 10th thru the last of July.

I love dance—I love music: that's what my work is all about. Enclosed is my resume. If you need more information, please write or call. I wish I had a typewriter.

Thank you,
Mark Morris

This resulted in a commission, my first real dance in three years. Things looked promising at first. They wanted to know what I was planning. I replied:

Hoboken, NJ, May 21, 1978

Dear Kent,

I can't answer all of the questions in your letter until I've seen the dancers I'll have to choose from. I'm doing what work I can and am prepared to alter my sketches to adapt them to the individuals. Here's what I can tell you:

Description—style

I am certainly influenced by several people whose choreography I admire very much: Eliot Feld, Lar Lubovitch, Jennifer Muller, Laura Dean. I also draw from my extensive involvement with ethnic dance. I take a strong balletic foundation for granted and from there I alter, distort, modify, you-name-it, to achieve the movement that most fully expressed my musical ideas. The music is tremendously important to me. The structure of this piece I'm unable to discuss until I've chosen dancers.

Music—Beethoven's trio in B♭ maj (op. 11) for clarinet, cello and piano.

No. of dancers—5 to 9.

I would like to request that my friend Page Smith perform the cello part. She is principal cellist with the Northwest Chamber Orchestra and has worked with me before. I admire her playing and she has a very good understanding of my work.

I'm sorry this response took so long. I just finished performing in Lar Lubovitch's NY season, had visiting family to entertain, etc. I'm available anytime in June and July. We can discuss that or other details when you call or write. Thank you so much for including me in this project.

Sincerely,
Mark Morris

I choreographed it on Tina, Winkie, and Ruth. The dance started with Tina running backward in a circle that got slower and slower until she stopped. I made her do it over and over and over again. "I should have known you'd be a perfectionist," she commented, with genuine regret.

In the event, the finished piece, on which I'd worked extremely hard, was almost saddled with the name *A $200 Dance*. I'd intended to use live music, and though we'd rehearsed with piano, cello, and clarinet, Pacific Northwest Ballet decided to pull the plug at the last minute because apparently we couldn't have live music. It was a budget thing, I seem to remember, about which there was miscommunication. I had been paid $200 (which wasn't very much money *at that time*) to work for two weeks on a dance, and then they took away my music. I was so angry that I decided to call it *A $200 Dance*, because that's how I think. Instead I found the word *Brummagem* (an old name for the English city of Birmingham and also a nineteenth-century expression for counterfeit coins, for which that city was apparently notorious), a title that referred to the commission rather than the theme of the dance or the music, "a cheap piece of shit that looks expensive."

My response to the musical dilemma was a little Cage inspired. I used a recording of the music and three radios playing at the same time to ruin it. Fine or stupid or both, depending on your point of view. But it was still a beautiful dance.

My friend Peter Wing Healey knew of an opening at Laura Dean Dancers and Musicians, so I auditioned. I stomped and spun for hours and I got the job. I had replaced Peter at Hannah Kahn's when he'd originally left for a job with Laura Dean. It all goes around. (And it still does. It's a world you like to try to make bigger, but sometimes you stick with the people you trust. Never a bad idea. Even when you want to kill them, at least you trust them to die.)

Laura's choreography managed somehow to combine everything I liked: Koleda, minimalism, conceptualism, trance, and always live music. That first piece I'd seen with Stevie, when he got mad at me, was *Song*, for singing dancers and Laura's own piano music (extremely minimal minimalism), which went on for about an hour, half of which was spinning in a circle in identical costumes. Incredible. Later there was an electrifying piece called *Tympani*, scored for two tympani and stomping.

Like everybody else, Laura, who made up one dance every two years, rehearsed in her loft, in that same area of Manhattan, in the teens. She'd been lovers with Steve Reich and had choreographed *Drumming* when it was first written in 1975. The work was exhausting, fully aerobic, hard. At that time the piece we were performing most often was *Dance*, six dancers stomping in concentric circles clockwise, then counterclockwise: sixty-four beats clockwise, the same counterclockwise, then thirty-two, and then sixteen, and so on. It took a long time to go through the whole system. Like Lucinda Childs, she set up problems and worked them through; when they were done, the dance was finished. Laura wrote the music, a lovely piece for two Autoharps, and us stomping, spinning for fifteen straight minutes in a circle, and singing. That's what I loved.

We toured France with her. The program of each show was two pieces of about equal length with an intermission; everybody was in everything. The older pieces had been precisely eighty minutes long, but she reduced them for touring on the smart commercial assumption that people probably didn't want to see dances that long. The funny thing was that, wherever we danced, the stage spacing was based on the original circle that fit in her loft as we'd rehearsed it. It didn't matter what size stage it was, or how big the theater, the dance was still done on the dotted lines from her apartment. There were no entrances or exits, the curtain would go up and you'd dance, and then you'd stop and the curtain would go down.

Then she started choreographing a new dance I felt was a little

Broadway, the key difference being that it was front facing. That's when I lost interest. I always wanted to dance in a circle.

ERIN MATTHIESSEN, one of Peter's friends, was also dancing with Laura. He was a Catholic like Steve, but devout rather than merely guilty. (His real name was Gary Cobb; he'd changed it as an homage to the writer and naturalist Peter Matthiessen.) We both found ourselves in Laura's company for a State Department tour, a long five weeks—six dancers, two musicians, and Laura—starting with two weeks in Auckland, teaching a workshop. We were treated very well, as you used to be by the State Department. (International touring depended on the State Department, and vice versa.)

New Zealand itself was the Land That Time Forgot: Dinosaur Country. I'd never seen such plants, and such vast expanses of emptiness, as if nobody lived there. Despite all this, the first person I encountered when we walked into an Auckland bar on the very first day was a beautiful seven-foot tattooed Maori drag queen. We were having such a wonderful time, and Erin—so handsome in his glasses (*all* my boyfriends had glasses)—and I suddenly went DING! We had sex for the first time in Auckland, and then we were lovers, done, and falling in love, and in love. And what places to start! The next stop was one week in Indonesia, when I was first woken up by the prayer call. I'd never heard the Muslim muezzin before. That was also where I found a little roach of New Zealand weed left over in my bag. Not the right place for that. Death sentence.

We had two weeks together in India, my first trip, the beginning of another lifelong obsession. First-time visitors either feel immediately welcome and at ease or in a terrible blind panic. Though it *was* overwhelming, I loved it. Of course men in India hold hands, because men rarely touched women in public, so Erin and I, now boyfriends, held

Laura Dean Dancers and Musicians in India, 1981.
Back row from left to right: Erin Matthiessen, me, Peter Healey,
Angela Caponigro, Laura Dean, David Yoken (musician), and Ching
Gonzalez. Front row from left to right: Paul Epstein (musician),
US State Department employee, Nurit Tillis (musician),
and Sara Brumgart. *(Holly Williams)*

hands without any self-consciousness. Laura and the people from the embassy were worried by this public expression of queerness. That's what it was, but it didn't matter.

I was familiar with a little bit of North Indian (Hindustani) music, but I'd never before encountered South Indian (Carnatic) music. And it was now that I first heard M. S. Subbalakshmi's singing—it blew my mind entirely. India's classical music, northern and southern, is like that of a more advanced planet; Western classical music is a petroglyph by comparison. It's a natural, practiced, and inherited ancient oral tradition. An Indian audience hears the first two pitches and, judging by that interval, knows the mode that it's in and probably even the duration of the piece. It's like a periodic chart of the elements.

I knew I needed more of that music, but it would be a decade before I was able to return.

ON MY WAY back from the airport, I met Tina coincidentally on the PATH train. "I have to tell you something so incredible that's happened to me," I said. "I've fallen in love."

Erin left his boyfriend and moved in with me. We were in love, and he would never dream of hitting me.

Promotional postcard for Dance Theater Workshop,
taken in Seattle, 1983. *(connie j. ritchie)*

Five

Gloria

I didn't just want to be a dancer. Doing my own work turned out to be practical because that's what was taking over my life. In the end, I had to get a group together because, frankly, who else was going to do my dances?

I WAS CHOREOGRAPHING CONSTANTLY.

Lar was my senior, but we talked about matters choreographic, and he welcomed contributions. Hannah and I worked more as peers, choreographer to choreographer. The specific reason I left Laura Dean Dancers and Musicians (after doing only three pieces the world over, each time with the same people) was a dance called *Skylight*, which later became part of the repertory. The music was in 11/8, a very fast 11, which I understood because of my experience with Bulgarian folk dance.

"Just do that in a canon," Laura instructed us, a canon being the device by which movements are introduced, then reproduced sequentially by other dancers a little later. "Start halfway through."

But you can't start after five and a half beats—she hadn't thought it out—and it dawned on me that I was spending time solving other people's problems when I should perhaps be solving my own instead, regardless of whether I had a company or not. A lot of choreographers, Paul Taylor for example, might say to their dancers, "I like *this*; now make it fit into the music." That's a legitimate way to work. But I didn't want to be the one having to work it out, making it fit, for anybody's dances but my own. I was happy to lend my skills to other choreographers, but I wanted to make up pieces for other people to dance.

Granted, I had neither the time nor the money—the two indispensable requirements to putting on a dance show (besides dancers)—so I started to make each part up on myself. If you watch any one person's part in *Gloria*—my first big dance—each one of them looks like me; they're each doing a thing I taught them to do, based on my body. I'd then arrange all the parts structurally, but it was still basically me doing every part, and at that point the only way you could have seen the dance done better than with my dancers was time-lapse photography of me dancing every role. As soon as I could, I started to make the dances up on other people so the moves were based less on my own anatomy or style. They were my preferences, of course, but no longer "do an impersonation of me."

So time and money were a problem, but I had enough courage and I had enough friends, so I had enough dancers. The urge, however, wasn't to start a company; that was a by-product.

Lar's rhetorical advice was "You're *not* going to start a company, are you?" He meant "It's a pain in the ass, it's impossible to raise the money, it'll drive you crazy, and besides, no one's that interested in dance." All totally true. Jerome Robbins once similarly warned me, "You're *not* going to choreograph a piece for the Paris Opera Ballet, are you?" I did, and it was a nightmare. Lar and Jerry weren't just being dismissive and unhelpful; experienced people know what they're talking about.

I WAS NOW A KNOWN professional dancer in New York; I taught Modern Dance at the Boston Ballet summer workshop and guest taught elsewhere. My own work seemed to be gaining some slight momentum, piquing the tiniest interest. I had a very modest reputation, about which I was somewhat modest.

Erin Matthiessen, Brockport, New York, 1988. *(Nancy Umanoff)*

Things were certainly vastly improved in Hoboken; home became homey. Erin was quiet and taught me Transcendental Meditation, and we went to a lot of shows together. We read poetry to each other; things were smooth. He even got a job dancing for my favorite, Lucinda Childs. Her dancers would arrive at rehearsal to find a chart for each of them, containing their instructions and sharpened number two pencils; they'd work out their steps and trajectories for the first hour, then she'd come in and put it all together.

Then Tina and her boyfriend, Barry Alterman, moved close by. They'd met working the same shift at the Häagen-Dazs on Christopher Street (when Christopher Street was the center of gay everything), united by a shared love of baseball and, more specifically, the Yankees. I met Barry at that same ice creamery. I liked a black and white malted, made a particular way with vanilla ice cream and chocolate syrup. The first time we met he gave me a scoop of chocolate chip, gratis.

Barry was interesting, cultured, smart, and taking acting lessons; we became great friends. He'd gone to City Ballet with his mother for years—he was always a bit coddled—and was a devout opera queen. He was also cute and in good shape. We went to the same gym, the Jack LaLanne in the Woolworth Building. (This is the time to mention that he once saw a turd bobbing gently by in the Jacuzzi.) He was the gayest straight man I'd ever met, completely comfortable with queers, with a voracious heterosexual appetite. (To this day, we're still sifting through the aftermath.) He was a good editor, a very good writer, and he took an immediate interest in the potential of a company, started helping me write grants, and even took the press photos we used for years. He was invaluable in helping me mobilize.

Tina and Barry became our neighbors and companions. We ate together, drank, exchanged books (there was an Iris Murdoch obsession), watched TV (*I Love Lucy*, *Dynasty*, and *Jeopardy!*, still a nightly ritual). It was every possible combination of friendship, with Tina, Barry, Erin, and me—not to mention Bobby and Donald; not a huge social group but tightly knit, with regular cameos from various friends from class, and colleagues from other companies. One thing: when Barry came over, he'd make straight for the refrigerator and eat anything he could find. We were all broke and I started to get resentful. We'd hide the cheese in advance of his arrival.

FROM THE VERY FIRST CONCERT, we were the Mark Morris Dance Group. The name came naturally. It was the time of the Patti Smith Group and the Wooster Group; those were the other "Groups." Everyone else had a "company," either that or "& Friends" or "& Dancers." I thought of it as more of a communal thing, though certainly not a "cooperative."

The first Mark Morris Dance Group concert was on November 28, 1980. I wrote the grant application to the New Jersey State Council on the Arts myself, and because I was possibly the only choreographer in Hoboken, I got $2,000—plenty—which I could use to put on a show in Manhattan, provided I also did a couple of performances, along with some teaching, at the Jersey City Museum. The grant paid the rent of the loft theater at the Merce Cunningham Studio at Westbeth, which was the right place for us to make an entrance. The space itself wasn't expensive, but once you'd rented it, you had to pay for everything and do all the work yourself. We couldn't afford anywhere to rehearse, however, so we used my loft with its terrible broken-up floor. Even worse, the building had once housed a sewing machine factory and there was still the odd needle lurking, a dancer's nightmare.

The group was made up of people I liked being with. It was Teri, Elvira Psinas, Ruth, and Hannah (so four from Hannah's company, including herself), Nora Reynolds and Harry (both from Lar's company), Jennifer Thienes and Penny from Seattle, Tina, and Donald from next door. We were all friends who became even better friends in the Mark Morris Dance Group. All dancers know each other from classes anyway, so this wasn't an unusual way for a group to come together. Besides, I was so confident in the dances, so sure of my choreography, that if you were there for the rehearsal, you could be in that part of the dance; I believed there was no way you could fuck it up.

Then there was the question of what to put on the program. Frankly, there wasn't a lot to choose from. *Dad's Charts* and *Castor and Pollux* (to more Partch, from *Plectra and Percussion Dances*) I made up specifically for the show (and in fact only finished at the technical rehearsal). *Ženska* already existed, as did *Barstow*, from when I was fifteen at Port Townsend. Those old dances were juvenilia, but then . . . I was still a juvenile. *Brummagem* had been previously commissioned, but this would be the New York premiere with my own dancers.

I'm not sure how many people were there: two nights sold out, capacity probably sixty or eighty. Some kind of audience was guaranteed, because all the dancers were known with their respective companies, so it was already something to see. Details of that first concert are hazy, though there is a video out there, shot from the far corner of the room. Penny helped me put it on; Hannah gave me advice. There was no live music in the show, zero—and you know how I feel about that—but then the Partch was more or less unplayable anyway.

I was busy, active, having fun, nuts in love, and I remember being excited about the show and feeling, in its aftermath, not let down. And it got us some bites. David White, who now runs the Yard at Martha's Vineyard, offered to present me the next year on a shared week—Split Stream—at Dance Theater Workshop, the hotbed of downtown dance (also known as the Economy Tires Theater, since it was above a tire repair shop), where he was then the executive director. I'd actually be paid to make up new work and put on a show. This felt like a speedy promotion.

Dance Theater Workshop was the first service umbrella organization of this sort specifically for dance rather than theater. It started a program called the Suitcase Fund, which provided companies with money to tour, and published *Poor Dancer's Almanac* (subtitled *Managing Life and Work in the Performing Arts*), a manual on how to put on a show, everything from applying for a grant to making a poster. It was part of an informal network of like-minded people and producers in different cities, a circuit of similarly sized spaces—little black box theaters that seated one hundred maximum. It was a bare-bones tour, but if you could get yourself there, they'd present you and you wouldn't lose money. We did that.

THE ATMOSPHERE in those earliest days of the group was the greatest. It was all about the collective. We danced together, traveled together, slept together, brought in clothes ("Everyone bring in whatever you have that's gray! Dark gray, light gray, whatever!") and made our costumes together, everything. It seemed like the center of the world, the most fun place imaginable. We'd go out after rehearsal, eat, then hang out, drink, and just keep drinking. Someone would inevitably ask for a quarter for the pay phone to make an excuse to their partner about why they weren't coming home yet. No one wanted to break the spell or to miss anything, because if you missed anything, you missed *everything*. No one ever wanted to leave that party.

The founding women—the goddesses, the pillars—of my company were Ruth Davidson, Penny Hutchinson, Teri "Winkie" Weksler, and Tina Fehlandt. The similarity was that they were all strong, brilliant, wonderful women and, best of all, great dancers long before I met them. These were liberated women in the pre-AIDS 1970s and '80s, when people had sex whenever they liked in a way that was simultaneously promiscuous and fabulously feminist.

From the ballet industry's point of view, Modern Dance was the refuge of the failed ballet dancer. At that time the consensus was that if you weren't good enough to become a ballerina, if you couldn't point your feet well enough, if you weren't the right shape, you became a Modern Dancer. It looked like it was changing for a little while, but amazingly, it's *still* that way. Modern Dance's response? Ballet is for infantilized airheads who are treated like children, behave like children, and have no thought in the world except how they can lose more weight. The "body shaming" was mutual. People (like those nurses who'd informed me I should do something else) certainly told me I'd never make it as a ballet dancer. Somebody else told me my ass was too big. Imagine what women have to put up with.

Imagine a female dancer. Before puberty, she's a promising, slender dancer, and suddenly, through no fault of her own, she becomes a woman. She gets tits, hips, and acne, and she's menstruating. (Ballet wants to prevent that, which is the reason behind those stories, which aren't entirely untrue, of amenorrhea and bulimia. You have to be skinny and small.) And that change leads to defeatism. "I was so promising," she thinks, "and now I'm the fat girl whom no one can lift. I can't do ballet anymore." So she gets depressed, feels demoralized, and immediately reports to Modern Dance. Tina remembers asking me why I wanted her, and apparently I said, "Because I like you,

With Tina Fehlandt rehearsing *Mort Subite*, Boston Ballet, 1986. (*Jaye R. Phillips*)

you're my friend, and you're big and you dance big and that's what I like."

Some dancers don't even believe they deserve to do *this*, because they were a failure at *that*. It's a fucked-up thing for women in dance generally. Ironically, Modern Dance is where the strong women are. There are many more women involved in its making: it's more intellectual, more political, more rigorous, and, occasionally, in the wrong hands, less accessible.

These four women were permanently attached to the company; men, on the other hand, mostly came and went. It's not just that the women were steadfast and true (though they were) or that they had greater stamina and a higher pain threshold (which they did). In fact, the steadfastness of the women might have been true of any dance company; I just liked working with women. They're usually better. Men, because of their rarity in the dance world, are a different story.

The pillar gentleman of MMDG in the early days was Guillermo Resto, a genius dancer of Puerto Rican descent who'd danced with a million other little companies, and was so modest about his genius that he somehow thought it was all a big mistake (though it is true that he'd got into dancing more or less by chance). Quite gorgeous, a beautiful Caravaggio with tousled black hair and a perfectly proportioned muscularity and virility, he was also a full sex devotee, one of those rare people who fucked everybody yet no one hated. From the moment we met, we were like evil twins. We both liked to drink, and we laughed so much, egging each other on and making each other so giddy that people wondered what on earth was wrong with us.

Though Guillermo believed we'd been married in another lifetime—either king and queen or king and servant—he was full-on straight, though he rather liked people thinking he was my boyfriend. (I always called him Queermo.) I wasn't afraid of straight men, as some gay men are, and Guillermo was both gorgeous and frequently naked.

We never had sex, although we kissed every once in a while. One time he apologized for not being more into it, and I asked him why he'd let me kiss him at all. And he said, "Because I love you and that's what you want. It's not *horrible*," he reassured me, "but it's not really my thing. I'd give you anything you need, short of having sex, and maybe even sex . . . but it just isn't me. I love you and if I was gay, I'd be gay. But I'm not." Enough, already! That's why I made up a dance to a Vivaldi cantata, *Love, You Have Won*, a mirror pas de deux for the two of us, in which we looked like matching altar boys. That was my saying, "I get it, you're not gay, but I love you," through the mirror to Guillermo.

He was also sensational in *Championship Wrestling after Roland Barthes* in *Mythologies*, in which he "fought" Winkie. When he finally stopped dancing, he tried his hand as my rehearsal director, but it wasn't for him. (It wasn't for Tina either. In fact, the only one who ever lasted in that position was Matthew Rose, whom I always trusted with my work.) Guillermo was, however, often a valuable liaison between me and the dancers, representing my point of view or explaining the ethos of the company to them, while standing up on their behalf to me. He saw his job as to make things better, to let me know if I was being too hard on someone. On top of everything else, Guillermo is genuinely resourceful, and he can fix anything, a great handyman to this day.

Rob Besserer, a very important eleven-foot (he's pretty tall) dancer and another gorgeous man, was a star, but never technically a member of my company, always a guest performer. He had a fabulous grace and suppleness, and a legato aspect to his dancing that sometimes read as *late*, perhaps because of his size, but looked beautiful. He had the knack of looking like he knew what he was doing while no one around him did, though in fact the opposite was often true. Donald Mouton, a Cajun from Louisiana, was charming, a natural. Keith Sabado, a Seattleite of Filipino descent, who'd danced for Hannah Kahn at the same time I did, was another very popular dancer, with (it must be said) extremely large feet. He still dances with Yvonne Rainer even now, one of the "Raindeers," as she calls them.

These are only some of the many great dancers I worked with in the first years. Some still work with me to this day, setting dances, teaching classes. I've been working with Penny, for example, on and off for nearly fifty years, ever since Koleda and *Barstow*. She still has a great creative imagination; the things she comes up with as a teacher—movement prompts and exercises to get the dancers to think another way—are so magical, and the students will do anything for her. Guillermo has been part of my life in some capacity ever since I first met him, other than six years off in the middle (due to a very difficult intracompany breakup), after which he reappeared in my office and started midsentence from six years previously. He hasn't cut his hair in twenty years now and is still incredible looking, though somewhat more like a bison these days.

Tina still sets dances for me. She was always a member of what I call the Step Police, those helpful dancers who patrol rehearsal to see if anyone is violating the rules of the choreography, or otherwise doing anything that might affect the purity of my intention, starting on this leg whereas I originally choreographed it for that leg. To the Step Police, the urtext must be preserved above all else, which requires an attention to detail that is extremely useful to me (even if I also refer to it as "squealing"). To this day, she's one of the few I trust to set my dances on other companies. Sometimes you need the police.

Other dancers go away and I never see or hear from them again. They want nothing to do with me or it or this.

And I get it.

ERIN AND I WERE FULLY into opera, listening to recordings, going whenever we could afford it. It was the beginning of the early music movement, the rediscovery of the baroque operas, which were now being recorded with period instruments for the first time. I found myself learning a lot about choreography by listening closely to Handel's astonishing musical architecture.

The first Dance Theater Workshop show featured the Vivaldi Gloria in D, which I'd sung back in Seattle at Franklin High, then listened to while tripping in Hoboken. It was one of the first pieces of early music I choreographed, and also the biggest dance I'd done so far. I'd known it as a huge choral and orchestral piece, but my interest was reignited by the conductor Christopher Hogwood's intimate presentation in a historically informed style with a smaller group of period instruments. It was as if that was the version I'd been waiting for.

A happy side effect of my use of early music was that it was helpful with people's initial impressions of me. No one else was dancing to old music or, perhaps more pertinently, *good* music.

Paul Taylor had a reputation for working with baroque scores—which he used as a grid, a waffle iron—but he had a tin ear. If there was a loud moment in the music, a big gesture inevitably accompanied it. He didn't like to work with live music, either, because it was too unpredictable. He liked to use the recording to which he'd made the dance up, right down to the pauses between the tracks on the record. People likened me to him—*Taylorized* me—but I can't say I ever took it as a compliment.

What is more, I was using legitimate music so that people who liked music might actually have something to listen to. Put it in context: Only ten years earlier there'd been no music allowed in dance at all. Then choreographers took to minimalist music, in which I had absolutely no interest whatsoever at that time. My use of music like, for example, Brahms's *Neue Liebeslieder Walzer* (which I choreographed as *New Love Song Waltzes*, composed for vocal quartet and piano, four hands) was therefore an insanity, but an insanity with genuine musical appeal. My choices were also relatively unpretentious; I have learned that I can only choreograph to music I like, though I can also learn to like a piece of music if I feel, for whatever reason, that I *should* choreograph it; but if I don't like something, the work will suck. Luckily, my taste is pretty varied. Nowadays a lot of choreographers use live music, and some of them use good music. It just wasn't the case back then.

Gloria was the first dance I choreographed where I divided the danced chorus strictly into soprano, alto, tenor, and bass so it matched the singing chorus exactly. The sopranos would be two women dancers; altos, a woman and a man; tenors, a man and a woman; and basses, two men. So when we rehearsed it, the dancers knew exactly what I was talking about when I said, "Tenors, you're late!" or "Sopranos, you're on the wrong foot!" I choreographed each of the four voices separately, one by one on myself, when I got back home from class in the city. The floor was so rough up there—with always the possibility of a stray needle—that I had to wear shoes. I'd put on the cassette of the Hogwood recording, referring to the score as well, and then with the sun beaming through the eight-foot windows, I'd get to work, listening until it was so in my head that I could make up the dance without the music. I'd later teach that part to somebody else and make up the parts around it.

All of the moves for *Gloria* are defensible from any angle, not just rhythmically, but also in their relation to the melody and text. The best example is Vivaldi's fragmentation of the musical phrases in the chorus "*propter magnam gloriam tuam.*" It's precisely what is visualized in the dance. You can actually read what's happening on the stage from left to right, in those parts, like the music.

There's very little in my dance that's a literal representation of the text because, although there is plenty of feeling, there's no real story in the "Gloria" section of a Mass, which is basically praising God in the highest in every possible way. So I developed smaller narratives within the dance, one of which we refer to as "The Little Crippled Girl," which introduces one of several healing motifs in *Gloria*. The "Domine Deus" section features four dancers, a family unit including two men and a woman walking with hesitant, pensive steps on a strictly defined path as they carry a woman on their backs. When they put her down, she can't walk unaided, only by supporting herself on their shoulders. Their walk is in a three, whereas *her* walk is in a two over three (technically called a hemiola), which, to people who don't know music, looks brittle and spastic. The solos of the various family members are filled with grief and hope. After they've left, the crippled girl gets up shakily on her own like baby Bambi and does a hobbled solo, a recapitulation of the themes we've already seen. As the music ends, she circles her arms as if they're tiny hummingbird wings—she does it so fast, you can almost hear them hum—and then she pops offstage backward and vanishes. One of the exiting trio looks back but too late: she's gone, raptured. I wasn't making fun of healing—actually, I suppose I unavoidably was, because depicting it in rhythm as a dance makes it seem funny—but these healings are, I hope, genuinely moving.

Another healing move in *Gloria* that happens singly and multiply is that of the faith healer leaning in, putting his or her hand to the forehead of someone who falls backward, healed. It's a gesture taken directly from Kathryn Kuhlman, the great televangelist faith healer of my youth. We watched her on TV back then, making fun of her billowing angel sleeves and her grand opening line, accompanied by swelling organ, "I *believe* in miracles!" (By which time everybody at home was in tears, already healed.) When she came to Seattle for one of her services, we got stoned and lined up with all of the Holy Rollers. Members of the congregation would go to the stage to be healed; she'd touch their forehead and they'd pass out. That was the big move. I loved that shit.

I've always been a big admirer of religion: the swindle of religion. I love the snake oil, healings, and miracles. I have water and dirt from all over the world. I love a magic charm. In Houston recently, I went three times to Joel Osteen's supermegachurch, so unwelcoming to the victims of Hurricane Harvey in 2017. There was terrifying, handsome, smarmy Joel in front of me, preaching to ten thousand people in an

Photo compilation of the Amen section from *Gloria*, Seattle, 2010. Top row: Rita Donahue, Noah Vinson, David Leventhal, Joe Bowie, Lauren Grant. Bottom row: Craig Biesecker, Bradon McDonald, Julie Worden, Michelle Yard, Maile Okamura. (*Johan Henckens*)

arena, with a rotating globe and a giant gospel choir sing-along—far more interesting than going to the ballet. If I were a single mother, I'd go every day for the free daycare, food, clothes, and air-conditioning. Of course, there's a catch; there's always a catch.

I know a lot about religion, despite being an atheist (without really wanting to acknowledge there's even theism—the argument isn't that there's no god, it's that there's no argument to be had). Atheists *often* know more about religion than believers. (I once helped to explain Mormonism to one of my dancers who is a Mormon but hadn't been paying attention as he sat in church with his big family, playing on his Gameboy.)

I love a good creation myth. Every single one is weird. I have no preference for, or sharper ax to grind against, any religion. Nor do I think Mormonism, Scientology, or any Branch Davidian is more absurd than any other religion; they're just more recent, no more or less bullshit. It's all the same propaganda no matter which terrible religion you call your own. I like the music that the Lutheran Church caused Bach to write. Hooray! It wouldn't have been composed otherwise. I love Jesusy paintings. I love a gorgeous cathedral. But I don't buy a bit of what's behind it. Not a scrap. It's the same with Indian religion. Will I tip this beggar to improve my karmic odds? Sure. I'll knock wood and touch the head of this deity or kiss the Blarney Stone. It's just like avoiding the cracks in the sidewalk. Superstition.

It's easy to see how religion works. Go to an Eastern Orthodox service where you have to stand for the whole thing. The incense is so intense and dizzying, the music so hypnotic, that you start to lose your mind—I love that feeling. An organ is tuned to the precise room it's in. Organs only have their full power in the places they belong, where you, the listener, are the organ's resonator. A recording can't replicate that because you can't feel it viscerally—it doesn't rattle your bowels—but if you're there and it's reverberating inside you, and you're looking at the light through that beautiful stained glass window: that is heaven. Add the smells, the language you don't understand, and the outfits . . . the overall effect is irresistible. Count me in! Even though I don't want to be counted in. A Catholic service in Latin is fabulous; the magic is lost in English because you know what all the words mean, rather like when opera is sung in English (if you can make out the words at all).

And I want to see it *all*. I've been to a Sufi mosque in Turkey, where I happily removed my shoes and washed my feet just so I could witness the dervishes spinning themselves into a trance. When we were working together on his musical *The Capeman*, Paul Simon and I went to a clandestine Santeria service in the basement of a Dominican family's house in the Bronx—the priest spat rum at us as he went into a trance inspired by Saint Jude, the patron saint of lost causes. A couple of years ago in Cambodia, some of us visited a little village outside Phnom Penh to hear revered musicians play music that exists nowhere else and hardly, because of the slaughter of an entire generation, even there. We were made very welcome by a regular old granny, then invited within a tiny temple that could fit no more than seven people, where kids sat on our laps to watch. This nice toothless old lady transformed into the possessed priestess, going into a deep trance, spraying arak from her mouth like a holy baptism. She chanted (not even in Khmer), grabbed someone's face, peered into her mouth, spun, then shook the children—violent and scary—as these old guys played unbelievably sophisticated music on instruments I'd never seen before.

It doesn't matter if you believe in it—I don't believe in any of it—but it happens. It's a fact. And it's powerful. Prayer (or "mindfulness") may not hurt, even though it's a waste of time. But I don't argue with any of it. I love magic. I love a sunset. I love a baby. I love the ideas and myths of religion, its trappings, though what I really love is the kindness of people who are devoutly religious and don't proselytize.

You can hear the religious in music. At a Trinity Church performance of a Lou Harrison piece, *La Koro Sutro*, last year, the choir held the first chord on the downbeat, unison with octaves, about four times longer than humanly possible, staggering their breathing so it seemed to go on forever. I felt it then. That's the embarrassing part of being so moved—because I do find myself frequently moved—by what I assume must be the Holy Spirit, although there is no God. *I feel it*. It's how you feel when the music is echoing through you in a church.

That's what I try to put into a dance like *Gloria* (which Vivaldi wrote at a time when you were either religious or dead): the thing that inspires me, that feeling, but also a choreographic representation of that feeling. I try to express it frankly and honestly.

I WAS CLAWING my way up the greased pole of a career. We performed three years running at Dance Theater Workshop, first sharing the space for a week, then having our own week, and then a two-week run on our own. The director of the Brooklyn Academy of Music, the great Harvey Lichtenstein, saw my work there and—perhaps on the back of an Arlene Croce piece in the *New Yorker*, "Mark Morris Comes to Town"—invited us to appear at BAM as part of the second iteration of the Next Wave Festival. The festival's name was itself riding the wave of new wave, the music of the time (because the term "avant-garde" was itself a little *après garde*), or perhaps the nouvelle vague of French cinema, and referred to the next new thing, which included, in choreographic terms, Bill T. Jones and Arnie Zane, Trisha Brown, and Lucinda Childs, not to mention, in the wider world of art, Robert Wilson, Philip Glass, Meredith Monk, and Laurie Anderson. This enviable company of artistes was more established than I, if only a few years older, and I was thrilled and surprised to be invited. Though *I* thought I belonged in such company, I honestly didn't think anybody else thought so too.

The *New Yorker* article ran at the beginning of 1984. I had assumed that it would be a group pan, or a collective mention of three or four choreographers of my generation, but it wasn't that at all. It was about me and my work only. In itself, this was bizarre, because Arlene Croce just didn't do that. She wrote about Merce and Balanchine; those were the artists.

We were somehow in the habit of doing one show in NYC and one show in Seattle a year, along with whatever other work came the way of a fledgling company, and what Arlene saw and reviewed was nine of the best dances I had made by 1983. Frankly, it was almost enough that she'd just *gone* to the show, but to have such major coverage bestowed was sensational. She described *New Love Song Waltzes*, a love dance with a lot of misunderstandings, as "purple," by which she meant that it was evidence of a young person just about to find what he was doing or, in her more beautiful phrase, "his moment of excess before the reining in that signifies the start of true growth"; I read this as a big compliment, basically saying that everything I could imagine was in that dance. (All I've done ever since is try to pare things down and clean them out.)

Two of the dances she saw and reviewed were set to country music, another favorite genre. I have a real fondness for hillbilly music, Western swing, country music, and the great duet acts from the 1960s and '70s. I loved Buck Owens, Loretta Lynn, George Jones, and Tammy Wynette. When people ask that classic question "What would you have done if you hadn't gone into dance?" I say that I would have made a great pedal steel player (but not out of any talent, I assure you; purely because of my affinity for country music). It's the authentic emotion that fully moves me; it has nothing to do with kitsch, though I realize why people think it's corny. My parents, being from Montana, hated that music; my mother, particularly, made fun of cowboys because the cowboys at the dances were dirty, smelled bad, and stepped on her feet. But we sang Appalachian music at Koleda, and Chad played those glorious Carter Family songs, including my favorite, "Over the Garden Wall." Radio stations actually played that music back in those days, so I was hearing new music by Dolly and Porter in the late sixties; then there was that craze of CB radio and truck-driving songs, Red Sovine's "Teddy Bear" and so forth. I had a *big* collection of those.

At On the Boards (the enterprising nonprofit performing arts organization and venue) in Seattle in 1982, we premiered a dance called *Songs That Tell a Story*, featuring the heartbreaking songs of the Louvin Brothers, their white country gospel. I'd always been very drawn to the sweet, intuitive harmonies of family singers, including the Everly Brothers, the Stanley Brothers (*all* the brothers), the McGarrigles, the McGuire Sisters, even the Lennon Sisters on *The Lawrence Welk Show*, so I obsessively started listening to and collecting the Louvins. Their clever tunes and harmonies drove me crazy, and it almost killed me to narrow it down to the four songs, the four little moral tales, required for that dance. In the end I settled on "Insured beyond the Grave," "I'll Live with God (To Die No More)," "Robe of White," and "The Great Atomic Power."

It was a difficult, exhausting dance with a great deal of gestural storytelling and a tight canonic structure. Of course because I'm me, we had to do it in jeans, real denim; of course they weren't stretch jeans; and of course I wouldn't allow fake jeans. No modern technology was allowed, nothing that made life easier, just as, in *Dido and Aeneas*, I'd wear a real tied sarong (elastic was forbidden) and a real chopstick in my hair—further constraints, in time, in motion, in dress. It had to be authentic: it's one of the key decisions. Often when I make up a dance, I begin with props and sets; but before long they've been edited out and there's nothing left but dancers and lights on an empty stage. My original concept for my big dance *L'Allegro* included a bunch of sticks, scarves, and flowers, but they were all gone by the premiere. The dance I'm working on now was going to have three stools; I choreographed it that way, then removed the stools. It was immediately better. They're still there, of course, their ghosts, integral to the piece, but not actually visible.

Songs That Tell a Story was first choreographed for me and a man and a woman, though by the time we did it for TV it was all men. It could be any combination really—the dancers are doing work that either sex could do. My political idea was that if everyone couldn't do it, it wouldn't be in the piece. (Later, however, I realized, more generally, that if I needed to, say, change a light bulb, we had to put the littlest girl on top of the biggest boy so she could reach it; it was like the Grimms' fairy tale "The Bremen Town Musicians," in which the characters have to reach something way up high and they stack up, the little ones on top.) *Songs That Tell a Story* was mimetic, illustrative of the Louvin texts (for example, in "Robe of White," a postman delivering news of a son's death to his mother), structurally impeccable, and theoretically perfect, though that doesn't mean you could do all of it. Some of it necessarily failed because I had set up ideas that, though perfect in my mind, were not actually physically achievable. As a random example, not in this dance, you can't make a cube out of people. When I tried to execute this platonic perfection—the human cube—with eight people, I found that it was not only not pretty but also physically impossible. They're people! Legs are longer and stronger than arms. Another example specific to *Songs That Tell a Story*: there's a canon in which the dancers are doing the same moves a bar apart (possible) and then two beats apart (difficult) and then one beat apart (impossible, because it requires the dancer to be in the same physical space as someone who is still occupying that physical space from the previous move). You can only get as close as you can. That (as far as the performers are concerned) is the frustrating part of those pieces from the period, the constraints. You can do anything as long as you accomplish this one thing that can't really be achieved.

The next year at On the Boards, we presented more country music: three songs for *Deck of Cards*—"Gear Jammer," a great CB song by Jimmy Logsdon, "Say It's Not You" by George Jones, and "Deck of Cards" by T. Texas Tyler. *Deck of Cards* was another somewhat humiliating dance, in three movements, one per song, the geometry of the choreography identical for each song. I choreographed it on myself, a woman called Pat Graney, a choreographer in her own right, and a remote-controlled truck. Pat, as a male soldier, wore a uniform jacket, hat, boxers, military shoes, but no pants; I wore a coral polyester dress and did my solo as a woman, dancing to "Say It's Not You," a fairly obscure song by one of our nation's finest singers. It's a very sad dance, barefoot, in a dress, that charts a progress of loneliness, despair, and desolation, a love hangover after a night of sex and drink. It wasn't a pretty dance. People laughed at it, of course, because I was wearing a dress. The star of the show, however, was the truck. "Gear Jammer" was a truck-driving song, so I felt there should be an actual truck in it. The truck's beautiful solo was so moving that it made me cry almost every night. Guillermo operated the remote control, which was tricky because he was offstage, the maneuvers were complicated, and remote controls simply didn't work well back then. The truck was meant to take the same path on the stage as the soldier, but sometimes it would just drive straight off into the wings . . . zoom!

Finally, "Deck of Cards," a list song. Everyone loves list songs, everything from Mozart's *Don Giovanni* list and Gilbert and Sullivan's "I've Got a Little List" to Hank Snow's "I've Been Everywhere," perhaps the platonic perfection of the genre. Every one of those songs in the musical *Hair* is a list. (I also love a ballad that multiplies, like "Froggie Went A-Courtin'." I want endless verses of brother, mother, daughter, sister, all waiting in heaven for me. I love lists.) *Deck of Cards* was danced by a woman dressed as a man, an accumulation both in song and in the dance, a form made famous choreographically by Trisha Brown in a piece called *Accumulation*—the thumb move, then thumb hand, thumb hand arm, thumb hand arm knee, etc., a long, satisfying sequence, and one of her very conceptual and brain-complicated dances people do to this day. It's a dance people remember.

On that same program was *Celestial Greetings*, danced to popular and beautiful traditional Thai music, and *Dogtown*, to the music of Yoko Ono. I'd loved her song "Walking on Thin Ice"—John Lennon had a tape of the final mix in his hands when he was shot; they'd just finished it in the studio that day—though I knew only vaguely about Yoko's career as an experimental artist. I liked the music very much— all screaming; we danced to the recordings of "Toyboat," "Extension 33," "Dogtown," and "Give Me Something"—and it's evident from the program of music that I wanted to do something contemporary. *Dogtown* was dog behavior, ass sniffing and mounting, and I chose the ugliest songs—as I was to do with the Violent Femmes for *Lovey*— because I don't like popular music that much. I find it soporific and numbing, so I need the ugliest version. I'd heard Split Enz in New Zealand, but the thing I loved about the music—its new-wave bounce and friendliness—was precisely why I didn't feel the need to make up a dance to it.

We called Yoko to ask her permission, and she watched a tape and generously gave me the rights to do the dance to her music for free. (And I've been charged $1,000 for playing five minutes of Gershwin on the piano at a college.) One movement had an evolutionary sequence because, at that time, the Krishna Consciousness people, the Hare Krishnas, were everywhere. At the airports, they always presented a diorama in a vitrine: a representation of karma, the complete cycle of life in a circle—fetus, baby, adult, ancient man, skeleton, repeat. I reproduced that for a thirty-second, twelve-bar sequence here—from flat out as an amoeba to adulthood section by section. The cast was mostly women, so we called it "Pancake to Woman," a canon of evolution. When we later did it on film for PBS, I had everyone wearing rubber gloves, which made it look unhygienic. It was a violent dance, but kind of funny.

As a gift, Yoko sent me a beautiful print of a drawing of John's. Later, not long after we arrived in Brussels, it was stolen from our office, a suspicious burglary that didn't make us feel more welcome than we were. Everything was all over the place, but nothing other than that was taken. We figured the print was what they'd come for. It had value, of course, but more sentimental than anything, because Yoko had given it to me. If anyone has that, I'd like it back.

ARLENE CROCE'S REVIEW also mentioned *The Death of Socrates*, premiered at Dance Theater Workshop in 1983, to music by Satie from *Socrate* (which we presented in its entirety in 2010). The music was impossible and I couldn't afford a score from Paris, so I just counted out the whole thing—and it was *long*. There was no way to know the meter half the time. The piano and the voice phrases don't match, because it's purposefully and famously climax-free and therefore without landmarks. And although it seems incredibly repetitive, it doesn't repeat at all. So all I could really do was count the number of beats throughout its eighteen-minute duration and, if I got lost in the middle, go back to the top and start again.

To choreograph it, I divided the piece mathematically, disregarding all musical phrasing except the beat. I broke it down into beats and sections so I knew precisely how long each part had to be. Every phrase of the dance is exactly the same number of beats, but danced either slow, medium, or fast, phrases that started whenever it was time to, which seemed fitting since there was no climax in the musical structure itself. This graphing out and division were techniques learned from the minimalists: Lucinda Childs, Laura Dean, and Steve Reich.

I love to work with a score—people ask me if I make charts and diagrams, but there already is a chart, called the score—and lengthy transcription without one isn't something I'd necessarily choose to do anymore. Sometimes, however, it worked better without. For example, there *was* a score for Partch's *Castor and Pollux*, but it wasn't readily available and the chances are that, given Partch's bizarre notation, I wouldn't have been able to read it. I was therefore forced to deduce that piece's beautiful, perfect structure—A, B, C, and then ABC all together, with time signatures alternating in sevens and nines—from extended listening. So I made up a dance that corresponded precisely to the music. And in that one instance, it was perhaps more precise than if I had done it from the score, because it was abstracted mathematically.

I had decided on *The Death of Socrates* partly because of John Cage's relationship to it. Merce choreographed *Socrate*, which is in three movements, the last of which, as you might expect, is *The Death Of.* Satie had said he wanted the music to be transparent and unimpassioned, "white, like how we think of antiquity" (before we found out that antiquity was originally in garish colors), so he ate only white food while he was writing it to get himself in the mood. Merce choreographed it but then found he couldn't get the rights, so Cage wrote a piece of precisely the same duration as *Socrate* called "Cheap Imitation." (I actually had to do the same thing later with some Messiaen for which the composer Ethan Iverson wrote a shadow piece. There was an evil widow.)

And the chart I made for *The Death of Socrates*, which I still have, was so beautiful. I set it for six men, so it's gay (but only because I said so and it has to do with Plato), and everybody had a system of a certain number of beats. The dancers had to count incredibly carefully, because their moves had no relation to the score except by beat. They wore beautiful short togas designed by Bobby Bordo, and his set—we actually had a set!—was a big drapery hung in curves in the same material as the costumes. The dance was based on a fake idea of the ancient, set at a symposium with lounging, grape eating, and amphora carrying. It was the first time Erin danced with me—he wasn't officially a full-time member of the company, but I needed men—and there is a beautiful photo of Guillermo and Erin dressed like Apollos, looking their very hottest in togas. Guillermo's was the first solo (part of a zigzag pattern in which the solos took place at the back of the stage, after which the dancers moved forward), Rob's was the last, and someone later told Guillermo it read like a love letter to him and Rob, because those were the two solos you remembered, the salutation and the sign-off.

In her review, Arlene Croce liked the idea but labeled the dance "inert," which is such a wonderful thing to call a dance. You couldn't even do an inert dance, though it's easy to have an inert idea. But of course she was right. It didn't develop; it couldn't; there was no arc, no narrative, none intended, by either Satie or me.

THE TRUTH IS THAT I read that wonderful Arlene Croce *New Yorker* article—the one that put me on the map, heralding my arrival in the City of Dance—just as I was leaving town on a plane back to Seattle, exhausted and tired of working (or not working) in New York City.

I didn't have any money—nobody ever had any money—and I wasn't earning much apart from the little I made making up dances or dancing. I was at least always in some show, and teaching. For many weeks a year, I lived on unemployment insurance, a lifeline for a lot of people underemployed as dancers (and as everything else), and I made sure I was working just enough to collect it. I spent hours standing on line to sign for my $200, lying a lot in the process. It was quite degrading and very, very helpful. I lived very frugally, semicommunally—we were vegetarians, rent was cheap—but New York was all too much for me. (I still believe it is, by the way, but I'm not moving anymore.) It was time to get away. I wanted to live somewhere nicer, see a little sky.

No single review, in however grand a publication, pays your rent, and I didn't have enough work. All I had was a great review, and the thirty-three dances I'd made up during my first stay. There was a job at the University of Washington waiting for me, so it wasn't as if I was leaving for nothing. I was to be an associate professor of dance for two years, teaching and choreographing, ballet and Modern Dance. Barry and Tina moved there too, to work with me. It seemed a more practical base for everyone. But I didn't like the job—a nine o'clock class every morning is too early. I taught workshops on my own to make money, gain notoriety. Whoever showed up to my technique class was in my next concert.

Erin got a job there too. We lived in a neat cottage in Wallingford, a block from Lake Union. I drove a Dodge Dart, an ex–police car with a searchlight, and I'd drive down lovers' lane to see what it might illuminate. Living there seemed like heaven, and it was. A little home was what I had thought I wanted, and it was good to be around my family and my very old friends. Erin and I were interested in all the same things; on Saturdays we got up to watch *Pee-Wee's Playhouse* together. We listened to music all the time, and though I did most of the cooking, I wouldn't say I was the more housewifely. We shared the tasks; it was much less fraught than with Stevie, because Erin, a tender spiritualist, wasn't in any way ashamed of being queer. We simply lived together in fond love. We'd even made the decision not to have penetrative sex (though I was never that into it anyway), even though we were monogamous, because we'd had sex with many people before and we thought that one of us might have HIV. If I encountered people doing anything unsafe, I turned evangelist: "Don't do that!" I was like Carrie Nation.

One immediate surprise, which somewhat galvanized the company, was that some of my dancers, more or less on a whim, decided to follow me to Seattle. They knew I was prolific, that I'd get straight down to work, and they knew that I'd be putting on shows, shows they didn't want to miss out on. So they flew out, on the admirable basis of "What's the worst thing that could happen? He doesn't use us?"

Everyone made arrangements where they'd be staying except, naturally, Guillermo, who had decided, unbeknownst to me, that since I was now living elsewhere with Erin, there'd be a spare room at the Morris family home, and that even though he'd never met any of my family, he could stay there. His plan was to get a cab directly from the airport, introduce himself, and ask politely.

That's precisely what happened, except no one seemed to be home to answer his knock on the front door. Peeking through the window, he saw Maxine glued to the television and, unable to get her attention, decided to let himself in, which he did, tiptoeing slowly forward so as not to surprise her. She found herself confronted by a dark interloper, desperately trying to explain who he was and why he was there: "I dance with Mark, he's probably told you about me . . ." Maxine covered her mouth with her hand, a gesture made not out of fear but embarrassment—she didn't have her teeth in. So she excused herself to go upstairs. Maureen came down and sorted everything out; Guillermo offered to do the cleaning in return for the accommodation, and moved into my old room.

But as I pieced together a life in dance—a show or two in Seattle, a miniature tour that hardly paid for itself, a workshop, or choreography for the Boston Ballet—I found myself heading back and forth to New York, where all my dancers (except Tina, and those briefly lodging at my mother's) were, as often as I was in Seattle. I tried hard to work from both coasts, but it ended up that Erin and I were living apart more than we were together. He said in retrospect that it was a little like *A Star Is Born* in that I was away and he stayed at home taking my calls. This led to eventual infidelities on both sides, and, after we'd broken up, he fell in love with a student, which is apparently what happens if you work at a college. Nothing brutal occurred; we never had a single fight; it was merely sad and difficult, but we were good friends, so no one felt the need for revenge. When I finally did move back to New York, he stayed in Seattle and taught there, and when I was invited to Brussels, I hired him as a dancer; we were always good friends.

When Stevie had moved to Santa Fe, I almost went. Coincidentally, Erin had previously lived in Santa Fe, and later joined a Catholic monastery there (the kind of thing that inevitably happens after you go out with me), Christ in the Desert, a silent Benedictine order. He was deeply interested in theology, not just the ceremony, and he'd always been quiet and calm—fake calm but still . . . Finally, he decided against becoming a monk, though he was a lay brother for years, before moving back to Portland and becoming a nurse. He retired recently at sixty-five. He remains adorable.

I'M AFRAID TO SAY, for those with a lurid interest in that private aspect of a memoir, that though this moment doesn't signal the end of my personal life *entirely*, I haven't had a real full-time boyfriend, or a live-in domestic relationship, since Erin.

I have sex, but rarely. I've had sex relationships, and long-term love relationships that didn't involve sex at all. It's nice when love and sex match up. Combined effectively, they work very well together—that's my preference—but it's also sometimes nice when they don't. Their combination isn't mandatory. If you're gay, there's an option to have sex be anonymous and unattached. Once one removes the end of "living together" as a goal (which I have, long since), one is left with various couples, some of which are sexual and some of which are not, but all of which have a serious emotional component.

My ex-dancer Shawn Gannon is a best friend, as is Isaac Mizrahi, the designer—but neither of those relationships is about sex. Isaac and I may have kissed once. I first met him, back when fashion was fashion and he was the new young thing, having our picture taken together at a gala at BAM in the early nineties, possibly for *L'Allegro*. He'd graduated from working for Perry Ellis and Calvin Klein to go out on his own, when he became very big, very fast. Living the life then of a very glamorous young designer, he was tall yet somewhat schlubby, baby-faced, adorable, and purposefully nerdy. He wore his pants unnaturally high around his waist and modeled kerchiefs, headscarves, and cravats. He was funny, clever with words, spontaneous, and combustible without being volcanic. Of course, you could just turn on QVC right now to find out what he looks like, and you'd certainly see a *version* of Isaac Mizrahi, though perhaps one with an exclamation point after his last name.

A few weeks after that first meeting, Anna Wintour, the longtime editor at *Vogue*, gave a dinner at which she sat Isaac and me side by side with the intention of setting us up. We never dated, but it was exemplary matchmaking because we became best, then lifelong, friends, and in a sense we've been dating (not to mention perpetually interrupting each other) for thirty years. We also met in other ways. I used to call an anonymous sex chat line—an expensive, by-the-minute, hookup arrangement. When you called in, a deep basso voice would say, "Okay. Let's go dowwwwn," and then you'd be connected to someone, with whom you'd talk for a little while, and either keep talking or move on to another of the 1,800 male New Yorkers, all cruising for sex in some form (mostly solo), looking for a good fit. One evening, this particular anonymous stranger seemed cute, and he thought the same about me, so as the conversation went on, we decided to meet. At some point the penny dropped and there was a long pause on the other end: "Hold on. *Mark?*" It was Isaac. He thought my voice had sounded familiar. I owed him a phone call anyway, so we talked on for quite a long time, just at much greater expense than usual.

With Isaac Mizrahi at the New York City Opera's Spring Gala, 2008.
(Patrick McMullan)

Darling Isaac and I have been somewhat coupled in people's minds, not only because we've collaborated many times, but because I made a cameo in *Unzipped*, the celebrated Mizrahi fly-on-the-wall documentary directed by his then boyfriend Douglas Keeve. At the time, Isaac had a beautifully decorated, very contemporary SoHo studio of unfinished plywood, poured concrete. (I remember asking his assistant, in all sincerity, what it was going to be like when it was finished. My mistake!) It was suggested they film a real design meeting for whatever project was then occupying us, which we agreed on, but in the movie we seem to meet by chance on the street. Isaac, who was just finishing up with Naomi Campbell, exclaims on seeing me—I was early, on my way to my scheduled interview, and they were running late—and introduces me to Naomi, whom I greet with the words, "You are my heroine; how could you not be?" Nevertheless, however fake it may look, that was a genuine chance meeting, if only by minutes. That may be as real as documentaries get. These days, my most consistent social engagements by far are the regular family dinners shared with Marjorie Folkman (who danced with me for many years), John Heginbotham, and Isaac himself. We eat, Isaac talks, and one of us pays.

Since Erin, however, I've never been interested in a live-in boyfriend, and there's only ever been he and Stevie, but I do like roommates, people with whom I can cohabit who aren't actual boyfriends: Guillermo, for example. I've always liked people to cook for, but I think what one needs is, in the Virginia Woolf sense, a room of one's own, and basically I advise everybody against living together as a couple. Nor do I like the institution of marriage. I love that people love each other, or agree to be together forever, but I'm a bit of a Marxist in seeing marriage as a property exchange or unpaid employment for one of the partners. I also don't like automatically to have to relate to people as couples once they're coupled. It's not good for two people to add up to a total of one person; they should add up to a *minimum* of two people. But that's just me. You can do whatever you want.

Someone I ended up having sex with two or three times over the course of twenty years? That's not a boyfriend. But then I don't need a definitive "relationship status" descriptor to put on a business card. Sex aged eighteen in the shrubbery of Volunteer Park, a few days a week, coming home high from somewhere, was thrilling and fabulous, but it was also a style. Nothing was better than New York in the seventies sexwise. And luckily I'm alive to tell the tale.

Barry once said that my perfect boyfriend would be someone I visited in prison. We'd both put our hands up to the Plexiglas that separated us and stare at each other. Longingly.

And then I'd leave and get back to work.

Rob Besserer, me, and Tina Fehlandt, *Mythologies* performance poster,
Manhattan Center Grand Ballroom, 1987. *(Tom Brazil)*

Six

Mythologies

O n the back of Arlene's article and our new "overnight fame" (and perhaps in hindsight it looks like overnight fame, but it certainly didn't feel that way), the group started getting invitations all over the place: the Kennedy Center in DC, SUNY Purchase, London, Paris, and beyond.

For the time being, I was bicoastal, wherever the work was. Either in Seattle, where I stayed with Terry Grizzell, a friend from First Chamber who'd also been with me in Port Townsend, in his apartment in the Central District, or in Manhattan with Rob, on Seventh Avenue and Fourteenth Street.

IN SEATTLE, I premiered my solo piece *The Vacant Chair*, the saddest thing I'd done, degrading in a way that gave me enormous satisfaction. It's also how I first injured my neck.

It was set to three parlor songs: first, George F. Root's 1862 Civil

War song (from Henry Stevenson Washburn's poem "The Vacant Chair"—"We shall meet, but we shall miss him, / There will be one vacant chair"—I cry just thinking that, let alone writing it down), then a setting of a poem well-known from everyone's childhood, Joyce Kilmer's "Trees" ("I think that I shall never see / A poem lovely as a tree"), and finally "A Perfect Day," a phenomenally successful sentimental ballad from the turn of the century, and one of the songs my grandma Mabel hummed quietly to herself.

My notion was to illustrate these three sections with title cards like a silent movie—Guillermo made drawings for me, at least one of which he had to redo every night because I tore it up. Between songs, I'd change the title card and then dance. But the point of horror is this: for the dance to the song "The Vacant Chair," I was clad exclusively in white briefs with a brown paper bag over my head, so other people could see my naked body but I couldn't see *anything* at all. It happened mostly in place, but I had to trust that I knew where I was because the dance, though not long or terribly complicated, was punitive and hazardous, including repeated violent throwings to the ground. Because of the paper bag, I might end up facing the wrong way or running into something. That was part of it. I was mostly naked, blind, and wearing ugly underwear. It wasn't sexy in any way. (Though there's always *someone* who thinks something is sexy.)

I was handicapping myself, partly as a constraint (I couldn't do the things that I normally could, for example, *see*) but partly out of showmanship—"You've never seen *this* done before." Failure was possible, as success was almost impossible. It represented a form of self-torture, but it was also ceremonial, a ritual, like much of early dance. Yvonne Rainer was the first to instruct someone, as part of her choreography, to "lean over until you fall down." It's a challenge, and there was a lot of this in my early dances, my heritage from early minimalism. Lucinda Childs set the rules and executed every possible variation. It wasn't an arc; it just stacked up until it was complete, which is when the dance stopped. My love of strict formal problem-solving came directly from my great appreciation of her work. And Bach's.

Besides, testing oneself is one of the basic pleasures of dancing, of choreography. Though my dances were very hard, structurally they were nothing tricky. Later, their beauty increased exponentially with their difficulty. The dances were always structurally sound, based on complicated systems. As the dancer, you had to keep track. Like my favorite painter and conceptual artist, Sol LeWitt, I was interested in establishing similarly strict rules and fulfilling them. That's what I like. If it was something repetitive, I rang changes on it, and even if it looked like a repeat to the audience, it wasn't. There was some slight ornament or change. These solos were so tricky that, at times, I had to have someone in the wings telling me how many repeats I'd done, because I couldn't simultaneously dance and count.

When *The Vacant Chair* ended, I tore up the blindfolding paper bag and faced away from the audience, so they could see my bare back, to dance the role of the tree in *Trees*. I became a tree—who doesn't love being a tree?—and those shreds of paper bag became falling leaves. There was nothing else to the dance.

The finale, *A Perfect Day*, was wild, spastic, primitive ballet; a tombé pas de bourrée that got bigger, louder, and more grotesque. The torture was that I would do the dance, then exit, go all the way around backstage, running as fast as I could to make my entrance at the end of the four-bar bridge, reenter, do the next verse—the same but *harder*—exit again, run all the way around, reenter (by this time quite breathlessly), and repeat even bigger and harder still, until I was completely spent.

It ended defiantly (and stupidly, I now think) with me knocking the music stand over. A mic drop.

The end.

THAT SAME YEAR, 1984, I was invited to the American Dance Festival in Durham, North Carolina, at Duke University as a choreographer. So much happened during those few weeks.

I took three dancers with me, Penny, Guillermo, and Erin. There were choreographers and composers from all over the world. We stayed in dormitories (it was summer so there were no students), it was unbearably hot, and I had a giant crush on Guillermo. Erin, on the other hand, had an affaire de coeur with a young milk-fed dance student. The young man in question was new, gorgeous, and smart, and though I had no right to be, since Erin and I were no longer together, I was jealous. I shouldn't say his name—he personally arranged with another author not to be revealed in her book about me, and I'm not going to out him—so I'll call him H. He was beautiful, so beautiful you couldn't quite believe it, straight and athletic like a wrestler. He even sported my preferential boyfriend look, fair-haired with glasses. (I wouldn't have necessarily been able to predict my predilection for glasses.)

After the festival, when Erin went back to Seattle, H moved to NYC to continue his studies and became *my* boyfriend. It was nothing as exciting as revenge, and there wasn't a plot, so I had nothing to feel guilty about. We just ended up together, and Erin was far, far away. H turned out to be a ravenous sex creature—I don't know if he was like that with anyone else, but we had sex on our very first date—and we were full-on frequent sex partners for a couple of years, though he never publicly acknowledged that kind of bond between us, which was a little manipulative.

In the end H left me for another of my dancers (female, because he was basically straight). I don't hold many grudges that way, but it was upsetting. I can confirm what everyone fears: homosexuals get no greater thrill than converting straight people (which is not entirely true, though I won't deny it was part of his mystery and appeal), but I was pissed with both of them, particularly her, and we had to live with it, even as we worked together. My tactic in that situation is to keep going because it's the professional thing to do. If anything, I'm so perverted that, rather than give that person the cold shoulder, they'll get a solo. There may perhaps have been a few tiny examples of torture built into the rehearsals in that particular situation, but it can't have been anything too bad, because that particular woman danced with me for many years afterward. We lived with it.

There have been a few other examples of rehearsal trouble, but it's not always because one feels sorry for *oneself*. Sometimes you may know something about one of your dancers that you're not supposed to know, behavior that disappoints or even horrifies you: an affair, a lie. The remnants of my Protestant work ethic mean I feel I have to work through it and keep working. Everything will pass—I don't ignore things, but in the Jesuit way I feel you should smile when you're sad. I'm good at persevering. (A collapse of a relationship between two of your dancers can also be heartbreaking and difficult. They're doing a love duet together, they hate each other, and you haven't understood the half of it.)

In Durham, amid all this intrigue and chaos, I choreographed a dance (to Herschel Garfein's music based on the madrigal "Four Arms, Two Necks, One Wreathing") for sixteen students and the four of *us*, each of us with our own solo and a corps de ballet of four dancers, which is pure Balanchine. For obvious mathematical reasons, I therefore called the dance *Forty Arms, Twenty Necks, One Wreathing*, a system-based dance for Herschel's complicated modernist music.

O Rangasayee, Brooklyn Academy of
Music, 1984. *(Tom Brazil)*

Remembering my trip
to India with Erin, I made
up a solo, *O Rangasayee*, to a
wonderful twenty-minute
raga of the same name by
Tyagaraja sung by M. S.
Subbalakshmi, and showed
it in the empty theater to
friends, people we'd met at
the festival, dancers and
musicians from Senegal
and India. (I heard later
that Merce was watching
from the back row.) It was
the first flowering of my
Indophilia, my first fully
"Indian" dance, made up
after only the barest ac-
quaintance on that first
short trip with Laura
Dean's company in 1981. How dared I? But there's a fine American
tradition of exoticism, and it all ties into early Modern Dance. The
Denishawn people (Ruth St. Denis and Ted Shawn, full Orientalists)
would have probably thought *O Rangasayee* a genuine Indian dance. But
I wasn't even trying to be consciously historical; it was just what I liked.
O Rangasayee contains much hand gesture, percussive footwork, torso
isolation, and facial expression, and if someone has never seen one scrap
of Indian dance, they might be fooled—by the music—into thinking it
a genuine Indian dance. There was a section about infirmity and death,
in which I stood on one leg, then distorted myself, as though I had ele-
phantiasis, and kept it up until I fell over, which cleared the stage for me

to do it again. These horrible contortions, my writhing, had no rhythm at all; they were based on the physical fact of curling up and twisting my form and face until I crumpled to the floor.

The dance and music of India underscored my strong native belief that music is, as the composer Lou Harrison said, "a song and a dance." As I was coming into my own as a choreographer, it was more firmly established in dancing to ignore the rhythm and the tune, but my dances were always tied to the music. I wanted that and still do. It's not an accident and it's not because I'm stupid. It's hard to do it. But that's how it should be. All my dances are related very directly to melody (raga), rhythm (tala), gesture (mudra), and facial expression (abhinaya), and you can learn a lot about them from the honesty and drama of Indian dance. The Indian artists in Durham liked *O Rangasayee*, which emboldened me to put it on our forthcoming show at BAM.

This festival was also the year that Twyla Tharp, whose early *Deuce Coupe* I had so loved, presented *Sinatra Songs*. It was meant to be a tough, funny Apache dance with the gun, the scarf, and the cigarette: he done her wrong, she shoots him, "Frankie and Johnny"–style. At least I think that's what she meant. The song was "That's Life," the dreamy gowns were Oscar de la Renta, and it was the most god-awful war between the sexes, a man roughing up a woman as she begs for more. She's on the floor in her ball gown, clinging to his leg as if trying to scale him, to that lyric about picking yourself up and getting back in the race, and he rejects her. As a newly vocal, queer choreographer and feminist, I hated it. I had already resisted the stereotypes of male and female behavior in dance, which is why I was out at that time when most queer choreographers weren't, and I wasn't interested in seeing that kind of lazy cliché reenacted. I found myself standing and yelling, "NO MORE RAPE!" That's what I said. I didn't boo; I didn't say, "Rape is bad." I shouted, "NO MORE RAPE!" just once and walked out. There was no place for the rape in that dance.

Afterward I found myself at the same party as the dancers, all friends of mine, though Twyla wasn't there. (It's sort of like we're played by the same actor; we never appear in the same scene.) A few of the dancers were hurt because they couldn't understand why I'd walked out, and I was sorry about that. They weren't too worried about Twyla, though.

It made the *Dance Gossip News*—not an actual publication—because no one did that kind of thing. Twyla and I have no contact of any kind and never have; we've never talked at all. I can't believe she was too annoyed about my heckling. She was used to controversy, and I would think that was water off her back. But for years after she wouldn't allow a piece of mine to be on a program with a piece of hers.

Once, at a party on the Upper East Side, I walked in and found myself face-to-face with her, then suddenly back-to-back with her. That dance is performed to this day, and I still hate it.

OUR FIRST SHOW at the Brooklyn Academy of Music—the one that made all the noise—wasn't in the opera house. It was in the modest ("flexible") Lepercq Space (now the BAMcafé), holding about two hundred people. This show comprised *Gloria* (which I decided to bring back, adapt, and improve), *O Rangasayee* (for which I wore a loincloth, my hands and feet painted crimson), and *Championship Wrestling after Roland Barthes*, a new piece Herschel had composed for me. He'd proposed something from Barthes's *Mythologies*, his musique concrète score recorded at wrestling matches. I went to the wrestling at Madison Square Garden several times in preparation, and I made up rules for a dance that could be done by anyone regardless of size and strength. Any two people could do the various falls and throws. It was precisely as phony as *World Wide Wrestling*, which meant I could pair Guillermo, who's big, with Winkie, who's little—it didn't matter. Rob, who is the tallest dancer, possibly of all, was paired with Donald Mouton. It wasn't that dangerous, but it was grueling, made to look as much like real (fake) wrestling as possible, in a ring implied by the magic of theatrical lighting. The dancers wore actual wrestling gear—singlets, belts, knee and elbow pads, and high-laced wrestling shoes—and their moves were wrestling moves, as the dancers variously jumped on top of each other, got each other in headlocks, and smashed each other's faces into the ground. Certain time limits were set, and it wasn't even necessarily decided who would win the various bouts. One section featured Penny and Winkie in superslow motion, their moves as exaggerated as wrestling but even more extreme because the women were partnered (though the audience had to pretend these partners were invisible). One dancer could therefore "hit" the other, who would then fly through the air backward, lifted by her partners. It was a fabulous,

Clarice Marshall versus Penny Hutchinson in *Championship Wrestling after Roland Barthes* from *Mythologies*, Cirque Royal, Brussels, 1989. *(Danièle Pierre)*

funny dance. (We later added more Barthes, danced versions of his essays on soap powders and detergents and striptease, and presented all three as *Mythologies*, first in Boston, where they got it, then in Belgium, where they manifestly and vocally didn't.)

When we premiered *Gloria* for Dance Theater Workshop in 1981, I hadn't choreographed the last Amen. False piety, perhaps, but I didn't feel worthy of it. For the same reason, I also hadn't choreographed the first movement ("Gloria in Excelsis Deo"), which I left undanced. The audience simply listened; it's why they're called an *audience*. I've often started dances that way—music first before the dancing starts. (Besides, it was safer. Back then you never knew if it was all going to work: lights, recorded music, dancing, all at the same time on the downbeat. We had performances where the show started and the wrong recorded music came on. Another great reason to use only live music, incidentally.) By the time of the BAM show, I'd decided that avoiding the Amen was a cop-out, even more pretentious than doing it. I also decided to choreograph the first movement. Two dancers advance on the audience during the instrumental introduction, then at the entrance of the chorus, an abrupt blackout plunges the audience into darkness (often thought to be a mistake), and the audience is left to listen to the rest of the movement. Previously, the dancers had started late and finished early; now the dance and the music were the same length. At the end, as the Amens are sung, all ten dancers spiral to the floor. They turn two at a time and land on their faces, cruciform *and* in a cross shape on the floor, as if the cross has fallen down because they ran out of nails. I subsequently realized I'd stolen that idea from a famous image from the Met's great production of Poulenc's *Dialogue of the Carmelites*, where all the nuns are lying prostrate before they're guillotined.

According to *People*, that legendary dance review magazine, this performance "stunned the dance world." In that same article, Donald Mouton mentioned a woman in the lobby with tears streaming down her face. I was "the hottest young choreographer in the country" (*Time*) and "the crown prince and long awaited savior of the dance world" (*Newsweek*).

I was also broke.

BARRY ALTERMAN'S and my business relationship *proper* began, according to him, when he saw me dance *O Rangasayee* at its official premiere in Montreal. He said it was "like finding out your friend wrote *Moby-Dick*." He started representing me part-time, a natural progression.

Barry felt that there were better models for us than the awful corporate ballet company model. His inspirations were the Living Theatre and the Grateful Dead, the socialist idea of keeping control of everything in-house, so that's how we went about it. Everything had to be consonant: what we were trying to achieve, the shows we were putting on, and the presentation of our company. As far as was possible, we weren't going to go through other media and other corporations to promote ourselves. We didn't use a letterhead. If you called us up and you got *anyone*, you got Barry, whom you'd just woken up. We didn't court publicity. We were aware that it was a cool calling card, but that wasn't the whole point. The Wooster Group did the same kind of thing, and they were an influence. I don't love the theater, but I love everything the Wooster Group does. Even when I don't like it, I *love* it.

It was groovy but inefficient and soon got out of hand. So we applied to Pentacle, a service organization that managed fifteen or twenty small dance companies that each had three gigs a year, at a time when we still had an average of two, one in New York and one in Seattle. A woman there named Nancy Umanoff oversaw our account, did our books, wrote the checks. We headhunted her.

At our first meeting, I was wearing mirrored aviator shades in which she could see only herself reflected. Back then, Nancy sported something of an Adrienne Barbeau haircut, sometimes with accompanying shoulder pads. (Slightly later we shared the same hairdo and you couldn't tell us apart: see below.) She also had the most perfect complexion imaginable; her skin was so soft, clear, and gorgeous. It remains that way to this day.

"I can't talk to you like this," she said tetchily. "Could you take your glasses off?" I did. I wasn't high; I was just showing up for my first business meeting.

Nancy had been a tough new-wave teenager, but by this time, with her background at Pentacle, she was responsible and logical, not to say a workaholic. Best of all, she was passionately interested and involved in grant writing, the part of the arts management that is completely beyond me. I couldn't do it at gunpoint, and she was already so good.

We asked if she'd do what she did at Pentacle, but exclusively for us.

Nancy and me in the green room at Cal Performances.

She wanted to know how much she'd be making, and we said, because we were business *geniuses*, "You know how money works. You tell us. Hire yourself. Make up your own job, and your salary." She did.

Nancy has worked with me, run my life and the life of the company, from that day to this. It was a perfect marriage. We were all around the same age—and making it up as we went along, but she was *really* making it up. She rolled her eyes periodically, about whatever was going on, but who doesn't? Nancy became the power behind the throne, but Barry was the public face of MMDG. He had many obvious talents, and he was also a great schmoozer, very brave at approaching people. They trusted him the moment they met him. He was charming and versatile, knew everything they knew about and could talk about it: dance history, gay culture, opera, baseball, anything. He's the reason I met Susan Sontag—they had somehow become very close friends—through whom I met Annie Leibovitz, who introduced me to the genius painter Howard Hodgkin (who became a frequent collaborator), and so on.

Nancy and Barry enjoy a working lunch, Berkeley, 2001.
(*June Omura*)

Barry tried to match me up with other artists for projects. Sometimes it worked and sometimes it didn't, but they were generally good ideas: Lou Reed, for example, though nothing came of it, and Taj Mahal, whose music I had loved as a teenager (though when I met him, I thought he was never going to leave). Barry also later talked me into working with virtuoso bassist Rob Wasserman and singer-songwriter Michelle Shocked, which led to the dance *Home* in 1993, as close to a disaster as we ever came. The two of them were so disorganized that I basically ended up producing the music; they simply couldn't get it together. Michelle couldn't manage much at all, and Rob—poor lovely man and rest in peace—was extremely passive. There was a section for Appalachian-style clog dancing, for which I wanted a fiddle breakdown; they said they could do it, which they could, but they couldn't do it twice, and I needed them to do it twice at *every* performance. One time in Edinburgh, Michelle showed up at the venue a day late for rehearsal, having had a big fight with her bad husband/manager, without instruments, no guitar or mandolin, without even her suitcase, wearing an airplane blanket as a poncho. The meter was running and she couldn't pay for the taxi. She'd run away from him and shown up in Scotland; it was nuts. Somehow it all turned out fine, but the experience nearly broke me. The dance was beautiful, but it wasn't the most blessed union.

Lovey was another foray into contemporary popular music—the Violent Femmes, suggested by Chad Henry, who always had great ideas. The Violent Femmes had a folk aspect I loved, the same thing I loved about the British folk-rock of Steeleye Span and the Watersons. The songs from their first two albums were so funny and terrible, so awfully bleak and dark, so I made up a dance.

My niece Amanda was attached to a baby doll named Lovey, in tribute to whom I named this piece, which included actual baby dolls, dolls that represented different characters, and a lot of unsavory inter-doll sex acts. This was perhaps my inner punk, but it was also funny. Besides, I've always thought punk, which I didn't take that seriously because I wasn't a junkie, was funny. I loved the Sex Pistols, but I didn't want a safety pin in my nipple. I preferred the cartoon version, the Ramones and Devo. The reaction was, as intended, equal laughter and horror. Early on, people booed and walked out, choosing to see it as a promotion of child pornography and abuse, though to me it was consonant with the horror-comedy of the Femmes songs, cautionary tales that made the audience very uneasy. The point was that the dancers interacted only with the dolls, and not with each other. If there was a message, it was that people should notice each other and perhaps be a little nicer. And believe me, you genuinely need to see Tina eating out a doll.

For "Country Death Song," the Femmes' classic about throwing a baby down a well, the dancers acted out the story like a Sunday school pageant. Some people think that too plain, too frank, and in some way not artistic enough, not fancied up enough; it's what an audience imagines it might do in the same situation, perhaps thinking they wouldn't have the wherewithal to come up with anything else. In other words, "Anybody could have done that." But it's all much more stylized than people imagine and emerges from a vast complication of other choices that I could have made, rather than simply from my genuine affection for simplicity. If it looks artless, that's down to artfulness. My method is similar to Chinese or Indian theater. In Japanese Noh theater, the actor might say, "I am in my village," and then, "I will now go on a journey," at which point he simply turns around 360 degrees and is then immediately on the outskirts of Kyoto, magic with no magic at all. What could be more beautiful than that? It's called theater. There was talk later of doing *Lovey* live with the Violent Femmes, but it's an old dance now and not one I'd care to bring back.

The *Lovey* rehearsals were the cause of my biggest fight with Guillermo. "I want your foot just to hang!" Guillermo remembers me shouting. "If you have to think of that as a flexed foot, then do whatever you have to do, but goddamn you, don't change my choreography and make it look like ballet! If you point your foot again, I'll break your leg!" In this instance, I'd asked them to do what they considered an impossible task: to jump, go horizontal, and then land facedown. No one could do it, perhaps because it was impossible.

I split rehearsals into three groups of four, one of which contained Tina and Guillermo. That group worked so hard, so recklessly, that I focused exclusively on them. I didn't want to have to coax things out of the others, to have to interpret things for them that this group understood intuitively.

Apparently, Guillermo's group was thinking, "We'll get the premiere to ourselves, because Mark will want the dance seen the best it can possibly be done. And we're the four who do it best." But that had never been my intent, and for the premiere, I added everyone else back in, despite the fact that the other dancers had only learned by osmosis. Guillermo was livid: "You fucked us over! We worked our asses off, truly thinking that our quartet would get to do the whole piece, and it ended up being twelve!" We didn't talk for some time.

I knew they'd killed themselves to do it, but there's only one star in MMDG, and it isn't even me: it's the choreography. Everything is in service to the final show, and Guillermo knew this. Once, on the event of someone being injured because they'd gone horseback riding on their day off, Guillermo yelled at an entire dressing room, "The only thing that matters each day on tour is your ten minutes onstage. If I have to understudy for someone on this tour, their leg had better be broken, because if it isn't, I'll break it myself."

There were a lot of casual threats of leg breakage in those days.

Opera, and its choreography, was another new avenue of collaboration fostered by Barry. Dance used to be an integral part of opera (or vice versa), right up until the early twentieth century. In baroque times particularly, there wasn't an opera and a ballet; there was a big night out containing both, a *ballet tragique*, an *opéra dansé*. If it's a story ballet or an opera, with characters and relationships, it's all coming from the music and the book. My first brush with it was Strauss's *Salome* (Oscar Wilde's play in German, an amazing piece of music) directed by Sonja Frisell in 1986 for Seattle Opera, who hired me to choreograph the *Dance of the Seven Veils*, the only dance in that particular opera. As a rule, in a production of *Salome*, a body double for the female lead is used for this dance, generally a bad ballet dancer, who doesn't even take all her clothes off, so we decided to have the actual Salome—the great English soprano Josephine Barstow, a wonderful woman, forty at the time—do the dance herself and actually remove seven veils, down to a thong. It was considered scandalous that she was topless. Salome naked? Big deal.

I'd originally gone to New York with the ambition to dance for the Joffrey. That never happened, but the same year as *Salome*, Mr. Joffrey himself was one of the first people to commission a ballet from me.

Robert Joffrey was—and I try never to say this about anyone—one of a kind. He was a sweet, brilliant, openly gay, Armenian American Seattleite. Elsewhere, it was Balanchine or nothing, but his was, for years, the only company in the States that performed the wonderful dances of the Royal Ballet's Frederick Ashton. Joffrey's was also the ballet of the youth movement, the psychedelic ballet, the rock ballet. His company was the first to stage reconstructions of old pieces: *Les Biches* of Nijinska and *Pas de quatre*, a Fokine ballet based on the four great ballerinas of the late nineteenth century (Lucile Grahn, Carlotta Grisi, Fanny Cerrito, and Marie Taglioni), in which they continually try to upstage one another. Joffrey also revived Satie's *Parade* with the Picasso costumes, shocking stuff and serious ballet history. Famously, he was also the first person to hire Twyla Tharp to create a ballet. She gave him *Deuce Coupe*, a masterpiece.

So when Joffrey asked me to make up a ballet?

Mr. Joffrey, I'd love to.

Rehearsals took place at City Center, and the music was Haydn's Cello Concerto in C Major, with costumes by Santo Loquasto, who'd been principal designer for Paul Taylor and Twyla Tharp for decades. In the slow movement, for what would normally have been the pas de deux, I opted for a lone woman instead of a boy-girl couple, which was considered very bold. There was a corps de ballet of male-female couples, from which one woman—the great ballerina Leslie Carothers—separated herself to do the pas d'une, as it were, a sad and lonely dance.

What could go wrong?

The punch line: I showed up relaxed and happy in LA for the world premiere at the Dorothy Chandler Pavilion, having just enjoyed a getaway in Hawaii with Terry. The New York rehearsals had gone perfectly smoothly, but I arrived in LA to find that my piece had been completely changed. It had *self-Arpinoized.*

Gerald Arpino, Joffrey's lover and partner (they were an admirable gay couple from early on), was a famous choreographer of contemporary ballet. He's given a hard time nowadays, but I learned a great deal from his work. (Particularly the "wipe," which means to me, in dance terms, a crowd of people who cross the stage, leaving one person behind to dance for a while, before the crowd passes again and replaces her with another dancer. He used that in every single dance.) But *Esteemed Guests*, as my dance was called, was now being danced as though he'd choreographed it.

If you look at old pictures of ballet, an arabesque (the definition of which is that one leg is lifted to the back) is low and dignified in the English Ashtonian style. The Balanchinian version is so high that you can't quite tell if it's to the back or the side. It's easier to do, because it's about flexibility rather than strength, but to me it's less expressive and inelegant. Arpino's version of an arabesque was contorted, like ballet is now, like *Dancing with the Stars*, where you stick your leg up so far that your pudenda are protruding farther than anything else. I favor (both for esthetic reasons and also because of the natural shape of the body) a horizontal line in the old-fashioned style rather than what I call "Swiss Army knife," which is too gynecological. *Esteemed Guests* had dealt in horizontal lines, pivoting in a beautiful way, but I returned to find it had been changed to fit the institutional style, because it was easier for the dancers, because that's how they danced. There wasn't a thing I could do about it, and no time to make any changes. I just watched, surprised and disappointed. (Nothing changes. I recently made up a lovely, fairly plain piece for ABT. I was asked where all the big steps were. I said, "They're in all the other dances you do, but they're not in this one.")

Esteemed Guests got an okay review from my beloved Arlene Croce, who wrote that she liked it, but "who doles out the names for these things?" I do, and I liked the title, but this was when I first learned this lesson: as specific and meticulous as I can possibly be when I'm making something up, the exigencies of the ballet industry tend toward a homogenization of style that can't be exactly what I want. This was to have major repercussions later.

———

Money was always tight. We worked for free a lot, and when we made money for a gig, I'd divide it up and pay everyone whatever I could. It was a big deal just to fly someone somewhere from Seattle for a show to perform for free. My work earned me my keep—just—but I've always lived the same way, so it's hard for me now to remember how much we were, or were not, making, and when we had enough to afford our own fax machine. It was hand-to-mouth, but somehow we survived.

A classic MMDG MEMBER UNIT COMMUNIQUÉ of the time, typed and xeroxed, written presumably by Barry and Nancy, read as follows:

> Much has happened: many deals, maneuvers, projects; many hours spent by your management team slogging through that smoke-filled swamp which is known by the cursed appellation: Show-Biz.

Then, under the heading ENQUIRING MINDS NEED TO KNOW!:

> As some of you might have noticed, we have a "cash-flow problem." There are basically three reasons for this:
> A. Late-arriving grant cash
> B. Current work which hasn't yet been compensated. (U.W., California, Jacob's Pillow, etc.)
> C. New and Special Expenditures due to the historical juncture.
> The first two reasons are self-explanatory and depressingly mundane, the third is interesting stuff.
> As we continue the extremely rapid transition from "alternative" performing spaces to major (and electronic) auditoria—and thus from poverty to economic decency—certain operating re-

quirements are being thrust upon us. These requirements and their attendant cost must be dealt with <u>now</u>. They cannot be put off for some future "better time." We must also act now if we are to seize the approaching high-visibility moment (Autumn = TV, Joffrey, BAM) and insure our future. In other words, we have to spend it to make it.

We just didn't have it. The communiqué ends on a slightly optimistic note:

> And, you know, we'll be OK with the bucks in a couple of weeks. Really. I mean it. No kidding. The check's in the mail . . .
>   SEIZE THE MOMENT
>   THE FUTURE IS BRIGHT
>   PERSEVERANCE FURTHERS.

An invitation—referred to in this communiqué—to present my work on the PBS series *Great Performances* was a very big deal. It was almost unprecedented, someone like *me* getting a show like *that*. My work was already being seen, I may even have been something of a hot property, and my company was great (because it wasn't only my company, it was also excellent dancers), but this was entirely unexpected.

My entire previous TV experience boiled down to the choreography of a commercial for Capri Sun, the famous "juice drink." I'd been offered a couple of grand to work for five days in the Puck Building. It was fun and helpful in that it taught me how to adapt dances for the camera, which would be useful for all the other TV shows I haven't been asked to do. (The secret is the wedge shape, because that's the camera's-eye view. Everything has to happen in depth to give the illusion of width. Now you *too* can choreograph for TV! You're welcome.)

There was a lot more dance on PBS back then, but there's almost zero now. In a way that's good. They showed Paul Taylor so many times, you wanted to kill yourself. Jac Venza ran the arts wing of PBS; his was the ultimate credit, a full second long, at the end of every art show on PBS for thirty years, and it was he who approached me. Jac produced and Judy Kinberg directed. She'd done a lot of dance, including *Baryshnikov on Broadway*, and I liked her and her work. The show was intended to be a sampler of my dances to date. Though I had a lot of say, the pieces were to be adapted for the small screen. I understood the need for editing, though I was very reluctant to amputate half of *Gloria*, a weird compromise. But I would have done anything to be on TV, and please note: I will choreograph any horrible movie in the world for enough money—it just doesn't happen. Some principles aren't principles, they're prejudices. Wayne McGregor choreographed one of the Harry Potter movies, and a recent Tarzan, and I should hope made a lot of money.

We shot for a full week in Aarhus, Denmark (a lot of dance was filmed there, Balanchine included), and it was the time of year when it's perpetual daylight; I'd never seen so many drunks. PBS wanted visuals, so I asked Bobby Bordo to make designs for everything, which meant that for the very first time the dances were done with sets. For my solo *Jealousy*, Bobby had the floor painted so it looked like an overhead special, a comic-bookey stage spotlight. I made up the dance because I was jealous of a boyfriend, or perhaps because he was jealous of me, I can't remember—jealousy was a topic, is the point, and I would certainly have been remembering and tapping into things I'd experienced with Erin. This Handel chorus, from the oratorio *Hercules*, features one of the first great mad scenes, in which the jealousy of Hercules's wife, Dejanira, is described as an "infernal pest, / Tyrant of the human breast!"—a dignified, passionate, and terrifying response.

Jealousy was perfect for the PBS show—a stand-alone piece, seven minutes. My programs at the time comprised small pieces, because that's what I could afford and rehearse and because that was the size of the company. I've always enjoyed making up "short story"–scale pieces.

THEN I BROKE MY FOOT. The right foot. It was in Ottawa, and I *ottawa*'ve been more careful.

I was warming up before *Pièces en Concert*, choreographed for Rob, Susan Hadley, and me. I jumped, landed, and rolled my foot—I always had glass ankles—and broke the fifth metatarsal. Cleanly, I thought. My full body weight was on it, and it sounded like stepping on a Styrofoam cup. *POP!*

Though I suspected it was broken, I optimistically iced it at seven thirty for an eight p.m. show. It was swelling so badly, however, that I had to call out to Tina, my understudy, "Do you want to do *Pièces en concert* tonight? I think I'd better go to the emergency room." They made the announcement ("Mark Morris will not be performing tonight . . ."), at which the audience groaned, and we all looked at Tina with the sarcastic sad face. She put on my costume, went in at the last second, and faked her way brilliantly through the part, including an improvised section in which she hadn't the faintest idea what she was doing. It was then we found out she was not only excellent under pressure, but a gifted natural comedian. The crew kindly nailed me together a cane so I could take a bow. I walked out as if I wasn't injured (a matter of pride), which led to a sarcastic remark in the paper the next day, along the lines of "Was he really injured?"

In the Ottawa hospital, an idiot put my foot in a plaster cast up to the knee. The next morning, I rolled onto the plane in a wheelchair; by the time I got to New York my foot was swollen out of the cast. I went straight to a highly recommended doctor, orthopedist to the stars, who gave me her considered opinion: "Oh, this happens all the

time; it's a dancer's injury, just a clean break of your fifth metatarsal."
She put me in a little boot, fiberglass cap, and I went back to Seattle,
walking on it. All seemed fine.

I kept teaching at UW, on one leg. Guillermo, my hero, came out
to help me. He'd carry me, on his back, up and down the three flights
of stairs at Terry's place. It was a workout for Guillermo, but less time-
consuming and hazardous than the alternative: crutches on the stairs
in the wet Seattle winter. Guillermo hated teaching but he'd demonstrate in class as I taught from a chair, on crutches, while he did the
heavy lifting, literally. I was quite successful in my role as an embit-
tered teacher. In my woeful crippled state, I'd throw the crutches
across the room, yelling, "Can't you do anything right? *Fuck You!*"
I meant it as a joke, but I was still throwing my crutches across the
room.

At my six-week checkup, my foot still hurt and felt lumpy. The doctor, an orthopedist for the Seattle Sonics, said it was as if I'd broken it
the day before. The New York doctor had misdiagnosed it as a clean
break, but it was a spiral.

My foot had to be rebroken.

I TAUGHT AND CHOREOGRAPHED in Seattle for a semester, during
which I made up a dance for Seattle Men's Chorus (which was of course
the Seattle Gay Men's Chorus, as all men's choruses were), *Strict Songs*,
to beautiful music by the composer Lou Harrison.

The chorus had a sign language interpreter in their concerts who
was a pleasure to watch: they had a lot of deaf queer fans. At their
Christmas concert at Meany Hall, the entire chorus would sign the
last verse of "Silent Night" without any singing. It was so moving that
the entire audience was in tears. So, being that I had a broken foot
and couldn't dance, I was inspired to start studying sign language, and

in fact became lovers with my sign language teacher, Kevin, a full-hearing guy who worked with hearing-impaired kids in the public school system.

Dennis Coleman, who directed the chorus, asked me if I'd make up a dance for them. Of *chorus* I would! I'd just heard Lou Harrison's music for the first time, and you either love Lou's music or haven't heard it yet. It sings and it dances, and it hit me like that first trip to India. It felt like home—strange, satisfying, and just right. It emerged that, coincidentally, Dennis actually knew Lou. I proposed a piece, *Four Strict Songs*, which I'd heard on an out-of-print LP (made in the 1960s by the Louisville Orchestra), set for 8 baritone vocalists and orchestra. Dennis asked Lou to increase the number of singers from 8 to 120 (which actually ended up, the program confirms, at 114). Lou loved choruses, his boyfriend, Bill Colvig, happened to be going deaf, and Lou, who had many deaf friends, was learning sign language, so he was attracted to the notion of the piece being signed. Bill, by the way, refused to learn sign language. He just said, "What?" and shouted at you. The first time I met Bill he fell asleep at the dinner table, his beard wicking up the soup.

Lou not only agreed to all this but came up for the week from Aptos, California, and attended every single rehearsal in his customary attire of red flannel shirt and bolo tie beneath long white hair and a white beard. He was kind, femmey, and potentially volcanic. I never saw him get really angry, though I could tell when he was frustrated—there was a quiet madness in his eyes. He'd written the text, based on Hopi Indian verse forms, in praise of the elements ("Here is splendor, here is holiness")—corny, beautiful, sung in English. Kevin translated the words to the songs into American Sign Language, and videotaped himself for me so I could learn it.

I was on crutches, hopping up and down on one leg, so the dance (which was for my company—we were technically bicoastal, though I don't remember how we managed it) was very one-sided and demandingly unidextrous. It was staged thus: 114 men singing on risers, along with a small orchestra, and in front of *them* my dancers, and in front of them the sign language interpreter. It was a very difficult piece, for which the performance of the music was itself a production. All of the instruments had to be retuned because, being Lou's, the music was not in equal temperament. Even the *piano* was retuned, not to mention the mixing bowls that were filled with water and used as percussion instruments—Lou's own nesting bowls, brought all the way from California, filled, then covered with Saran wrap to keep them in tune.

I dedicated *Strict Songs* to the memory of Liberace. I'd gone, for kitsch value, to see him perform on his final tour at Radio City Music Hall, but I found myself genuinely moved by his performance and generosity. Best of all, Lou and I hit it off instantly and became friends, collaborating many times on remarkable projects.

THE FINAL SURGERY on my foot was extremely painful, but properly done. They opened it up, ground the bone to make a paste, and put in a screw, the full length of that fifth metatarsal.

I rerecovered for another six weeks, angry and miserable because I'd been disabled, in a job I didn't like much, having just endured a slow, sad breakup, frustrated and alone in winter . . . in Seattle.

I still have the screw in my foot. I could have had it taken out, but I'm rather attached to it.

With Peter Sellars and Peter Healey, in rehearsal for *Nixon in China*, 1987. Courtesy Houston Grand Opera. *(Ava Jean Mears)*

Seven

L'Allegro

The company's next defining moment was a direct result of the director Peter Sellars.

We first met in 1986—all in all, an eventful year—at SUNY Purchase when the wonderful Christopher Hunt was running the PepsiCo Summerfare. Peter was presenting *Così fan tutte*, one of his three Mozart–Da Ponte productions (the others being *Don Giovanni* and *La Nozze de Figaro*), a watershed of contemporary opera production. He was slightly more advanced in his career than I, not to mention two annoying years younger.

"Mark Morris! Mark Morris!" Peter screamed in the lobby as he rushed over, surprisingly small in stature with a very distinct, slightly elfin face. The straw-broom hair has always been the same, sticking straight up, tight on the sides and high in the middle, like wheatgrass one might buy for a cat. He's been cutting it himself without recourse to a mirror for probably forty years. "I love your work! We have to work together!" Christopher introduced us, and Peter suggested there and then that we team up for a version of the musical *The Pajama Game*. That was the first conversation we ever had. We liked each other immediately, though we hadn't seen much of each other's work. We knew. We're close friends to this day.

Peter is the most optimistic and appreciative individual. If anything, he's overly appreciative of *everything* in *everybody*. He embraces people all the time, cries freely, and has the amazing ability to make the person he's talking to feel like she's the only person in the world who matters at that moment. Someone who once sang baritone in the back row of the chorus in Salzburg in 1991 remembers him warmly, because Peter will have taken that person aside and made him feel special. None of it is a con trick. It's just who he is. Of course he's also incredibly opinionated, observant, and knows bullshit when he steps in it. He can also participate fluently in the language of the international art and theater market, which is a real skill. People are devoted to him, as am I, steadfast.

Like Yo-Yo Ma, he deflects. If someone tells me a show was great, my response might be, "I thought it was too!" To me, that seems regular. It doesn't mean I'm saying my performance was great, and indeed I may not even have been in it, but I feel fully able to say, "Thank you! I was watching too! You're right!" That's conversation. Yo-Yo, however, would more likely say, "I'm glad you liked it. Do you play an instrument? Tell me about your lessons." Whereas Peter would say, "I had nothing to do with that; the room is filled with fabulous artists." Of course he had everything to do with it. The truth is we're all saying the same thing but in different ways. However, Peter and I are quite direct with one another. Before I see something of his, he's bound to let me know, "You're going to hate it!" Sometimes he's right. He once said a show of mine—I don't remember which one; there may have been several—was the most boring thing he'd ever seen. I've certainly said to him, "That made me sick. Why are they crying onstage? I want *me* to cry! I don't want them to cry!"

Peter is very hard on himself physically, surviving basically on a diet of coffee and ice cream. I've only seen him sleep once, in my apartment in Brussels, as a result of which he missed his train; perhaps a clue as to why he never sleeps. He loves color and he dressed in extravagantly African clothes for a long time. The bathroom in his apartment is like a pirate's booty boutique of bright, shiny baubles. In fact, the only thing that annoys me about him is when people occasionally ask if I got my habit of wearing necklaces from Peter. No. I've been wearing beads, ornamental rather than religious, my whole life. People still confuse the two of us, supposing that we work in the same way. We don't.

Our first collaboration was John Adams's *Nixon in China*, which Peter asked me to choreograph. John Adams, whom I knew as one of the founding fathers of contemporary American music, was still writing the opera, while the great poet Alice Goodman was working on the libretto. *Nixon* was a production of Houston Grand Opera, though we auditioned dancers in New York; bizarrely, almost nobody showed up, so I used everyone who did.

Peter had a regular crew of collaborators, artisans of the very highest quality with whom I'd be working for the first time and with whom I'd work many times after. *Nixon in China* had nothing to do with MMDG. There were ten dancers: a corps of four couples and two principal dancers for the reimagination of my beloved *Red Detachment of Women* that is an integral part of the opera. The whole preparatory six-week period was in Houston.

Of the singers, several, including James Maddalena (the original Nixon) and Sanford Sylvan (Chou En-lai), came from Emmanuel Music in Boston, run by Craig Smith at Emmanuel Church, whose choir sang the Bach cantata cycle, the appropriate cantata for each Sunday of the liturgical calendar, which Craig conducted for twenty years straight, starting the cycle over every few years: unheard of in America. All Peter's first operas (before he was in the big houses) were with Craig's singers, some of whom, like Lorraine Hunt Lieberson, became big stars because of this association (and their own brilliance).

The music for *Nixon* was gorgeous and extremely complicated; the meter changed almost every second bar.

"Do you really need this one-eighth bar of rest?" I once asked John. "Isn't that basically the same as a breath? Or a comma?"

"It has to be there," he assured me.

He certainly wasn't writing for singers to feel good about themselves, but he hadn't written much for voice yet. That's not to say he didn't do it well; he did it very well.

The Red Detachment of Women is written into *Nixon* as part of the argument, this being the show that China chose to present to the traveling Nixons. In the opera, the Nixons interrupt the show and enter the story of *The Red Detachment*. It's a surrealist moment, and Peter wanted certain things to happen, which of course I did because I was working for a director; you do what he wants in order to tell the story. Given my love for that dance, I was the ideal choice as choreographer, though neither Peter nor John could possibly have had any idea of my long-standing attachment to the *Detachment*. To make up a twenty-minute version for only ten people, for a three-hour ballet normally danced by one hundred, was a challenge, but I decided not to look at the source material at all, relying only on my memory of it on TV in 1972. The weird thing is that it remained so vivid to me (as it had when I referred to it in *Barstow*) that I was more or less right.

And somehow Adams had made *Nixon in China* funny, which wasn't easy. When Pat Nixon is touring a factory with three female interpreters, the workers show her a figurine of an elephant.

"This little elephant in glass brings back so many memories . . . ," she says. "Tell me, is it one of a kind?"

"It has been carefully designed by workers at this factory," the interpreters cheerfully reply. "They can make hundreds every day."

Nixon in China was controversial, partly because its subject was alive—the libretto drew from writings and diaries—and partly because people had assumed that Nixon would be depicted as a buffoon.

DIRECTING AN OPERA MYSELF was an obvious step I was ready to make, and Seattle Opera was the first to ask. The opportunity came the following year and was the second of two jobs for them in twelve months, the first being to choreograph (and dance in) Gluck's *Orpheus and Eurydice*—they chose to use the English name—directed by Stephen Wadsworth. This was the Paris version from 1774, originally in French and called *Orphée et Eurydice*, in which Orpheus is a tenor; later, I did two separate productions of the earlier Vienna version from 1762, *Orfeo ed Euridice*, with an Italian libretto and the hero an alto. This was a much bigger undertaking than the work I'd done for their *Salome* of two years earlier, with a lot of dancing. I had terrible bronchitis, perhaps pneumonia, and I could scarcely even move, let alone dance. I can't remember being that sick before or since.

The opera I then directed was Johann Strauss II's beloved *Die Fledermaus*, which was an almost entirely enjoyable experience. Back then, and it may still be true, the chorus at Seattle Opera was part-time. They worked day jobs and sang in the evenings. I decided that the chorus (rather than professional dancers) should themselves do all the dancing at the central New Year's ball, so I spent my evenings teaching them the various polkas, waltzes, and social dances. It was funny and realistic, though—granted—Viennese people of that period might well have danced better than the Seattle Opera Chorus after a two-week crash course. One woman had a broken leg, so she sat on her own at the party and got drunk.

The cast was first-rate, featuring the well-known baritone Dale Dusing, but the opera was sung in English. I can't now remember whether this was Seattle's particular policy or whether Strauss, like Stravinsky, liked his operas performed in the dominant language. The problem is that when operas are in English, you understand them, if anything, slightly less *and* you realize how silly they are. My expensive idea was that, since we were singing in English, we should have German supertitles written in a fancy, beautiful old Gothic script. *Verboten.*

What most disappointed me about the experience, however, in my naivete, was that though I was hired to direct, it wasn't to be, *couldn't* be, my full artistic vision. The sets were rented from this company, the costumes borrowed from a different production.

It was a success, but everyone likes that opera anyway.

THINGS WERE MOVING FAST. *Die Fledermaus* premiered on May 7 in Seattle, and by the end of the month, I was back at ABT at the Metropolitan Opera House in Manhattan for another premiere, my very first collaboration with Mr. Mikhail Baryshnikov (henceforth known as "Misha"), an association that led to an enduring friendship that began just prior to our European adventure.

I'd seen Baryshnikov dance for American Ballet Theatre with the great Gelsey Kirkland, when she'd refused to do the curtain calls on some point of bouquet etiquette and they'd stopped bowing together. His recent appointment as artistic director of ABT had been a great coup because, far from being some individual from arts management, Misha was a glamorous defected dancer, working in partnership with

Charles France, a brilliant, eccentric, corpulent, flamboyant major-domo, and very much the Barry Alterman of that company. Charles did the things Misha couldn't.

It heralded a revolutionary, brilliant period for ABT. They hired choreographers who weren't from Balletland, most famously Twyla Tharp, with whom Misha worked many times when her work was at its finest, though he also imported David Gordon, famous from Grand Union at Judson Memorial Church, and Karole Armitage, known for her punk esthetic. Downtown went uptown. There was a spirit of adventure and novelty that's now long gone. Outsiders were doing interesting work for ballet companies that wasn't, like nowadays, just the spawn of the company itself.

I went to meet Baryshnikov in his box at the Met during intermission. "I want you to do a dance," he said, like someone doing a bad Russian accent, "and I want to be in it." He moved fast, talked fast, and interrupted himself a lot. I was quite surprised at his diminutive size— everyone looks so much bigger on the stage—and taken with his beautiful blue eyes. I don't know what he'd seen of mine at the time, but that was pretty much the gist of the entire conversation. It was a very exciting prospect, not to mention a good gig.

We worked together for the first time on a gala AIDS benefit at the New York State Theater. I choreographed a short piece, *Drink to Me Only with Thine Eyes*, to music by Virgil Thomson, beautiful études, almost impossible to play, fabulously and technically bizarre. One is called "Double Glissandi," where you, the pianist, do slides in parallel octaves with your small finger and your thumb, ripping your fingernails off in the process; "Pivoting on the Thumb," where your thumb stays and your fingers move; "Oscillating Arm"; and "For the Weaker Fingers" (the fourth and the fifth, as you probably assumed). There was another where one hand was in three and the other in four, and then they switched halfway through—a hemiola, difficult and beautiful. The pianist who'd be ripping her fingernails was my old Eliot Feld accompanist and page turnee Gladys Celeste. The dance was originally for three couples, mostly principals from ABT, big-shot dancers, because Misha wanted to be in it, and of course I wanted him to be in it too.

That's how I got to know him. In the early days, he was a little intimidated by me, and communicated only through Barry. At one of our early meetings, I asked him why he was using that funny accent—not the Boris and Natasha one, the *gay* one. Was it because he thought that was how I sounded? I was a new type of queer to him, not one of the fops he was used to working with, all of whom were in love with and fawned all over him. I told him not to talk gay, so he stopped.

I wasn't used to working with stars of *any* magnitude, but I wasn't worried about his star factor. There was no question of "and now Mr. Baryshnikov will come out and do his giant solo," nor did he want that. It was always going to be a group dance, though in fact I did have him break away to do a very tricky series of pirouettes (though I then also had another male dancer do exactly the same moves).

I'd actually call *Drink* "postmodern" in its composition; not something I often say. It's logical conceptually, meticulously built in its math, and a piano ballet (which is already a funny idea, invented by Balanchine). There wasn't a broken column or video monitor or any other cliché of postmodern dance, but it was postmodern in its references to the full, classic lexicon of ballet-moves partnering and pointe dancing—yet without any climactic arc.

When a new version, fleshed out and expanded, with twice as many people and twice the music, premiered at the Met, I wanted the piano onstage. The stage of the Met is too big for almost all ballet, so instead of putting the piano in the corner, I positioned it dead center and the whole dance happened downstage. Only once did anyone venture behind it. The audience was hardly aware that there was forty feet of deck we weren't using.

Misha soon left ABT, but through our excellent experience together, we'd become friends. Since he was living in Croton-on-Hudson in a full family relationship with Lisa Rinehart at the time, he kindly offered me his Manhattan loft as a New York pied-à-terre. Then, at something of a post-ABT loose end, he even came to join me as a guest artist in Belgium, where we did *Wonderland*, and learned a solo of mine called *Ten Suggestions*.

Rob and I once went to Christmas dinner at his house. We ate mescaline, then we all ate the goose. Guillermo was there too, naked as he often is. He'll take off his clothes at the drop of a hat: between the elevator and the front door of your apartment, if you're lucky.

THAT SAME YEAR, 1987, Gerard Mortier, the Flemish director of the Théâtre Royal de la Monnaie, the Belgian national opera, was in Stuttgart to see Peter Sellars's productions of *Ajax* and *Così fan tutte*. We were on tour there and, on Peter's recommendation, he came to see a show of mine, a mixed-repertory program of which one of the pieces was *Gloria*. We'd had intimations that the Monnaie was looking for a new dance director, and we knew Mortier was in the house.

The strange thing: due to an injury to one of my dancers, I was making my own debut performing in *Gloria*, faking my way through somebody else's part. The truth is that though Mortier trusted Peter's opinion, he didn't know too much about dancing. (I get a lot of work that way—I know music *and* dancing; often they just know music.) Mortier was partly ignorant about my work, partly desperate—he needed a new choreographer immediately—and extremely trusting of Peter, so he took the entire company out to dinner afterward, dubbed me "*un homme de musique*," and on the strength of that one performance and Peter's recommendation, announced, "Come to Belgium tomorrow. I would love to install you."

Mortier was taking a big risk, partly because I was a new thing to him, from—if you like—the Peter Sellars esthetic, but also because I was nothing like what was currently happening at the Monnaie. The Belgians were used to a particular kind of dance, a kind of dance of which I had already tired. As Mortier himself once said, "Brussels was never a city of dance, it was a city of Monsieur Béjart."

Maurice Béjart, the previous choreographer at the Monnaie, had finally stormed out, heading to Lausanne after twenty-seven long years, partly because of various financial disagreements, but also because he didn't feel appreciated, which he probably wasn't. However, it may have also been that Mortier, who had good taste, had finally decided that Béjart's work was simply crap, which it had been for many years.

But there had been a moment when his choreography was exciting. Back at the opera house in Seattle when I was young, it was the sexiest, most glamorous thing I'd ever seen: the men nearly naked, faces vividly made up, hair wild. I was shocked, the way everyone is the first time they see men in tights at the ballet. I hadn't seen that much ass even on somebody naked. So as a teenager I liked Béjart; then as a grown-up I hated it, and it remains crap to this day—insane, grizzly, ghastly, vulgar stuff. You think Hermann Hesse and Ayn Rand are wonderful when you're young and . . . they're not. Béjart's famous version of Ravel's *Bolero* featured fifty horny men in a circle around a huge table watching as his big star, and presumed lover, Jorge Donn (giant hair, makeup, androgynous), did a seductive dance thereupon. The whole thing was porny-corny, hugely distasteful, and shamefully fabulous.

When I moved to New York City, there was my expensive night out to see Béjart's company, Ballet du XXe Siècle, perform Lar's wonderful *Marimba*. Very soon afterward, I was in Lar's company myself, dancing that same *Marimba*, and I realized that Béjart's had been the most repulsive, crazy, strung-out version. Yet I can't deny that its over-the-topness was appealing at the time. The other music he choreographed, *Le Marteau sans maître* by Boulez, was way over Béjart's head. He was a big ham who liked grandiose sounds, but he had no real clue about music. (Mortier later noted that Béjart used music for his spectacle, whereas I served the music, which was true.) Béjart himself didn't dance in his shows, but he often appeared in them, generally in the role of the crazy ringmaster, the poet, the seer. When we first got to Brussels, there were all these out-of-date billboards of a goateed Béjart doing this certain mysterious, pensive expression, his finger to his chin. There's a moment in *Dido and Aeneas*, our second dance in Brussels, where, at the end of the Sorceress scene, I did that same expression. It was a tiny quotation, a reference to his ridiculously smug look on that poster. Nobody got it but it made me happy. I was not above making fun of him.

I can't even remember whether I subsequently ever met him, though I don't believe there would have been any particular animosity between us. He did say something slightly patronizing along the lines of "Let the boy do whatever he wants." But I said a few things about him too.

The real animosity came not from Béjart but from the country of Belgium itself.

FROM THE START, the very thought of Brussels was thrilling, the prospects amazing.

Mortier was very extravagant, very generous, and totally ruthless. Either he got his own way or he didn't do it. For example, he was announced as the new head of the New York City Opera, its new savior, in 2007, but then decided not to take the job when he found out they'd sliced his budget in half. He wasn't easy but he was great. He'd do anything to make a show he wanted to happen, happen: "Your dreams come true *now!*"

Mortier had been hired in 1981 to put the Monnaie, and more generally Brussels, on the map. That was his job and his thrill. He was a master politician, and, from his point of view, there was no way he could lose by hiring me. It was either going to succeed magnificently, for which he'd get all the credit, or go down in flames, and my failure would be big news. He never pulled the wool over anyone's eyes. He always did what he believed, hoping it would work, and he knew precisely the power of publicity and controversy. I was aware that I was a controversial replacement, and that was fine with me, while also somewhat terrifying.

We had a glimpse of Mortier's power one night in Bruges after dinner. Mortier had asked me to drive back with him in his car, and I'd asked Guillermo to accompany us. It was the middle of the night in the barely lit streets of Bruges: a white hippie boy with long hair in shorts walking next to a businessman, followed a few steps behind by a dark-skinned man with long dreads, apparently a bodyguard. Guillermo pulled out a joint (some hash rolled up in tobacco), caught up, and handed it to me. I took a hit and offered it to Mortier, who demurred.

At that moment, an unmarked car swerved in front of us to cut us off, almost hitting us. Two cops got out. They can't possibly have smelled the dope from the car, so they must have been observing us, presumably thinking they were witnessing the biggest drug deal in Bruges's history. I freaked out, as did Guillermo, who stood back to stamp out the evidence. Mortier didn't miss a beat, calmly going over to confer with the driver. When he returned, the cops left. We asked what had just happened. "Well," said Mortier, "I told him who I was, and I told him that if I didn't get satisfaction from his commander and from the prefect of Bruges that I'd have them fired." And that was that.

I was mortified. Mortier . . . was Mortier.

He was a complicated man, slight, mousy, and somewhat effete. He had a manicure every other day in his office, and there was some secret room, an inner sanctum to which I was rarely granted access: who knows what happened in there. His eyesight wasn't great, and he was obsessive-compulsive and highly phobic, suffering from a kind of preemptive claustrophobia that meant he'd never allow himself to get into a situation in which there might be the vaguest possibility of claustrophobia. As he walked down a corridor, he tapped the walls like a blind man. At least it meant you could always hear him coming.

Mortier's longtime partner was Sylvain Cambreling, the Monnaie's music director, but he also liked to surround himself with very beautiful men. His assistant was gorgeous; his chauffeur was gorgeous; everyone was gorgeous. In fact, the gorgeous chauffeur told me that they were once stuck in gridlock in a tunnel somewhere, when Mortier had a panic attack, opened the car door, got out, and started running toward the light at the end of the tunnel. The driver had to chase him down and get him back into the car.

I loved Mortier.

AFTER THE MEETING IN STUTTGART, Barry and I took an emergency diversion to Brussels, where Mortier wined and dined us. We took a car to Amsterdam to see the Monnaie's ornate production of *La finta giardiniera*, a clumsy but charming opera that Mozart wrote aged about eleven months.

Mortier really just wanted *me*, and since he was laboring under the misapprehension that he'd discovered me, he thought that he could hire me alone, that I'd hire Belgian dancers, that we'd all live happily ever after for the next couple of years, and fuck my entire company and the management, Nancy and Barry. He wanted somebody cheap and malleable. I was comparatively cheap, but he hadn't realized that I was far from malleable. So there were various negotiations, courtship trips, not to mention a tense summit meeting with my company in Berkeley. Mortier was talking to me in French and English.

"Write this down, write this down," he brusquely told Nancy, who refused.

"You don't understand," I said. "Nancy isn't my secretary. She's me, if I knew what I was doing."

In fact, Mortier needed us so badly that we ended up getting everything we wanted, including keeping my company and management intact. I'd hire more dancers: we'd go from twelve to twenty-four. It was all in the details. We worked on the change of name from Mark Morris Dance Group for a really long time, which was a contract point, a big deal. We tried every possible nonsense variation. (I even suggested for a joke that we change it to Ballet du 18ᵉ Siècle to send up Béjart and my love for baroque music.) The one we ended up with—Monnaie Dance Group/Mark Morris—didn't make a great deal of sense, but we'd removed everything that didn't absolutely have to be in the name of the newly formed company, reduced the equation, and that's what was left (that and a virgule). Everyone was happy with the compromise: alliteration and an elegant logo.

We agonized over the decision and finally decided, why the hell not? We were getting lots of work in America, but we weren't making lots of money, and we liked the idea of official status as an arts organization, which moving to Brussels would immediately achieve, whereas if we stayed in America, we wouldn't be on that schedule. Up to this point, we'd perhaps done fifty dances, and although we used live music as much as possible, we'd only (aside from the TV work) done one dance with anything as extravagant as a set. This was our chance for only live music and all the décor we could imagine. So we finally agreed. We were on our way to Brussels.

When it happened, it happened fast.

I immediately felt two things. One, this is going to be great. Two, I've been set up for something weird.

To START WITH, we were given our own building.

Thirty rue Bara was a giant warehouse, far from ritzy, on the wrong side of the tracks in an industrial neighborhood that had seen better days, beyond one of the two train stations, the south one, Zuid. You were already on the way out of town. It was a fifteen-minute downhill walk from my apartment, right across the station concourse, where people were enjoying their first beer of the day at nine in the morning. The building itself had served many functions over the years, but most recently it had been Béjart's own studio, Mudra (named after the hand gestures of Indian dance). It was a deep rectangle, like a U, with a full scene shop in the back, where all of the sets and props for every one of the Monnaie's huge, extravagant, expensive shows were made. The two wings were divided by a one-lane road so trucks could come in to load the scenery that they'd then transport to the theater, fifteen minutes away. On one side of the rectangle, there were two stories containing a canteen and offices; on the other, a bathroom with scary showers that had nondraining soap dishes (a bad omen) and some dressing rooms. There were several rehearsal studios, one of which was raked at five degrees to replicate the actual theater. Americans aren't used to dancing on rakes, so this drove us crazy.

It seemed outlandish, getting our own building—we could hardly believe it—but the place was such a big mess of a loft building, more like being outside than in, impossible to keep clean and impossible to heat. We fixed it up as best we could, sealed it for warmth, but it was a

Office window with pulley message
system, 30 rue Bara, Brussels, circa 1988.

losing battle, like bailing water out of a sinking boat. We were near a brewery, so there was the overwhelming smell of yeast, not to mention the waft of chocolate from the Côte d'Or chocolate factory. Yeast and chocolate. Believe me, you don't want that combination every day. And there were pigeons everywhere, pests, making that horrible sound, shitting everywhere. The night watchman would pick them off one by one with a shotgun.

I bought junk furniture for my weird, beautiful office, the window of which looked right across at our secretary's. We strung a pulley message system between us that we used to communicate when we didn't want to walk down and across and up again. We decorated as we could. Halfway up the stairs hung a beautiful 1960s postcard that I'd had enlarged, a little African American Cub Scout, with the message "You can always do better here," an inspiration to everyone and the most pathetic thing in the world. In the studio, there was a flag that now has a negative Tea Party connotation, the chopped-up snake from New Hampshire, "Don't Tread on Me."

We were housed in nice apartments until we had the time to find something of our own. First I found myself in a gigantic, sterile place on rue Africaine; then I rented a beautiful apartment on a park—three bedrooms, big kitchen, balcony on the front and the back, and room-mates all the time. Guillermo was the constant, while others came and went.

One of the best of the new recruits, Hans-Georg Lenhart, had come from the Folkwang University of the Arts in Essen, the art school that had been started by one of the founders of *Tanztheater*, Kurt Jooss, in the 1930s and then became Pina Bausch's, so Hans-Georg was trained in her style. He was a wonderfully clear dancer—probably ten years my junior—who became a vital component of the company for the Brussels years and beyond. He was adorable, very publicly and physically affectionate like Guillermo, and the two of them lived with me for quite a while. I did all the cooking and they did all the cleaning (and the eating).

THE PRESS CONFERENCE WAS DRAMATIC. It was my first appearance, supposedly just my saying hello to Belgium. Coincidentally, it was also my first ever press conference. There were the usual ponderous questions, and I said all the right things about what an honor it was. Then one casual remark did it. One of the journalists asked me my philosophy of dance.

"I make it up and you watch it. End of philosophy."

No one had ever asked for my philosophy of dance before—in America, there's no philosophy of dance and no one would ever bother—and that's what came out. The assembled company of Belgians, who had settled back in their seats expecting me to expatiate for thirty minutes, were shocked. They were used to Béjart, whose work was all very well thought out. He'd been providing thirty pages of program notes for every new dance. (Wagner was to blame for all that.) While my answer was meant to be funny (though the joke fell flat), it was also true. Come to think of it, it still *is* my philosophy.

Someone then asked me if it was queer for a choreographer to use the music rather than the movement as the starting point, and I answered, "Well, I am a queer choreographer." It was another turning point. Béjart was the gayest thing in the world, and they didn't mind him. The difference is that I actually said I was gay, whereas the policy in Belgium was strictly Don't Ask, Don't Tell. Mortier was sitting beside me, rubbing his hands with glee.

Then, when they asked me specifically what I thought of Béjart, I made a comical face of horror. Of course that was the picture they used in all the newspapers, with the headline NON, JE DETESTE BEJART! They say there's no such thing as bad publicity, but maybe that was imprudent. It bit me straightaway.

Another true story: *Vanity Fair* almost immediately sent a writer, Charles Siebert, over to trail me for a week. I said some supposedly bad things to him that made it into his article, one of which was "Béjart's work is shit. . . . On my worst day, with the worst hangover in my life, I could never do anything that bad." (Although I did add the proviso "Well . . . maybe in the future." I'm not a monster.) One night, we were at the opera house with King Baudouin and Queen Fabiola, the royal patrons, in attendance. As we were leaving, people were shouting, "Vive la reine! Vive la reine!" and when asked, I said I thought they were talking about me. I certainly didn't have anything against the queen, so perfectly ornamental with her Maggie Thatcher hairdo, and in fact, I was happy to bow down before her, delighted to be invited up to her box to meet her.

As I left, I did happen to say to Charles, "Best blow job I ever had." He had the good taste to leave that out of the profile.

WE HAD THREE MONTHS to prepare for our first performance. Mortier had said we could do anything we wanted.

"What's your dream show?" he asked.

"*L'Allegro*," I replied, without needing to think.

L'Allegro, il penseroso ed il moderato was a very popular piece in Handel's time that disappeared for a couple of hundred years; the first version I'd heard was a wonderfully rough-and-ready recording on early instruments by Banchetto Musicale, rustic and fabulous. It was the perfect time to go for baroque in Europe because of the many great early music conductors and players just starting out in Holland and Belgium—for example, Philippe Herreweghe and Marc Minkowski, both great artists, superior to most of their American counterparts. Mortier hired Craig Smith from Emmanuel to do the music for *L'Allegro*, so he and I set about devising the performance edition of this music. It was complicated.

L'Allegro was to be by far our biggest and longest production yet. I had previously suggested it to the Boston Ballet—my company dancing *with* their dancers—but Bruce Marks, the artistic director at the time, would have been taking a sizable risk on me to make an evening-length dance with the Handel and Haydn Society, the big period band at that time, and it didn't work out, due to both lack of money and lack of interest. However, because of this possibility, I'd started imagining the project—the band above the dancers in the air in the baroque style—and before we even moved to Brussels, we were working on *L'Allegro* at a summer residency in upstate New York at SUNY Brockport.

L'Allegro, il penseroso ed il moderato is a pastoral ode from 1740 based on the poetry of John Milton, who had written "L'Allegro" and "Il Penseroso" separately, though they are invariably paired, about one hundred years earlier. Handel had the good idea of interleaving the two poems to contrast the happy, mirthful man (*l'allegro*) with the thinking, melancholy man (*il penseroso*). These two moods also represented the inner and outer states of man—public and private, pensive and gregarious, friendly and hermetic—so, for example, there's the lark (the happy bird) in "L'Allegro" as opposed to the nightingale (the sad bird) in "Il Penseroso." Unfortunately, *Allegro* and *Penseroso* weren't enough for the Age of Reason, and Handel also had the not-quite-so-great idea of balancing this debate with an extra poem, "Il Moderato," by Charles Jennens, the *Messiah* librettist, an extra act with just as many arias and choruses. A record of the entire thing is about half an hour longer than our version, featuring a dull series of *Moderato* numbers, for which the poetry is noticeably less good.

I had decided that I wanted the show to end with *L'Allegro* as the dominant idea, the winner of the debate (partly because I'm a cockeyed optimist, but also because I simply wanted to end it happy—that's show business!), so we reordered some things and cut a few things. *Moderato* didn't really apply, because the Thinking Man and the Having-Lots-of-Fun Man cancel each other out, so no one really needs the Boring, Stupid Man Who Doesn't Do Anything without Being Told: the dialectic implies moderation without actually having to present it. I therefore decided to more or less ignore *Moderato*, except the two highlights, the duet "As steals the morn upon the night" (the only duet in the whole piece) and "Each action will derive new grace." I reimagined these so that no one watching would imagine they were from an argument for moderation. (I almost used a third, a very ornate aria for mezzo and a cello obbligato, but it turned out to be too difficult to play.)

Armed with that structure (which wasn't too far out, just a bit of replacement and shifting), knowing it would be in two acts—dark in the first half, lighter in the second—we went to work.

Considering that half the company was new, in a giant studio with a new team, stagehands, a big staff, and assistants to assistants, we worked fast.

Hundreds of people had come to the auditions from all over Europe, even from Mudra, Béjart's dance school. Most of them were terrible, but we were able to find the requisite number. Then the issue became "how many *Belgians* have you hired?"

It turned out I'd hired *one* Belgian. *I hadn't looked at their passports.* And this lone Belgian, Olivia Maridjan Koop, was a woman of Indonesian descent, so she didn't even count to some Belgians. No one had ever mentioned that it would be more politic to pick more Belgians, but I can't honestly say that I'd have picked more Belgians just to keep people happy. *And* there were problems even with the dancers I'd picked, though it wasn't necessarily their fault. I wanted it to be barefoot dancing, the honest origins of Modern Dance, and neither ironic, bad ballet nor historical reconstruction. The dancers who'd come with me—Penny chief among them, because she had my folk dance background—knew how to do the required stuff plainly, but I now found myself with newer dancers who didn't know what I was after.

One of my little casting jokes was that the longer you'd been in my company, the more you were featured and the more dancing you did—see above for the underlying rationale. Everybody was in all the corps work all the time, but if you were Penny, Ruth, Keith, or Tina—among the lifers who'd come with me from New York—you got a big part. And the dances were so lovely, whether ethnically inspired—a Highland sword dance, a Walachian dance from Romania, and an old Croatian dance (simply jumping)—or made up. There was the Stupid Men's Dance, as we called it (in act 2, where they slap and then kiss each other), which followed perhaps my favorite piece of my own choreography, if I'm allowed to choose: the Dream Dance, where Olivia floated up like a balloon, the men made a forest, and the women escaped. Then there was the Kleenex Dance for all the women, a very hard dance, meant to be a Busby Berkeley crane shot. The Walking Dance ("As steals the morn") is based on a harvest dance called a *bujenec*, originally done by virgins arm in arm in the fields of Bulgarian Thrace (and not in front of an audience). The leaders of the two lines symmetrically nod to each other, turn right (the Thracians would have been improvising these patterns), and the lead girls carry a huge sheaf of wheat, the others follow her—and that's the whole dance, tracing patterns in a field. The first time they do it in our version, they do up-down, up-down. The second time they do it, a recap of that same pattern, they go down-up, down-up: totally different and very satisfying. It's an abridged repetition and ornamented in a slightly different way, which is what baroque music itself is all about. As I told the *Vanity Fair* writer, "Even if you can't read music, if you really listen and you're somehow accidentally moved by something, that's why, because of a tiny, tiny secret thing that was plotted out in the structure. One reason I make dances is to trick people into hearing music better."

Paul Lorenger, Penny Hutchinson, Raphael Brand, and Joachim Schlömer in "Day's Garish Eye" from *L'Allegro*, Théâtre Royal de la Monnaie, Brussels, 1988. *(Klaus Lefèbvre)*

The finale of act 1 of *L'Allegro* is six quartets—twenty-four people—doing symmetrical square figure dances, which then become lines, then circles; six, then four, then two, which magically become one very slow circle. Then there's a joke, or what people see as a joke. Paul Taylor used a step all the time, common in musical comedy, where the man picks up the female beloved as if she were a baby. He might rock her like a kitten in his arms. It's a tired old trope—"Don't worry your pretty little head about that"—and I wanted to redeem it, not quite to do its opposite, but to fuck with it. So in *L'Allegro*, the dancers form a big circle, and the women pick up the men, carry them around like babies—everybody chuckles—and then the men pick up the women. The women are protecting the men, which is maternal, and beautiful, as if the men are boys who've fallen asleep in the back of the car on the way home from the drive-in, and are being carried inside by their parents. The music accompanies the lyric "By whisp'ring winds soon lull'd asleep," and that's a beautiful way to fall asleep. Everyone needs to feel he's being carried inside by his parents. And that horrible cloying, degrading move, that weak person/strong person dynamic, was redeemed for me by placing it in that new context. Twenty-five or so years ago, this was radical; now it's classical.

I WANTED *L'ALLEGRO* TO BE, and knew it had to be, a big stage production. I'd chosen it not just because the music is gorgeous, but because it's not a linear narrative. Most of Handel's oratorios are biblical and most of his operas (of which every single one is great) are mythological, lengthy, and complex character-driven narratives. *L'Allegro*, on the other hand, because of Milton's poetry, is evocative as opposed to purely narrative, so it afforded me a great deal of variety in the realm that dance does best. In particular, Handel's musical word painting is spectacular—the music is specific, but the situations are vague—and the music is much more (I hate to use the word) "accessible" than Bach, but equally genius. Handel is Bach's equal, Telemann not too far away.

I'd worked with Adrianne Lobel on *Nixon*, so I asked if she'd design the sets. She immediately came up with brilliant ideas, based directly on Josef Albers, Mark Rothko, and other color-field painters, to make an identifiably abstract series of looks. Her central idea was to divide the stage in depth—the Brussels stage was very deep—and she started showing me a million options in slide form, watercolors, drawings of all different color relationships, proposing many different ideas, most of which we ditched, ending up with twenty-one drops (which are opaque) and scrims (which are translucent gauze), a huge project. I had to choreograph with the drops and scrims in mind: were they see-through or not? Would we dance between them? They offered infinite combinations both choreographically and in perspective (once you bring in a drop, you can't do anything upstage of it because the audience couldn't see the dancers—it became a visual-spatial puzzle, how the scrims changed the look of the drops). You can imagine a line of eight people, on a heavily raked floor, dancing in and out of sight lines among these obstacles.

Working with Christine Van Loon, the costume designer, I decided that I wanted the costumes based on the beautiful William Blake drawings for *L'Allegro*. Adrianne wasn't wild about that, alongside her color-field idea, but I hate to see the sofa match the drapes in a show's design. The world simply doesn't work like that. The costumes were beautifully simple, a tunic or Grecian drape based on early Modern Dance of the barefoot variety.

My original, impractical idea was that the dancers would, one at a time at regular and precise intervals, change their clothes throughout the evening, and that the palette would therefore brighten imperceptibly throughout the show, the reverse of leaves in autumn. But everyone was dancing all the time, and there was simply no opportunity for constant quick changes. A simplification of this idea, however, did work. We'd go from muted-colored costumes in act 1 to brighter colors in act 2. Everybody had two costumes: the darkened version in act 1 might be a dark green with a deep orange beneath, and in the second half, a lighter green on top of a pale yellow. It was the same with the men in their very expensive dyed silk chiffon shirts. The two *Moderato* dances feature every dancer, without any drops or scrims, on the perfectly white empty stage, colorless to this day.

My original inclination was that there would be props. I wanted the sticks and kerchiefs of Morris dancing, sticks to hit and hankies for ladies to wave, or for gentlemen to brandish in a folk-dancey way. I was also thinking of bigger baroque stage machines inspired by the greatest opera movie ever made, Bergman's *The Magic Flute*—not only the greatest music film, but also perhaps the greatest ever single production of an opera. *That*'s what I wanted: the cranked spiral of the ocean, the thunderstorm rumbling, the mechanical shrubbery. Bergman's *Magic Flute* was filmed in the Palace Theatre at Drottningholm, the residence of the Swedish royal family in Stockholm, where all the real baroque devices were still in use; our production used zero of those magnificent contraptions but simulated their effects through dance. That was as much of the baroque (and one could equally say Bunraku) spectacle as I wanted, those artifices and illusions that could take us from springtime to snow in the simplest, most beautiful way. And that's what Adrianne achieved, with a strip of grass, a strip of river, and a strip of sky, a vision enhanced by the genius lighting design of James F. Ingalls.

Adrianne might agree this was her best work ever. We had a big budget and lots of time, and the Belgian scene shop realized it beautifully. She had several weeks with the full crew in the theater before we opened—you can only imagine what that costs. That's quite usual in Europe, though unheard of in the States. The Metropolitan Opera House in New York does sixteen operas in rotating repertory, so they're always on an insane schedule, loading out and loading in overnight for the next show. European opera companies do it by season, *stagionale*. They perform one show for weeks, then close for a spell to put on the next show. Consequently, you have the luxury to rehearse at length in the actual theater in which you'll be performing, to build the sets there, fit them perfectly, and perform the same show multiple times instead of rotating.

This production is where I first came into contact with Johan Henckens, who's worked for us ever since (and been married to Nancy). But the truth is that everyone on their crew was helpful. They were glad Béjart was gone—they'd hated him—and I seemed like an easy mark. Everything was so extravagant that there was a luxurious week of rehearsal for the set *alone*, complete with a pianist in order to synchronize it to the music, to see how far to fly the trims, how fast to bring that black thing down in front of the pink thing so both were still visible, whether it should touch the floor or not. It gets dangerous when three or four things are flying in and out at the same time. You had time to iron out the problems, to make sure the backdrops weren't too close together, thus avoiding that undesirable moiré effect and so on.

It was all magical luxury. There were technical rehearsals, orchestral rehearsals, rehearsals with lights, rehearsals with costumes, music-only rehearsals; all of the rehearsals that come before the final dress rehearsal, which, in Brussels, is open to the public. In fact, the possibilities for perfectionism were endless, and at some point, we had to draw the line. When it was finally time for me to watch, it was immediately evident that certain aspects were too complicated. The dancers needed more clearance overhead; they couldn't dance that far downstage, even though it suited the design. You couldn't really know these details until you got in there, however true to scale the maquette, the model of the set we'd used as reference.

The pressure, the deadline, the atmosphere, the importance of it . . . none of those were daunting, though they were facts. What was daunting was the project itself, trying to corral all these various things, because, having made all the decisions (on everything from the edition of the music to every step of the dance), I was really *alone*.

In the theater at dress rehearsal, there was a production table, lighting, computers, people communicating on walkie-talkies, an orchestra of thirty, a chorus of twenty-nine, twenty-four dancers, a crew of one hundred, wardrobe, makeup, videographer, sound balance, my management, publicity people coming in and asking, "Do you mind if I . . . ?" to which I might respond, "No, get out of here quick or I'll kill you." And in the middle of all that, me with a microphone saying, "*Stop!*" at which everything ground to a halt and I'd say, "Okay. Let's go from bar number 622 in big number 7, from . . ." And then someone had to translate it into Flemish and French.

It had been a fraught and very complicated project, and I knew I'd tortured the dancers. I get very engaged and agitated when I work on something new. I can be curt, blunt, even cruel sometimes, certainly, but that's not anger. Screaming, shouting, chasing people around a room: that's excitement and it's usually good. Occasionally I might even yell, "Can't you fucking do *anything* right?" That's excitement, not anger. Anger is when I speak very quietly and don't talk at all or just . . . stop.

But there wasn't a huge personal crisis. I was both happy and miserable and working very hard. We'd discovered that Brussels wasn't only dank and cold but creepy, and we quickly noticed and felt the xenophobia and misogyny that would make anyone targeted by them feel awful.

There was one Flemish poster everywhere, silhouettes of stereotypes of "colored" people with a long-suited, cuffed, authoritarian arm telling them to GO HOME. Leave Brussels to the white people, was the message. There was a general air of defeat among the population, and they certainly made us feel unwelcome. It didn't hit me getting off the plane, but it didn't take long, and *L'Allegro* stands as a testament to the agony. All the strife is in it, yet somehow it ended up heaven.

THE THÉÂTRE ROYAL DE LA MONNAIE, the building itself, was elegantly beautiful, one of the great theaters, like La Fenice in Venice but less gaudy. It was either called the Théâtre Royal de la Monnaie or, if you were Flemish, the Koninklijke Muntschouwburg—De Munt for short. (In fact, part of the laboriousness of it all was that everything had to be in two languages to placate the Flemish and French camps. They even annually flipped which was top and bottom on the letterheads and the logos on the side of the company trucks.)

Mortier had updated the theater, put a multipurpose party room on the top floor (the Salle de Sandwich, we called it) with a suite of offices below, and commissioned the lobby floor and columns from Sol LeWitt, my favorite artist. The ceiling is by Sam Francis, the wonderful painter. It was already a million-dollar extravagance, and Belgians just thought, "What the fuck?" The combination of Sol LeWitt and me was too potent. They looked at his work, as they looked at some of my dances, and thought, "There's nothing there." On opening night, Belgian dancers were passing out white carnations outside the theater. We were told these meant "I wish you would die." Maybe it meant "Never come back to this theater." Either way, the flowers weren't positive, a protest against the fact that there wasn't one Belgian dancer, except the Indonesian Belgian, and that I was not a Belgian choreographer. The popular vote had been Anne Teresa De Keersmaeker, whom

I childishly called Anne Teresa De Tearjerker, when I unwisely criticized her work thus: "All you have to do here is not wash your hair for a week and then sit onstage and act depressed and you've got it. *Magnifique! Formidable!*" The irony is she's a good choreographer and I like her.

Despite all the noise and distraction that night, *L'Allegro* was a huge success. The reaction was rapturous. Mortier immediately understood its quality. I was relieved and very proud, and I still am, though I am thankful that enough time has passed that it is no longer seen as my defining work. For a long time after, the default critical response to a new piece of mine would be that "it doesn't hold a candle to *L'Allegro*." Well, I'd done *L'Allegro* already. The project also had the advantage of helping get a big chunk of baroque music out of my system. And it's still a success everywhere we do it, and we still do it all the time, through many years, many dancers, many singers, many conductors, and many theaters.

My theory on its success is that it's what the audience for dance thinks it doesn't want but is in fact dying for: people simply dancing to music, responding to music, doing what the music makes them (or me) believe. *L'Allegro* isn't "You'll never get this because it's too sophisticated and esoteric for you." Nor is it "We're doing something that's physically impossible for humans to do." It's just people dancing to music. That's not to say it isn't extremely difficult to put together and perform. Neither is it, like the proverbial six-year-old who could have done that Picasso, "Anybody could do that," which is how some people see my work to this day.

It's anything but simple, but it looks simple and natural. My decision, my esthetic, is to make the complicated look simple. First, my dances are *hard*. Everything starts on the wrong leg and turns in the wrong direction. Much of it is counterintuitive and initially awkward. You have to find a natural way to solve it. When people first learn a dance of mine, they might say, "Oh, this is so easy, we just run over there." And I say, "No, you're running in a counter-rhythm, and the stress has changed, and your feet aren't flexed or pointed"—the only two positions that people know—"they're natural and relaxed." In general, dancers expect instructions to toggle between all or nothing, but in my world there's a gigantic range of modalities, a kinetic energy that isn't just full force or zero, turgid or flaccid, on or off. I'm very facile at making up dances—I can come up with a dance in one second—so in order for it not to be the most obvious thing right away, my default is to start with the opposite ("The music sounds like spinning, so let's lie on the floor facedown and twitch"). My thought is "Everyone would do this, so let's do *that*." It's partly experimental and partly so the audience is able to dishabituate itself from its normal expectations of dance and dance traditions. It won't be quite what the audience expects from the music either, if they know it (which is one of the reasons I often choose obscure music).

L'Allegro isn't difficult music, however. It's consonant (in that it isn't dissonant) and relates directly to the dancing—that in itself was a little transgressive in contemporary dance—and the dance relates directly to the music and the text. I'm not afraid of the obvious, as someone once *kindly* said about me. I do what I do on purpose; it's not an accident. That's what I want to see and what I want to do. I don't want someone dancing *at* me, I want them dancing *for* me. I want them to dance as the music plays and I watch and listen. That's our relationship.

With perspective, I can see that *L'Allegro* is the summation of my old style: hippie and Isadora Duncan, but conceptual, argued, and constructed. I still love working on and watching *L'Allegro*, whereas I have little interest in some other older dances. I cry. I love the music so much.

—————

YEARS LATER, IN JULY 2014, we finally had the chance to film *L'Allegro.*

We'd always thought it would make a beautiful film, but it had never happened. There had previously been some well-shot segments in the British TV arts program *The South Bank Show*, and the director, Nigel Wattis, had an idea to do part of it for Channel Four, filming some of it outside and blending it like a crazy fantasia. For example, at the beginning of the solo that opens the second act, *Gorgeous Tragedy*, the curtain would rise to reveal Ruth standing on a cliff by the ocean, and then when she turned around, she'd be in a theater on a stage. I'm not generally in favor of exterior dancing, but this seemed imaginative. Scouting locations, looking for old-timey villages with greens, bosks, and ha-has made for dancing, we ended up in the Greenwich observatory, its floor checkered black and white like a chessboard. The director's inspired idea was to make a sprung deck of that floor, put it on the actual floor, and do the Walking Dance—"As steals the morn"—on the facsimile. It would have been beautiful, but there wasn't enough funding, and the whole thing was shelved.

But we never gave up, because we don't, and suddenly, a mere twenty-five years later, the opportunity arose for us to shoot it with PBS as a coproducer. Mortier had already invited us to perform *L'Allegro* at Madrid's Teatro Real, where he was now the artistic director, perhaps the greatest opera house in Europe, a beautiful nineteenth-century jewel box with the added advantage of state-of-the-art recording and filming facilities. We were going to perform it anyway, so why didn't we shoot it there? By the time we made the film, Mortier had died. It was complicated.

We'd previously had a hit in Madrid with *Mozart Dances*, and when we found out we'd be returning to do *L'Allegro*, it was suddenly very "now or never" to raise money, specifically for the costumes. Christine Van Loon's once-beautiful chiffon costumes were dead; they'd been replaced years previously in off colors and cheaper fabrics, but even these replacements were patched and threadbare. They wouldn't survive the scrutiny of high-definition film. Nor would the set: there were mends and smudges everywhere. So we resorted to a crowdsourcing campaign. This would pay for "272 yards of silk chiffon for 52 costumes . . . , 78 yards of lycra for 26 leggings, skilled small batch dye processing to match the 18 original colors, 26 leotards and seamless undergarments, professional costume shop reconstruction of the original patterns, labor to build the new costumes."

Confirmation of the filming *finally* came through. We were going to do it over three live performances and two extra pickup sessions (because you can only film so much when there's an audience), one where we did the whole dance (at eleven in the morning, which is universally agreed to be the best possible time to dance in full makeup and costume by no one) to a recording of the orchestra the night before, with all seven cameras in position. It was eerily silent without a houseful, so I cheered the dancers on from the wings in the giant empty theater. The film crew was francophone, the theater was all Spanish, my dancers were English speaking, as was the conductor, Jane Glover. It was intense. Although the sound didn't turn out great, there's nothing I don't love about the film.

L'Allegro itself keeps changing over the years—I don't change the piece, but the piece changes because at some point every single dancer is new. The parts have been passed down genetically, dancer to dancer and through me, in the oral tradition. A new person learns it, exactly the same part, the only difference being that every person in the world dances uniquely. For example, the solo that opens act 2 (*Gorgeous Tragedy*) was originally Ruth Davidson, one of the greatest. Yet she was so worried by one particular turn that, though perfect at every rehearsal, she fell down at every performance, if not on her ass, then coming out of the move with a stagger, a *thrilling* stagger; she even went to the length of spraying her soles to make them more slippery for the turn, though of course that only made her more self-conscious. Years later, Maile Okamura did the same part. The text of the dance (meaning the choreography) was exactly the same, and Maile was able to do the same turn, two times around, with relative ease. A dance critic said, "Maile is so beautiful, but I miss Ruth. Her version was so tormented and dangerous-looking." That was because Maile didn't fall down every time she did it. Does that make her a better dancer? I don't know. She's doing the exact same dance, just not falling down. Succeeding generations of dancers have different skills. It was perhaps just disappointing that someone could do it as *well* as Ruth.

L'Allegro is even better than I thought it was when we first presented it in Belgium. And I thought it was great then.

AS FAR AS BRUSSELS was concerned, everything went to shit soon after that first show.

With Ruth Davidson and Jon Mensinger in *Dido and Aeneas*,
Théâtre Varia, Brussels, 1989. *(Danièle Pierre)*

Eight

Dido and Aeneas

had a big salary in Brussels (with 60 percent income tax), health insurance for my entire company (a big deal), fabulous orchestras, and a great stage. I was so excited to work in a beautiful, perfectly proportioned proscenium theater; I'd always seen my work like that, even in the black box of Dance Theater Workshop, which is why *Gloria* had translated so well to an opera house.

Mortier himself was always helpful, making connections and introductions: "Have you met this conductor?" "Have you heard this singer?" I had a great experiential education at his hands. I don't entirely bury myself in my work—I watch TV, read books, and cook; I socialize, I have fun; I'm pretty healthy for a crazy artist—but I realized this was my empirelet, and that basically I could make up the rules and do what I liked. In America, we'd been skimping and saving; now we could do whatever we wanted. But it was weird. Though we were separate from the opera house, we no longer had autonomy. Everything had to be approved by Mortier and the board and the accountants, and *everything* was a struggle. There were fights; everything had to be planned far in advance; there was very little room for spontaneity. I could do everything I wanted; it was just a very different way to do it.

For example, Nancy had a secretary for the first time, Marina, the daughter of the secretary of a man called Deschrijver, who had approval over all the budgets. Yet Marina couldn't get us a meeting with him, even via her own mother. The only way was to get Mortier to intervene, which only ever happened at the last moment. It was like that with everything all the time. Yet, despite the fact that no budget was ever refused or cut, we couldn't get a simple pay raise for Marina. I could add a $100,000 backdrop, with approval, but I couldn't get a twenty-five-cent increase in salary for Nancy's secretary. It was deeply sexist, in the same way that they couldn't accept that Nancy was my manager.

It soon got petty. Nancy had to redo entire budgets purely because the Belgians couldn't read her ones. She drew a 1 like we draw a 1, a straight vertical line, but they wanted the Belgian upside-down V. We were computerless back then, so the budgets were quite beautiful works of art in their own right. Luckily she already crossed her sevens.

The Belgians may have been happy to see me go after the press conference, but *L'Allegro* was an undeniably great show and they loved it. The next wave of reaction was "Have we somehow been duped? Was it really that good?" Classic media stuff.

The crime was that I was American and not highfalutin enough: no philosophy. At home, I see myself as somewhat conservative; in Belgium, they thought I was an American moron. Forget *homme de musique*; I was *homme sauvage*. Over there, it was peak postmodernism, broken columns and video monitors, which I'd always hated. They saw my dances as art brut. "That's dancing? They're not doing anything. They're just running around barefoot." They thought there was no story, no subplot; but of course there was. It just looked too natural to them, like children playing.

When we brought *L'Allegro* back a year later, people realized they were no longer supposed to like it. The public changed its mind. Between these two *L'Allegro*s, we had a controversial hit, Purcell's *Dido and Aeneas*. I imagined it would be my last ever dance.

I'D ASSUMED I was going to die in a few years from an AIDS-related illness. I knew a lot of people who already had: an early boyfriend, close friends, people I'd had sex with. I knew people with Kaposi's sarcoma, wasted, damaged, and dying. I'm not a hypochondriac, but I didn't need a test; besides, tests weren't very common then anyway. I knew I was going to die and didn't need it confirmed. During *L'Allegro*, Erin fell hopelessly in love with a beautiful young dancer who died of AIDS shortly after. Tall, skinny Jon Mensinger, on whom I used to choreograph my moves for the Sorceress in *Dido*, died later, rapidly. At one point, people were dropping dead all over the place. Why not me? I wasn't a "top" or a "bottom" either—those are bullshit terms—nor was I ever into bad drugs, but I suppose I was lucky (it's all luck in the end anyway), because I'd had sex with hundreds of men in many ways, over many years. I'd been a gay radical, all in favor of the promiscuity afforded by the 1970s—it was very important to me—but I learned that I didn't have anything like the depth of experience others had. I was a virgin compared to some, even though I'd fully enjoyed myself.

As someone with narcissistic tendencies, I presumed that I was HIV positive. There was no particular evidence. It was pure weltschmerz. I can laugh at it now, but it wasn't a laughing matter at the time. It was heavy and intense, and I very melodramatically and monodramatically decided that the next dance would be my last. My thought was, for my swan song, I shall do the tragedy of Dido, and I shall be Aeneas and I shall be Dido. I shall be the cause of her death, and I shall be her dying, and it will be only me. I was dancing marvelously and freely then, and I wanted to do a big, dramatic one-man show, and my original thought was a solo with me doing all the parts. Nuts! But that's how I started thinking about and working on *Dido*. There's even photographic evidence from a shoot with Annie Leibovitz, which accompanied a *Vanity Fair* article. We'd been intending to go to Malta to shoot me like Isadora Duncan at Cape Sounion (where I'd realized I'd lost my ticket on my European trip), but we ended up taking the pictures at her studio in Manhattan. They were my studies for Dido. In the photos where I'm naked, I'm Aeneas, and when I'm Dido, I'm in a drape. The dance was based on those pictures as much as anything else. My mother had one of them up in the dining room for years, shockingly revealing her son's penis. Nancy and Barry thought the photos too drag-queeny, and perhaps they were. *Dido* stayed that way, despite the fact that it no longer remained a one-man show.

IT WASN'T THE FIRST TIME I'd associated Purcell, blood, and mortality. In 1985, I premiered *One Charming Night* at Dance Theater Workshop. Like everybody else, I'd just read Anne Rice's *Interview with the Vampire*, which I loved. Her work may have gone downhill from there, but that was a great book, as erotic as her pornography. Vampirism is always bubbling under, then over—the films *Nosferatu* and *Dracula* were in my veins, as was a great tragic song by Buffy Sainte-Marie called "The Vampire"—but this Anne Rice revamp was everywhere, the zeitgeist, though I'd never have made up a dance based solely on my enthusiasm for a book. It doesn't work that way, and besides, the dance ended up having little to do with the book. My inspiration was the music.

I had a residency at Robert Redford's experimental Sundance Institute, an exclusive summer intensive for composers, filmmakers, choreographers, and designers. I went with Winkie and Herschel (working on *Mythologies*), and there I started on *One Charming Night* to a recording of some Purcell songs, unrelated except inasmuch as they were by Purcell, and I made them into a suite. The four component songs were "Be Welcome Then, Great Sir," "One Charming Night," "Hark! The Ech'ing Air," and "Lord, What Is Man?" To me, they were diabolical—two religious, two not—deeply Christian, and

With Teri Weksler in *One Charming Night*, Jacob's Pillow, 1986. *(Tom Brazil)*

unsettling. They were all about love and sex and death, like everything is. I decided to set them as a classical-style pas de deux, meaning a duet, a solo, a solo, and a coda—the seduction of a very young girl by a very old vampire.

I started work with two ballet dancers from Mormon Utah's Ballet West and Winkie, my assistant, and then I learned it and did it with her. It was a difficult, virtuosic dance, based on baroque dance and early ballet in a delicate style rarely seen (or attempted) anymore, and very sexual, an intimate and ultimately awful dance with full bloodsucking orgasm. I sucked the lifeblood from her throat, then I slashed my wrist and fed it to her. Finally she became immortal, flying off my shoulder to eternal life, to the final "Alleluia!" Though structured precisely like a nineteenth-century pas de deux—the same basic story and identical in the tempi and the choreographic content—everything else was wrong in this tale of abduction, murder, and transformation.

No one could do it as well as Winkie and I, and though I danced *One Charming Night* with several other female partners, nobody ever danced the part of the vampire except me, so when I stopped dancing, it vanished from the repertoire. Until recently. I finally found someone I trusted to do it: Dallas McMurray. It's a heavy-duty artistic responsibility to take on a piece like that, but he'd progressed to a point where he could handle it. I've never met anyone with his rhythmic accuracy. He's as good as I was. He isn't necessarily interested in choreography, nor does he seek big solo attention, but as a dancer he can do anything immediately. For him to learn it that rapidly and for Winkie (whom we'd brought in to set the dance) to drill it that hard was very challenging for both of them.

Although *One Charming Night* was about the orgasm of blood mingling, and despite the fact that it was at the time of AIDS, the dance wasn't necessarily about AIDS. Not everything *was* until it later turned out to have been. The inspiration for *Dido and Aeneas*, however, certainly was.

I'D KNOWN PURCELL'S OPERA for many years, but the Lament kept coming around to me, particularly the still-chilling cover by Klaus Nomi, the German new-wave singer. (He also recorded the Cold Genius aria "What Power Art Thou" from Purcell's *King Arthur*, which I later directed for the English National Opera.) I'd even given it as an assignment in the very first choreographic workshop I ever taught, at Harvard Summer Dance in the mid-1980s.

In the version of Virgil's original story in *The Aeneid* that Nahum

Tate (real name Teate) extrapolated for Henry Purcell, the story of Dido and Aeneas goes like this. There are only five scenes:

The Palace: The Trojan War is over. Aeneas's destiny, as decreed by the gods, is to found Rome, but he has become obsessed with Dido, queen of Carthage. Her sister and confidante, Belinda, and other optimistic courtiers urge her to enjoy her good fortune, but the young widow Dido is anxious. Aeneas arrives to ask the Queen, again, to give herself to him. Belinda notices with relief that Dido seems to be capitulating. Dido and Aeneas leave together. Love triumphs.

The Cave: The evil Sorceress summons her colleagues to make big trouble in Carthage. Dido must be destroyed before sunset. Knowing of Aeneas's destiny to sail to Italy, the Sorceress decides to send a spirit disguised as Mercury to tell him he must depart immediately. Since Dido and Aeneas and the rest are out on a hunt, the witches create a storm to spoil the lovers' fun and send everyone back home.

The Grove: Dido and Aeneas make love. Another triumph for the hero. Dido senses the approaching storm. Belinda, ever practical, organizes the trip back to the palace. Aeneas is accosted by the false Mercury with this command: "Leave Carthage now." He accepts his orders, then wonders how to break the news to Dido.

The Ships: Aeneas and the Trojans prepare for the journey. The Sorceress and her witches are pleased to see that their plot is working. Once Aeneas has sailed, they will conjure an ocean storm.

The Palace, again: Dido sees the Trojans preparing their ships. Aeneas tries to explain his predicament and offers to break his vow in order to stay with her. Dido is appalled by his hypocrisy. She sends him away and contemplates the inevitability of death. "Remember me but forget my fate." Dido kills herself on a pyre made of all the possessions that he's left behind.

Postscript: The next book of *The Aeneid* begins with Aeneas looking back on Carthage from his ship to see a ribbon of smoke rising from Dido's immolation.

Tragedy.

MORTIER WAS THRILLED with the idea.

The solo version would have probably been a good dance, but the simple reason I didn't do it was that I realized how hard it would be, in purely visual terms, to make out with myself. There's that joke move where you stand with your back to the audience and put your arms around yourself, which of course I tried. That's *pretty* good but I thought . . . maybe not.

So I decided to make it for multiple dancers, as the show ended up, with me as Dido—good part—*and* the Sorceress. I had previously intended to be both the man and the woman, to symbolically fuck myself to death, but now I was a man playing a woman (two women, in fact), which was, as far as some people were concerned, equally insane and complicated. The Belgians even mistook it for misogyny.

My immediate impulse was to choreograph from background to foreground. Think of it like a painting. The first thing you do is the background, the mountains and the sky, then you do the trees and the deer, and last you put in the Mormon family having a picnic by the stream. So I started with the back and moved forward. First the corps or the frame (the chorus), the eight to ten people in the back; then, in front of them, the costars, Belinda and the second woman; and then, closest to the audience, the principals, Dido and Aeneas.

It's set in Carthage (now Tunisia), but I wanted it to have an Orientalist look, a Western idea of Eastern exotica. I based the moves on Indian and Indonesian classical dance—that's the language of Dido, both of the hands and the feet and of the stage grammar. All of this demanded a certain flatness of dimensions. People say, "It looks like it came off a Greek vase." No. The images on those vases are dancers being represented two-dimensionally. Nobody stood like that; it's just how the artists managed perspective on a circular surface, to show those dancers painted flat. So it wasn't "come to life," it was kept dead.

The cast was finalized at twelve people, everyone in full view all the time. I wanted full ceremony, where no one, including me, was off duty for one second. We never left the scene. For one hour, each dancer was either watching the ceremony or participating in it. Everybody dyed his or her hair black. The makeup was black kohl eyeliner, early Martha Graham: pale powder, scarlet lipstick, either red, black, or gold nail polish, and golden earrings. Beautiful. The dance could only be done in sarongs—designed with Christine Van Loon—because that was what I had choreographed it for. We had to rehearse the whole thing in them, and develop a particular Javanese-inspired "sarong walk" to keep from tripping on our skirts. There was no shortcut to putting them on either, long pieces of fabric that hardly stretched and had to be tied. No new technology was allowed. Even my hair (often described as "glorious" or "flowing," by the way) had just a chopstick stuck through it, no barrette. It was uncomfortable, ceremonial in a way I associate with South Asia, not punitive but a ritual ordeal. There was so much time sitting still, watching from the side of the stage in a strictly formal pose, that you thought you might pass out, sweat dropping rhythmically off the tip of your nose. You couldn't have a drink of water, fix your hair, or go to the dressing room. The actual dancing came as a relief.

The performance space was the Théâtre Varia, a big empty room where we built the stage from nothing. The set featured a ramp up each side, with a vertical square at the front that framed the audience's view. Robert Bordo, who'd been recently working on cartographic images, designed the décor. The band was on the floor (i.e., there wasn't

Dido and Aeneas film shoot, Toronto, 1996. *(Cylla von Tiedemann)*

a pit), and the court dances were highly formal. (If you don't like my work, you'd call it "schematic"; otherwise it's "formal.") Every move was text related, nearly every word of the text acted out, gestures matched directly to words to clearly illustrate the story. A lot of the gestures derived from American Sign Language, but a lot of it I concocted, so as far as a hearing-impaired person is concerned, Dido makes either perfect sense or none at all.

That may need a little more explanation.

I've always maintained, and it's not so original, that one communicates with one's hands. Nondancers hardly notice or care about fifth position of the feet but understand a lot through the dancers' hand gestures. In everyday communication, hands and faces communicate the truth, and can be the tell for a lie. It was something I started to take note of when I was stuck in Seattle, studying sign language (so something good came out of breaking my foot after all).

There were so many words in *Dido* and so many of them repeated—*L'Allegro* is the same way—that I'd started to develop explanatory signals. In *L'Allegro*, for example, every time anyone sang "come," the dancers did the ASL gesture for "come." When the word "here" is sung in *Dido and Aeneas*, the dancers pointed to the ground. Some gestures were therefore strictly ASL, others were adaptations, while still others—for example, the gesture for "fate," which appears many times in *Dido*—I made up entirely. That particular gesture, with strongly splayed fingers, was hard to do, but very good for tendonitis (both causing and relieving it).

In the *Sailor's Dance* in *Dido*, and many times after, the word "never" is accompanied by the ASL version, the top of a question mark on a diagonal. The dancers make that gesture in sailorish fashion every time that word pops up, and their facial expressions make sense of it whether you immediately understand it or not. The gesture for "mortal wounds"—one of the most memorable—became akin to "ripping your guts open and their spilling out," though this was faux Graham rather than ASL. I've always personified Cupid in my work by the gesture of taking an arrow from a quiver and shooting it with a bow—it's funny and accurate—so this "sign language" is part of how I communicate generally, but in *Dido*, it's more than that.

Peter Sellars does it too. He calls it "Peter Sellars's School of Dance"; I call it hand jive. If you assign a gesture to a word, and the chorus is singing in counterpoint onstage and does that gesture at the right moment, it makes an interesting visual composition. So in *Gloria*, in those soprano, alto, tenor, bass sections, when everyone is doing the move with the text or the rhythm—they don't necessarily have to be illustrating the text, but their move accompanies a particular word—it makes it automatically as contrapuntal to look at as it is to listen to or to read.

When I later staged Prokofiev's *Romeo and Juliet, on Motifs of*

Shakespeare, my "sign language" was taken from a great early Italian book called *Gesture in Medieval Art and Antiquity*, a treasure trove of fascinating drawings of the various fuck-yous of yore—*stronza, malocchio*, elbow biting. That was the source, with variations, of the aggressive confrontations for the various crowd scenes. And for *Layla and Majnun*, more recently, I studied Azerbaijani and Georgian folk dance, in which the women always hold their hands in a certain way. There's a similar hand position in ballet, as if you're holding on to a piece of paper with two fingers, the idea being that it doesn't betray any sign of strain. But I've always liked to see the physical work, the strain.

I like what hands mean.

I DANCED Dido and the Sorceress. The Sorceress is as chaotic and horrifying as possible. I would almost use the word "camp." It's meant to be cruel: she's an evil woman who wants Dido dead.

While I set the Sorceress on Jon, I made up Dido on Ruth. Having made the change of focus from all the parts being myself, I no longer wanted it to only be about me. I'd gone from "This is how I feel, I'm going to die" to "I'm not even in it as I make it up." And then I put myself in the part, into those moves I'd choreographed on Ruth and Jon, and that's why it worked, because it wasn't just me feeling sorry for myself anymore. And that's basically good, because . . . no one's interested.

But Dido was very hard, probably the most demanding thing I've ever asked of myself. Every dance I've ever made up is difficult, but this was by far the most difficult, and I used to kill myself on a nightly basis. Dido itself is one of the great roles, and I felt an amazing sense of puissance performing it well, alone. Before I started the Lament, I always paused for a few seconds, an eternity of silence in a theater, as if to say, "Stop everything! Watch and listen." I had the audience's rapt attention in a tiny point of focus, something every child is familiar with.

Another big element of course was the ancient, worldwide theatrical tradition of men playing women's roles. It didn't mean I was a woman inside or I wanted to be a woman. In fact, when you're a man doing a woman's role, what you have to avoid is any type of caricature, and generally therefore you don't do much different. You make yourself feel different, and if you have command over your interpretative abilities, it's not a problem. But it was for the Belgians. They interpreted my Dido as my insult to all women (and presumably all men too). The press called it "a hideous spectacle." One of the headlines was ALL OF BELGIUM STANDS SPEECHLESS BEFORE THIS DISASTER! They couldn't work out the tone: pathos or parody? It was a violation of decorum, a "bad transvestite act," tasteless, debased. Another review referred to me as "*une Didon dodue*," a chubby Dido. Why, thank you! The august English dance critic Clement Crisp once said I had "the delicacy of a Duchess fording a trout stream." I think that was about me generally, rather than particularly as Dido. I took it as a compliment.

Later on, when I stopped performing the role myself, it was great to see a woman dance the part of Dido, though when I first brought it back, I split the part between Amber Star Merkens and Brady McDonald because I didn't necessarily think either of them could handle it. I was just being protective, both of myself, because I was so exceptionally close to the role, and of them—it's a racking part, physically demanding, emotionally distressing, and you're dead in every way by the end. Both Amber and Brady took it over on their own, and recently, Laurel Lynch—who's big, a little butch, and a great artist—danced the part. I don't see me in it at all anymore. I don't even care. I was only worried, because I was a good performer, that the people who followed me wouldn't be able to pull it off. But they could. And that makes it a good piece of art that can be replicated without nostalgia. It still works.

And when the Belgians saw my Dido, they heard the passionate voice of Lorraine Hunt Lieberson. It was a real collaboration between the two of us, a dancer and a singer creating a single character. (She alternated the role with another wonderful mezzo, Mary Westbrook-Geha.) When I'd first met Lorraine, she wasn't even a singer, she was a violist; then she was a soprano, then a mezzo-soprano, then a giant superstar mezzo. Her spirituality at the time was very angel-crystal-unicorn—I'm sure you've intuited that mine is not—and I loved her.

I have two terrible stories. She gave an unbearably great recital at Carnegie Hall—Handel and Haydn arias with Philharmonia Baroque. When it was over, I waved to her from the audience and swiftly made my exit into the corridor. But just as the door locked behind me, she sang another encore as I was trapped listening outside! How dare I leave too early? The final time I saw her perform was *Les Troyens* at the Met, one three-act opera that seems three evenings long. The production was boring, so I left before the last act, before the whole Dido finale, no less. Tragically that was the last time she performed it. She died not long after of breast cancer. I wish I'd stayed.

She was to have been the star of my version of Gluck's *Orfeo ed Euridice* at the Met in 2007 if she hadn't died. That was going too far! She could have just said she didn't want to. (People have told me never to say that again, but she'd have laughed. Besides, now it's down in print, so I've said it forever.)

AMID ALL THIS FUROR over *Dido*, we tried to cheer ourselves up in any way we could. An anonymous notice appeared on the call-board.

We are currently in negotiation with Touchstone Pictures . . . for a feature film to be based on the company and its experiences in Brussels. This casting list is <u>tentative</u>. If you have serious objections to the actor assigned to your part, please write a list of 3 actors who you think should play the part . . .

Here are the highlights so you can better picture people depicted in this book:

YOUNG MARK MORRIS	Ricky Schroder
TEENAGE MARK MORRIS	Robby Benson (I corrected this to "Dweezil Zappa")
MARK MORRIS	Roy Scheider
BARRY ALTERMAN	Judd Hirsch
NANCY UMANOFF	Cher
GERARD MORTIER	Jackie Mason
MIKHAIL BARYSHNIKOV	Rob Lowe
RUTH DAVIDSON	Belinda Carlisle & The Go-Go's
TINA FEHLANDT	Linda Evans
PENNY HUTCHINSON	Shirley MacLaine
HANS-GEORG LENHART	Matthew Broderick
ERIN MATTHIESSEN	Kirk Douglas (Matthew Modine)
JON MENSINGER	Michael J. Fox
KRAIG PATTERSON	Diana Ross

YOUNG GUILLERMO RESTO	Prince
GUILLERMO RESTO	Omar Sharif
YOUNG KEITH SABADO	Sabu
KEITH SABADO	Toshiro Mifune (Linda Hunt)
DONALD MOUTON	Phil Donahue
LINDA DOWDELL	Carole King (Tom Hulce)
MAXINE MORRIS	Maureen Stapleton
MAUREEN MORRIS	Julie Kavner

When it came to Show Number Three, *Mythologies*, developed from *Championship Wrestling* at BAM, *Le Soir* ran the headline MARK MORRIS GO HOME, in English, of course, on the assumption that I couldn't possibly understand it in French. (The Flemish-language paper predictably responded with MARK MORRIS PLEASE STAY.)

Mythologies was the turning point: "How dare you use Roland Barthes as source material? You're American!" This show earned us the headline THE PATHETIC FRAUDS OF MARK MORRIS: ENOUGH! I understood the cultural background and the depth of the negative reaction, the context of the booing, but I hadn't been plotting to offend; it wasn't "proactive," as people now say. I never once thought, as they imagined I did, "I dare you to like this"; I only ever thought, "I like this and I hope you do too." I'm always trying to do something I've never done before. It's as simple as that. I may naturally be an agitator, but Mortier hired me to be me, and I wasn't doing anything freakier because we were out there. However, a lot of the booing was directed at me personally. Bear in mind that I was also naked, completely naked, in *Mythologies* and that my nakedness wasn't meant to be sexy. If anyone expected the nudity to be erotic, they were sorely disappointed. It was just nakedness, unglamorized exposure, the facts—unashamed, unembarrassed, and uninteresting.

It was then I started to push back.

Belgium is bizarre. The French Belgians are more French than the French, and their papers were more conservative. They hated me most. The more intellectual and progressive papers were actually the Flemish-language ones, and although the Flemish didn't like me much either, they at least defended my right to exist. So it was basically the French and the Flemish fighting each other via me. I found myself cannon fodder between the two halves of Belgium: MOMMY! DADDY! YOU'RE TEARING THIS FAMILY APART! The Flemish spoke Flemish, French, English, and maybe German, whereas the French spoke French and couldn't be bothered to speak anything else, like in Quebec. (On a side note, I later did two ballets for Les Grands Ballets Canadiens. I decided to give them non-English titles, so they couldn't be translated into French. Why? Because, despite being *vive la France!* in every possible way, I am French resistant when it comes to Quebec. I called one piece *Paukenschlag*, the actual German name of Haydn's Surprise Symphony; the other ballet was a beautiful piece for strings by Donizetti, choreographed in shapes of five. I called it, in Latin, *Quincunx*, because I love a quincunx, that beautiful geometric pattern like the number five on a die. When I saw the printed program, they'd renamed it, to my horror, *Quinconce*, the French spelling. Thank you, everyone in Quebec!)

Of course it hurts one's feelings to be booed at curtain calls; it upset me personally because I wished they'd liked the show. I don't gain power from being booed, so I bowed as though I was having roses thrown at me. It's a point of dignity and I tried not to do it sarcastically. I accepted it. In that situation, "Fuck you!" isn't in my nature.

However, I did resort to "fuck you" once at a big fashion gala evening at the Monnaie. It was a luxurious environment, 20,000-franc tickets. Nobody cared about us, the show started late, and everyone was drunk and laughing during the performance, perhaps a little derisively. For the curtain call, I came out in Bermuda shorts and zori with fake money that I'd found in the prop room and I threw money on my company: a joke. That was me trying to survive within a very tight system.

BRUSSELS—WHICH I ONCE HEARD described as "a city habitually underrated by tourists"—was a rainy, depressed, dog-shit-all-over-the-streets kind of city, always monochrome, light or dark gray. We were uncomfortable, and every weekend, if we could afford it, we'd leave for Paris or Amsterdam, where we'd check into a cheap hotel, go to cafés and smoke pot, then eat delicious Indonesian food, walk around, or go for a bike ride. Then we'd come back to work and stay in our cute apartments, go to the fabulous market, eat out, associate with each other, and that was it. We went shopping at the PX on the army base, because some of the women in the company needed cranberry juice for their bladder infections; that's where we bought peanut butter, Advil, and other American necessities.

I never really translated the money I was making into dollars. It was Belgian francs at the time, and I'd just take out money and spend it. I'm not generally an overextravagant person, but I was extravagant in Brussels, because the food was great and I didn't notice how much I was spending—a lot, all the time. Mortier's largesse was incredible: fifteen people for a lunch meeting three hours long with five bottles of great wine at the best restaurant in town. In light of that experience, we'd think, "I loved that restaurant Mortier took us to! Let's go there every night!" One particular Belgian beer was 12 percent alcohol.

After several weeks of people vomiting in cabs on the way home, we switched to Stella.

I was vegetarian until I moved there, but now we found ourselves in Brussels, with its beautiful old-school French cuisine, where the restaurants had a table on the street outside displaying their wares, a beautiful Netherlandish still life: a dead pheasant, a fish, some pomegranates, a lobster, and a haunch of venison. That's when I embraced actual food again, at places like Chez Richard, with its simple plank tables—a delicious green salad, a kilo of *moules frites*, followed by an incredible steak topped with a piece of Roquefort. Every night dinner was fabulous fresh food, be it a great Lebanese restaurant or the fancy creepy French restaurant Comme Chez Soi. I still tell people to go to L'Ogenblik—"The Blink"—a brasserie with sawdust-covered floors, where we ate twice a week. And Aux Armes de Bruxelles, where *everything* was served with ham and endive (Belgium's other great export besides Béjart, as I apparently once claimed in an interview).

After rehearsal at rue Bara, we'd often go to a place at the station called Au Relais, which served my favorite dish, *un portion mixte*, toothpicks of cubes of sausage and cubes of cheese with celery salt. One evening, a whole gang of us was sitting at one of the long tables, Misha right next to me. This very drunk Belgian guy came up, said something like "Mark Morris, you are shit" in English, and poured an entire beer into my lap. I was almost certainly drunk too, but at the moment I realized exactly what he was going to do, I remember thinking, "Okay. Go ahead then." Why did he do it? I was speaking English and I was gay with long hair. That may have been enough. I don't know whether this was really linked to any huge offense my dance caused, though Nancy remembers that was *precisely* what it was about. I just thanked him.

I was tired of being on display, tired of being harassed, so I started hiding out in my house, cooking and eating at home. I'm told Belgium is now less homophobic, xenophobic, misogynist, and intolerant, but back then it was like the Eisenhower 1950s. I should put that in perspective: it wasn't like Spain under Franco. In Belgium, they just didn't like you and made your life as difficult as possible. The cops were thugs. If you were black or brown, you were stopped every three days, if not daily, and it happened to Guillermo, being among the more memorable in appearance, all the time. Invariably, a cop would stop Guillermo and then be surprised on finding that he was working for the Monnaie (and probably earning more money). The cop would have a computer record of every previous time Guillermo had been stopped, all without subsequent arrest. One cop asked why it happened so often. "Why do you think?" said Guillermo with a shrug. "And next time I'll have been stopped that many times, plus one." If you were a woman out at ten at night waiting for a bus, the car would cruise by and ask you to show identification. They'd make you empty your bags onto the hood of the car or onto the street. It was constant, and that's when I stopped walking to work (and it was only a fifteen-minute walk). I started taking taxis because I didn't want to be harassed. It was horrible. They hated everybody: Muslims, Americans, Africans. Nancy used to leave her apartment and cross the street diagonally, so she didn't have to walk all the way around a traffic circle. The police would stop her, then escort her around the right way, purely to humiliate. Dancers would show up at rehearsal in tears.

The nearest I ever got to jail was when I was busted for possession of marijuana. I'd come back from Amsterdam with a little nugget of pot in my pocket that I'd forgotten about because I was high. When we arrived at the train station, we were greeted by dogs, policemen, sirens, everything except handcuffs. I had to agree to let them search my apartment, where they found a pipe and some pot. Barry and I were thrown in a holding tank for three or four hours. They even took our shoelaces and our belts as if we were planning on suicide. It was ridiculous. They taunted us with the phone call: "In America, we know you get a phone call when you get arrested. Well, you don't get that here." The officer on duty typed up the report purposefully slowly. I was incensed. But I was also nervous. The arrest would have been a giant scandal. The newspapers had already told me to go home; then I get arrested for pot and I'm in jail? I was probably very close to losing the job. In fact, they let us out and there was never a whisper. Whatever Mortier did, it was all very hush-hush. However, it left me somewhat paranoid for the rest of our stay, particularly because the cops now had the right to enter my apartment whenever they liked without a warrant, and even *more* particularly because Guillermo was living with me, providing hash (which he'd buy in the Moroccan quarter) to some of the dancers.

The arrest was the straw that broke the camel's back. I gave up at that point. And by giving up I mean I went *right* back to work.

MY OLDER DANCERS, the original company, had always had an option to stay for one season and then go home. Several of them did. It was a big deal. Some of the dancers would have preferred to be one of twelve, rather than one of twenty-four. We'd doubled in number, and the mood wasn't particularly good. There was a division between the old and the new dancers.

Barry's theory, when things started to go wrong, was that we'd come to Belgium purely to destroy the company. But people didn't leave morosely; it was more like "This isn't for me." Some were near the end of their performing careers; some just missed home; some had or wanted to start families. Susan Hadley's husband had accompanied her but couldn't find work, so they left; Winkie went home to her husband, Kenny, to get pregnant. Tina decided to stay on the basis that she wasn't going back to anything, and remembers the second year as the best ever for her, personally and in dancing terms. I could have gone home after a year, but I didn't want to. But no one said, "We quit. Fuck you!" It was organic but it did change things.

At one point, Nancy started posting the number of days remaining on the call-board so we could count down, because everyone was so looking forward to the whole experience being over.

THE FIRST PIECE was *L'Allegro* and the last was *The Hard Nut*, also a hit. It was the three years in between that were rocky.

There was *Mythologies* and the semi-joke horror show dance that was *Wonderland*, with a ninety-five-piece orchestra that had to rehearse for weeks because of the density of the Schoenberg music, *Five Orchestral Pieces* and *Music for a Motion Picture*. My idea had been to make up a piece for five people (to include Mr. Baryshnikov), based on stock Hitchcockian noirish types, that had nearly no dancing, just great impenetrable music. I wouldn't claim it all made linear sense, but it was scenic: venetian blind lighting, fedoras, shadows, all the things that are happening in my head as I listen to the marvelous Bernard Herrmann's scary, jagged strings on Hitchcock soundtracks. But the music was Schoenberg, which is even scarier.

It's a beautiful dance, but we only ever did it once more (at BAM in 1990, to a recording), because the whole point—a joke, funny only to me perhaps—was to see how much money we could possibly spend on the orchestra and how little dancing we could get away with. The style in Europe at that time—*Tanztheater* (a word you can only translate into English literally) at the hands of Pina Bausch and her protégés—was violent, high impact, and precious little dancing. She was a brilliant artist, but the work of her protégés held no interest for me, and that's what I was parodying with this dance of few steps and maximum angst. I was supposed to dance in *Wonderland*, but I got plantar fasciitis and Keith replaced me, so I actually never once got to do the piece, which almost made it perfect. The logical conclusion of "as little dance as possible": no dance at all.

We followed the sublimely huge with the ridiculously silent. I choreographed *Behemoth* with no music, because I wanted to see whether I could. Trisha didn't use music at all for many years—a lot of people didn't back then—and though that wasn't my prime interest (because I'm so reliant on music to engage me), I thought I'd try. It turned out that I could.

The evening's program was called *Loud Music*—the joke being that *Behemoth* had no music at all—for which I made up two new dances (the second being *Going Away Party*, to recordings of Bob Wills and His Texas Playboys). Normally I have a score "in hand" so I can fake making something up, if only to kick-start myself, but for *Behemoth* there was nothing, not even a diagram. I worked for a few weeks until I had what turned out to be about an hour's worth of "material" (as we in the business call "moves"), all of which was very rhythmic and very organized. There was no particular story being told, but there were sections that I reordered, editing as I would normally do, ending up with a forty-five-minute piece for maybe a dozen people, called *Behemoth* for its length and weight. We did it at the Halles de Schaerbeek, a covered market around which all the streets were shut down for noise. Every night on the dot an ice cream truck went by, broadcasting "Whistle while You Work" into the silence. All the dancers were counting to themselves, trying desperately not to trigger each other into laughter. It is a tense, weird dance. A critic suggested it was about mental disorders, because there was some repetition and some shaking. It wasn't.

There was nothing unsatisfying about that experience, though it's true that I've never done silence again. I like music so much; I can only *just* do without it. Music complicates things for choreographers, most of whom are just choreographing to a beat or to an atmosphere anyway, as opposed to the actual music as it is composed. We once programmed *Behemoth* between the two *Liebeslieder Walzer*, beautiful Brahms split in half by a forty-five-minute silent intermission.

MEANWHILE (AND NOT DIRECTLY because of *Wonderland* and *Behemoth*), things had been getting very bad with Mortier and my management.

He and Barry had learned to hate each other. They loved taunting each other. They *tortured* each other. Barry refused to learn French, and didn't understand a word, whereas Nancy took the Flemish route because of her husband-to-be. Once Mortier was walking down the corridor in our office, tap-tap-tapping his way, presumably to see Nancy. He was so nervous to be in the corridor that he walked into Barry's office by mistake, let out a shriek, and fled. They were no longer on speaking terms. At the end of the first year, while we were on tour, he'd refused to renew their contracts, and Nancy tells me that at the very tense meeting where he finally agreed to compromise, he signed the contracts, then immediately ripped them up to show how little he cared. I don't remember, but that's a fabulous thing to do.

Things got even worse after an interview in the London *Times* in which I described Belgium as racist, sexist, homophobic, highly conservative (much as I have done above), and, in short, somewhat fascist. The headline in *Le Soir* the next day was the French for MARK MORRIS SPITS IN THE SOUP AGAIN! (MARK MORRIS CONTINUE À CRACHER DANS LA SOUPE!) I received the following letter, originally in French, from Robert Wangermée, the president of the Monnaie/De Munt, on March 29, 1990:

Dear Sir,

In a meeting that took place on March 28th, the Board of Directors became aware—much to its members' surprise and dismay—of certain remarks you made about Belgium, which appeared in an interview with the British newspaper The Times dated March 23rd.

The Board of Directors has charged me with determining whether you actually made those remarks and, barring any denial on your part, I'm to convey the Board's extreme dissatisfaction.

I should add that if you have such contempt for the country that welcomes you, the Board would not object to your prematurely terminating your contract with the T.R.M.

I look forward to hearing from you regarding the issues raised in this letter.

Respectfully yours,
The President

I counted to ten in French and chose my words as carefully as I could:

Dear Mr. Wangermée,

Thank you for your letter of 29 March.

First let me say that I am sorry if I caused anyone to take offense because of remarks attributed to me in The Times. It is never my intention to sow discord and I sincerely regret any discomfort caused by The Times article.

It is unfortunate of course that The Times writer chose to excerpt out of context these brief remarks from a wide-ranging two-hour interview. The societal ills to which I made reference (racism, sexism, etc.) are present in every Western democracy (not just Belgium as the article infers) and I think any honest and justice-seeking person would agree. And I have been repeatedly quoted on the record as criticizing these same problems in the United States.

I am a choreographer, however, not a speechmaker, and that is how I must be judged. Since coming here in the fall of 1988 at the invitation of De Munt/La Monnaie, I have created many works which have won widespread international acclaim and praise for Belgium, its national opera, and its director M. Mortier.

I am most grateful to Belgium, my adopted country, for affording me the opportunity to work freely, independent of financial and political interference. I will continue until the conclusion of my contract in June 1991 to make dances to the best of my ability and serve the cause of art.

Sincerely,
Mark Morris

It was a close one. I stayed.

NANCY RECENTLY FOUND an MMDG Communiqué from the latter part of the Brussels period. The tone sums it all up:

We have come to a critical juncture. A mountain has erupted in the middle of the road. New paths must be created.

The move to Brussels was attempted to satisfy certain specific needs:

1. A permanent studio facility.
2. Higher production values (i.e. live music).
3. A better financial package for the dancers.
4. An end to the American Modern Dance conundrum of scanty rehearsal–long tour.
5. A home.

All of these were realized to a greater or lesser extent. And they remain valid goals. Of course, every action, no matter how small, unleashes a myriad of unforeseen consequences. And moving to Europe was no small action.

Barry then listed the positives—the dances, the meeting of new people, the lifting of the perception of MMDG to a higher level— before moving on to the negatives:

> A. The yielding of final power and control over our finances and futures to an institution which does not and <u>cannot</u> understand what we are and what we need. (We are everything to us; we are only the annoying and troublesome Dance Division to the Monnaie.) . . .
>
> B. The hiring of some wrong people and the lack of mechanism to part ways with them. . . . This has contributed to a malaise which, while not pervasive, is undeniably present.
>
> C. Lack of flexibility. This is ironic, as a prime goal . . . was greater latitude in the choosing of projects and venues. . . .
>
> This current situation is bankrupt and cannot be salvaged, there is no fight to be had in this situation, only dissolution and construction. Contexts must change, and the task here is to identify the ideal and realize it as closely as resources and circumstances allow.

There then followed much speculation about the identity of the ideal: how many dancers, where to base the dance company in the future (London was an early idea). The communiqué ends:

> I'm running out of ribbon so I can't write anymore. Mao: Great disorder under Heaven: the situation is excellent.

With Mikhail Baryshnikov and Linda Dowdell,
Brussels, 1989. *(Nancy Umanoff)*

Nine

The Hard Nut

One of the haunts where we gathered to drink and vent was a downtown theme bar called Le Cercueil ("the coffin"), a candlelit funeral home, complete with casket tables with flowers, skull tankards, and Gregorian chant on the sound system. During one late-night conversation, Misha, Rob, Guillermo, Barry, and I came up with the idea of my choreographing one of the big Tchaikovsky ballets: *Sleeping Beauty*, *Swan Lake*, or *The Nutcracker*. *The Nutcracker!* Why not? We had an orchestra and a budget at our disposal. When Mortier had first asked me what I wanted to do, I'd immediately suggested *L'Allegro*. Done. So I proposed *The Nutcracker*. It took one wonderful year to plan.

My first exposure, as an adorable child, had been everyone's: Disney's *Fantasia*, the music's most exquisite realization. Later, when I was fourteen, Chad played me the LP of the whole *Nutcracker*, not just the suite as in *Fantasia*. I'd never heard the tarantella before—it was often cut, as was the coda of "The Dance of the Sugar Plum Fairy," and what remains of the score is presented out of sequence—so to hear it straight through as an orchestral performance was eye-opening. I was hooked.

My first experience of the music as a dancer, on the other hand, had been humiliating. At sixteen or so, as a student with First Chamber, I'd toured the rest homes of Seattle with a nine-person version of the suite. Our version of the Chinese dance was an exact rip-off of *Fantasia*, so we were mushrooms, our costumes a dome-like phallus, a heavy umbrella. We squatted, then stood up and opened. Traumatic.

In 1892 in Saint Petersburg, the Mariinsky premiered Tchaikovsky's *The Nutcracker* on a double bill with *Iolanta*, a one-act lyric opera of his that was then lost for years. The miracle was that they share precisely the same orchestration, except for a newly minted instrument, the celesta, first unveiled in this production specifically for the Sugar Plum Fairy's dance. It was, as you can imagine, a lengthy evening. Ironically, it was *Iolanta* that was the big hit, whereas *The Nutcracker* disappeared for years without a trace.

The first American production was William Christensen's for the San Francisco Ballet in 1944—we don't know whether it was good or not, though it was well reviewed—and it was because of this production that *The Nutcracker* became a comparatively recent Christmas tradition. The production now known as the "original Nutcracker" is later: Balanchine's from the late 1950s—the first "full" version I saw, very good if a little dull. People take that as the Bible, the one against which all others are judged, without necessarily realizing that it is itself a weird hybrid, including an interpolation from *Sleeping Beauty* in the score that doesn't belong at all. I therefore decided that I'd use the full original score without a single note missing, at Tchaikovsky's original metronome markings. In Brussels, they'd give it the fullest attention. I wanted my version of *The Nutcracker* to be interesting, fun, beautiful, scary, and sexy, but above all . . . I just wanted it to make *sense*.

In most *Nutcrackers*, act 1 is boring—a Christmas party—and act 2 is confusing, and then it's over. The general reaction, beyond "Oh, we saw some pretty ballerinas!" is incomprehension: "Why is it over? What just happened?"

In fact, what does the audience even see? To start with, they're not seeing E. T. A. Hoffmann's original 1816 story *The Nutcracker and the Mouse King*; they're seeing a libretto based on Dumas's greatly sanitized bastardization of 1844, *The Story of a Nutcracker*. In Tchaikovsky's ballet, act 1 is generally set in an upper-class drawing room in the late nineteenth century in Düsseldorf, Deutschland, or some fictional Mitteleuropa. There's a Christmas Eve party peopled by dull adults who scold and swat their fake-naughty children. The centerpiece is the arrival of Drosselmeier, a crazy magician relative, who brings presents—a drum for little Fritz, a Nutcracker doll for Clara, who apparently loves nuts—and delights the kids with cheap magic shop props, including a windup doll. The naughty boys gang up on the adorable girls, and the Nutcracker is broken. The guests yawn simultaneously, and it's bedtime.

Clara can't sleep and comes downstairs. She's miniaturized, the tree becomes enormous, the Nutcracker turns into a soldier (but still a toy), and there's a big fight between the mice, who live there anyway, and the toy soldiers who are gifts under the tree. The Nutcracker murders the Mouse King, Clara faints, and the soldier becomes the Prince, a human being. It makes absolutely no sense, and *that's* when there's a big pas de deux between a snow lady and a snow gentleman. And curtain.

For act 2, we're magically in Candyland or Confiturenburg, where there is much excitement about the arrival of the little boy prince and Clara. The Sugar Plum Fairy, self-appointed hostess of the Kingdom of Sweets, welcomes them, and the Prince mimes a précis of act 1, for those who can't remember or don't understand what happened before the intermission. Then they sit down and watch the rest of the show, a travelogue of snacks and delicacies from around the world: Arabia is coffee, China is tea, Russia is candy canes, Spain is chocolate (probably much to the chagrin of Belgium), and so forth. Then there's another big pas de deux, and off they fly in a sleigh.

That's it. It never goes back to the party. It's basically two different ballets that make no sense together. Or, in fact, apart.

My first inclination—in my quest for a coherent story—was to turn to Hoffmann's 1816 original, *The Nutcracker and the Mouse King*, which Marius Petipa (Tchaikovsky's librettist and choreographer) evidently considered way too bizarre for the late nineteenth century. I couldn't possibly have predicted that it would deliver on every thrilling level, and I wrung everything I could out of that gothic, creepy story to put into my show.

The synopsis, therefore, for my back-to-basics version—for which I decided to use the snappy title *The Hard Nut* (the name of the story-within-the-story in the original, which is *The Nutcracker*'s origin myth and the kernel of the tale)—was:

ACT I

Dr. and Mrs. Stahlbaum's annual Christmas Eve party. Their children, Fritz, Marie, and Louise, wait in the den. Party dances: polka, hokey-pokey, hesitation, stroll, bump, waltz. Friend of the family Drosselmeier brings animated toys that he's made. He gives a Nutcracker to the children. Fritz breaks it. The children fight. Dr. Stahlbaum changes the subject. The guests go home. The family goes to bed. The housekeeper cleans up.

Marie can't sleep and comes downstairs to see if the Nutcracker is resting comfortably. At midnight, she is frightened by rats. Everything in the room grows to giant size. G.I. Joes led by the Nutcracker battle rats led by the mutant Rat King. Marie kills the Rat King with her slipper. She falls unconscious. The Nutcracker is transformed into a young man. Marie is tucked in. A worried Drosselmeier makes his way through the blizzard.

ACT II

Marie is in a fever. Drosselmeier comes to see if Marie is resting comfortably and tells her one of his stories:

The Hard Nut

Once upon a time a King and a Queen had a beautiful baby girl named Pirlipat. The Queen's old enemy the Rat Queen threatened to ruin little Pirlipat. The nurse and the cat were left to guard the baby at night. While the nurse and cat slept, the Rat Queen destroyed Princess Pirlipat's face. The royal family was horrified by the sight of their formerly beautiful daughter. The Rat Queen explained that the Princess would regain her beauty only after a young man cracked the hard nut, Krakatuk, with his teeth and stepped backward seven times. The King commanded Drosselmeier to find the hard nut or face decapitation. Drosselmeier set off in search of the hard nut. He traveled the world for fifteen years before finding it back at home.

The ugly teenage Pirlipat watched as one young man after another attempted to crack the hard nut. The last one to try was Drosselmeier's own nephew. He succeeded. On his seventh step backward he stepped on the Rat Queen, killing her. Pirlipat became beautiful and rejected the young Drosselmeier as he started to become ugly—like a nutcracker. . . .

At this point Marie interrupts the story and offers her love to young Drosselmeier. Mrs. Stahlbaum acknowledges her daughter's new maturity with a flower dance. Everyone in the world joins

Marie and young Drosselmeier in celebrating their love. The two go away together forever.

EPILOGUE

Louise and Fritz are sent to bed.

My first thought was to employ Edward Gorey as the designer. I'd worshipped his work since I was thirteen, and when we met, he was wearing his legendary uniform of fur coat and sneakers. He loved dance and liked my work, and he'd recently designed *Dracula* on Broadway; it was perfect. But I paused. I feared it was the wrong generation, the wrong society, too penny-farthing. I didn't want it to be gothic or creepy and kooky in the Addams Family way, though I love both Gorey and Addams. I needed a different direction.

Barry, a comic book nut, showed me Charles Burns's *Big Baby*. I'd read Alan Moore's *Watchmen*, and I'd loved Bill Griffith's *Zippy the Pinhead*, but I was by no means a devotee of comic book culture, which had been around in its groovy new form for some while. I was friends with Lynda Barry, of course, and loved the work of Matt Groening— same period, same Northwest noir—but Burns's linocut style referred to a much older and more frightening world, the missing link between *Reefer Madness* and *Eraserhead*. We were from the same neck of the woods, had contemporaneous childhoods of *The Flintstones* and Disneyland (when it was genuinely scary), and we therefore shared an esthetic. Barry contacted Burns; we met and I was very enthused. It was love at first sight.

My other collaborators would be old favorites, lighting designer James F. Ingalls, set designer Adrianne Lobel, and costume designer Marty Pakledinaz. I remember shopping at the now defunct Toys"R"Us in Manhattan with Adrianne for the kids' Christmas presents, all the crappy toys they don't need. (Someone gets an ugly sweater—the joke there was that we actually used one of Nancy's *real* sweaters.) That was the team of criminals gathered for one last Belgian heist: Burns, Lobel, Ingalls, Pakledinaz, Morris. We started synchronizing our diaries and lining up meetings every few months, all over the world—coincidentally, always glamorous cities too. And at these meetings, we came up with ideas as Charles sketched away, and Marty imagined the costumes in Charles's style. Then we'd disperse, work, think and re-collect.

I didn't want it set precisely in my family's Seattle home in the 1970s—we were all in our thirties, remembering that time—but I was already entertaining autobiographical thoughts. Mrs. Stahlbaum would have elements of Verla, and there'd be a touch of Uncle Jim about Drosselmeier. At one point, we were debating whether we should have extreme makeup or even possibly masks. Marty remembered my saying, "This is my company's goodbye to Brussels. I don't want to hide their faces." We'd go out proudly. Besides, if we'd used masks, it would have been as dead as everybody else's *Nutcracker.*

The Hard Nut, BAM, 2010. *(Stephanie Berger)*

WHEN I STARTED MAKING the moves for the party that takes up all of act 1, I assigned partners; everyone was in a couple—she's with her, these two have been married for twenty years, and so forth. I was the lone drunk, the only sad single at the party. I'd put on the music and we'd improvise with cups and chairs, starting to flirt, and I'd specify things I wanted to happen, like the stroll dance, the hokey-pokey (the suburban version of folk dances from my parents' time), the bump, and the promenade. As we improvised, people developed relationships. At one point, I asked Penny, "Could we run into each other now, and you maybe hand me a drink?" And she said, "No, I can't; my husband's over here and we just had a fight and now I'm coming on to this lesbian over here and we're just about to . . ." And I said, "Fine, forget it! I'll find somebody else." Everybody had a whole life they were living, a fabulously detailed track they were on, of relationship and business, much of which remains. You steal a package when you leave; you play the guitar because you're the hippie folksinger; you're the gay one wondering who else is gay; you're the people who think they're interesting but they're really not; you're the kooky couple who doesn't fit in; and you're the one who cries all the time. These decisions became absolutely strict structurally.

The set design has to be done before you can start blocking the moves, and Adrianne had the wonderful idea to make everything backward. In *Giselle*, to use a classic example, the peasant girl's house is down right, and her bench where she picks flowers and courts boys is down left, and there's a ramp at the back that goes off to the forest. *The Hard Nut* would be the exact opposite of prevailing stage logic. The front door is upstage left, and the bathroom is downstage right beyond the TV. The whole set is beautifully phony, occasioning a lot of pretend peering around to see who's at the "front" door. The large portals that frame the stage are round. In the Hoffmann, when Marie emerges from the sleeve of her father's fur coat, she finds herself in a magic pristine winter wonderland. In Brussels, the stage had the sumptuous visual depth afforded by its rake, dangerous to dance on but offering a beautiful telescopy to the eye, which gave an even more penetrative fallopian depth to the designs—"sleeve of her father's fur coat": hello! The themes and the set were married from the start.

"The Waltz of the Snowflakes" at the end of act 1 is a high point, as the dancers endlessly leap across the stage, flinging snow. I wanted the tutus Marty designed to look like frozen snowflakes, and he went through a million photographs to find the perfect snowflake, before I reminded him that it didn't matter because all snowflakes are *famously* identical. We put as much work into the snow itself as anything else, auditioning every different kind of fake snow yet invented, thinking at first we might be able to get away with some of the crew throwing snow down from above the stage (though it was easy to predict that might look a little underwhelming). And we knew we needed shitloads of snow. The next idea was confetti that the dancers themselves threw. I coincidentally already had them doing the hand movements of "throwing" in the choreography, so we added a fistful of confetti each time. The snow is stored in cardboard boxes in the wings, and the rule is to enter the stage with your hands full and leave with them empty, *every single time*. It's part of the choreography. And it's intense. There's a real skill to holding and throwing it, to avoid its clumping in the sweat of your palms. Then the entire intermission is spent vacuuming the stage.

Narratively, the main problem is the story within the story in act 2 that gives my dance its name, as Drosselmeier goes around the world looking for the nut, Krakatuk. In other versions, there's a lot of dancing candy, and the poor kids, for no reason I can think of, have to sit there and watch this boring ballet, usually from the back too. (Why aren't they in the front, where they can actually see it?) In my version, Drosselmeier asks the people from different countries about the nut. They reply, "I don't know what nut you're talking about. I don't speak whatever language you're speaking!" and do their national dance, which we made as amusingly obvious as we could. There's Spain with a female bull and the Frenchiest France you can possibly imagine. The music tells you the whole story. I was the original beautiful Arabian princess, covered from head to foot, tattoos on my face, sunglasses, and a veil. (However, you can't dance without the use of your eyes, though I suppose I did manage it in *The Vacant Chair*, so I lost the glasses.)

Some other fun facts: no one ever goes to the bathroom at parties onstage, which is why I emerge from the bathroom with toilet paper stuck to my shoe. And everyone gets stuck on the cross-sex casting—the maid (played for a quarter of a century by Kraig Patterson), a woman playing Fritz, of course the beautiful snowflakes—and every year straight males in the audience find Mrs. Stahlbaum, played by John Heginbotham, disquietingly attractive. The makeup is so disguising that there's no way to know who's who, which makes it unique in our repertory. Nobody looks like himself, and in that way, it's like a Broadway show, which is also why it's not the moneymaker some might imagine—the crew is twice as big as the cast. There are only thirty-three dancers in the show, but backstage is even more hectic than onstage—the makeup and costume schedule requires military precision. As a performer, there are certain other performers you might never see at all during the entire production, depending on which track you're on. Originally, there was a central globe (already a replacement for Charles's first idea, a gigantic science-fictional throbbing pink brain), but I suggested a Mercator projection map instead, which seemed more appropriate to the period. There was a conscious *Wizard of Oz* influence in the spiral vortex (used when Marie goes in and out of fantasy) and the way the production switches in and out of color. The prologue is in black and white, then the children change and come back in the same costumes but in color. No one *ever* notices.

There were a couple of terrible wrong turns. The production is full of rats: the dancing rats, a Rat King, and the remote-controlled rats (which never used to work consistently; we've finally figured them out). There's a battle between the G.I. Joe soldiers (come to life under the tree) and the rats, which are all female dancers because I wanted sexy bare showgirl legs, so they're vicious mean killer rats with great gams. When I got to creating the battle itself, I wanted it to be somewhat *Apocalypse Now*, so I had the soldiers raping the rats, fucking them and killing them. Perhaps I was going stir-crazy in Brussels as the date of our release got closer, but at rehearsal, I found myself going full Brando, shouting, "Rape her! Kill her! Fuck her!" until I stopped to think about it for a second. "Wait . . . who am I, Béjart? Am I becoming the enemy? Do I really want to see a rape onstage? That's why I booed Twyla!" It was a blind alley, one I skipped down for some time. Mercifully, it became the more palatable version it is now.

At the end of my version, Marie stops Drosselmeier's story—"That's enough, I'm fine now!"—and that's when she and young Drosselmeier fall in love, actually as people. Some complained about the ending, finding it anticlimactic that they didn't have a longer duet. But they don't have to dance anymore: they're together, young people in love, dancing forever. It's their apotheosis and the show's over. They just get to make out. And that's as it should be. Almost every dance performance I see is overchoreographed; sometimes I long for a little *less*.

Misha was meant to dance the role of Fritz, the asshole son. Jon Mensinger was the Prince, Young Drosselmeier, but when I started working on it, Jon got very sick (and ended up dying, as in fact we all do). I promoted Misha to the Nutcracker, but during rehearsal Misha blew out his knee, so Bill Wagner, his understudy, did the part first.

According to Belgium, *The Hard Nut* liberated me to be my vulgar American self—everything they'd disliked about me from the beginning. I'd wanted to go out with a bang. The surprise, however, was that it was very well received, and not only out of the country's relief at my imminent departure. *L'Allegro* had been a smash at the start, though there was backlash. Between these two big hits, the work was largely dismissed, and it had stopped being fun. I prefer fun.

THE HARD NUT was the last full "Mark Morris" production in Brussels, but two months later our Belgian experience came full circle back to Peter Sellars.

The Death of Klinghoffer—John Adams's second opera and the other Adams/Sellars/Goodman/Morris collaboration following *Nixon in China*—was a co-commission between the Monnaie and several other opera companies, some of which never presented it. The opera itself concerns the real Leon Klinghoffer, a Jewish American businessman, who, on a cruise with his wife in the Mediterranean in 1985, was shot and thrown overboard in his wheelchair by a group of misguided and terrified young Palestinian terrorists who didn't know how to hijack things: a terrible situation. Somehow, despite the few people represented in the actual opera, a complicated piece both dramatically and emotionally with a stunningly subtle libretto, the terrorists came to symbolize the entirety of the Palestinian people, and by association Muslims, and there was immediate controversy as to whether it was anti-Israel or pro-Palestinian, and whether it painted the terrorists in an overly generous light.

I'd first met Alice Goodman as the librettist of *Nixon in China* when she was very pregnant with her daughter Alberta; she wasn't an Anglican priest yet, she was a Jewish poet who had fallen in love with and married the great English poet Geoffrey Hill, thirty years her senior. She and I spent wonderful times together in the few days that we crossed paths; she was feeding me books and also Geoffrey's poetry. I visited them several times when they were in Cambridge, Massachusetts, after Alberta, my goddaughter, was born. I have a portrait she drew of me when she was five that depicts a black cone, a spiral, titled *Old Tornado*. She said that's what I reminded her of. Geoffrey seemed to like me, though it was at first hard to tell, because he was perhaps the most daunting person I ever met: shaggy, grumpy, quite impossible. I couldn't tell much about Geoffrey and Alice's relationship, but they were clearly very fond of each other. She took care of him when he was dying.

Alice wanted someone to bounce her ideas off of, and I found I was getting her texts for the choruses of *Klinghoffer* before she even sent them to John. I sat on them because I'm not really one to critique someone else's poetry, and besides, I hadn't realized that I had a say. These choruses, so concise and fabulous textually, were somehow inspired by her appreciation of my *Dido and Aeneas*, which she'd seen in Boston, with some of these same Sellars singers. So I'd suggest something, and she'd work on it and then send it on to John. It's possible this process even delayed things a little.

Unlike with *Nixon*, the dancers for *Klinghoffer* were always meant to be *my* company; John was writing the opera knowing I was going to choreograph it, sending me music as it was being finished, in MIDI (i.e., synthesized digital) form—absolutely the worst way music can ever sound. But that was the least of our problems.

George Tsypin was designing the sets. The entire edifice was sprung metal, the tension such that if a single bolt came loose, the whole Erector set would burst apart. This self-standing structure was conceptually beautiful but so dangerous. It's my job to protect the people I'm working with, and I told Peter that my dancers were *never* leaving the floor, that I wouldn't have them dance on the scaffolding. If he wanted to stage singers up there, fine, but no dancers. I also insisted that my dancers wear shoes: any debris on that floor (metal shavings, screws), and they'd be fucked.

The story itself demands wheelchairs and guns, so because I'm me, I asked Peter if he'd consider using neither wheelchairs nor guns. A show about wheelchairs and guns doesn't have to resort to wheelchairs and guns. So I wasn't happy when, on the very first day of rehearsal for the presentation of the designs, there was a fleet of wheelchairs and a table laden with a considerable arsenal. But we kept winnowing away at them during rehearsals, and opening night featured one sole wheelchair for Leon Klinghoffer (played by Sanford Sylvan), who was actually in a wheelchair, so that was somewhat unavoidable, and a few guns wrapped in fabric; gun-shaped gifts.

I choreographed only the choruses, which were written specifically for me. Peter, as is his wont, used my dancers as doubles for the characters—the dancing Mrs. Klinghoffer, the dancing Palestinian Terrorist—and I didn't take part in that at all. I've never liked that device. If he wanted to take my moves and use them elsewhere in his staging, then of course he was welcome, but it was distinctly agreed that I wouldn't participate in the character doubling, and there was no acrimony about it whatsoever. There were a lot of beautiful, complicated choruses anyway, and the rest of the time the dancers huddled around, scared passengers on the cruise ship, the *Achille Lauro*. Ironically, I therefore got credit for one of the best-remembered pieces of movement, apparently the most moving part of the show, when Klinghoffer's body falls over the side of the boat in a wheelchair. Peter staged it with Klinghoffer's body double, one of my dancers, Keith, lowered on a wire from the flies onto a tarpaulin that somebody then slowly dragged offstage. This was attributed to me, but Keith worked on it with Peter separately.

Dancers learn music from hearing it over and over. They generally know it better than the chorus and orchestra. On tour in Vienna at the Messepalast (a big horse stable of a theater), the orchestra, under the baton of Kent Nagano, who took the music at breakneck speed, broke down in rehearsal. As the band ground to a halt, my dancers (to my delight, and Kent's dismay) kept dancing and singing, because they'd been doing both for months, and that's what they'd do to keep going if it were one of our company rehearsals. Kent was trying to get everyone to stop, but my dancers were still spinning and singing at the same time: fabulous.

Klinghoffer was a very pleasurable and satisfying experience, but controversial simply because it didn't say "Death to all Palestinians," which made it pro-Palestinian. The controversy was far deeper than *Nixon*, because the Klinghoffer family, the daughters, got tangled up in it, and protestors (including Rudy Giuliani) were still demonstrating against the opera in 2014 when it received its first performance at the Met.

The first productions arrived with a prologue consisting of a thirty-minute scene at the Klinghoffers' friends' house, where they're having coffee and talking about the news and their friends, the Klinghoffers. This presentation of everyday privileged New Jersey Jews was very much part of the controversy, for reasons of its possible anti-Semitism. I didn't much like it either, but for structural reasons. This half-hour slice of life might have made a good one-act opera, but it started the show quite wrong. I wondered whether I should mention it, and finally I felt moved to. It turned out everyone agreed, and it was cut. The opera now started with the chorus of exiled Palestinians as the downbeat of the piece, the chorus singing directly at the audience, a powerful beginning. It had been a mistake of balance (as though perhaps John was writing it in sequence); now the symmetry was much better. I thought the opera was very well argued and in no way anti-Semitic.

Alice and John had big fights. She and Peter had little fights, because he doesn't fight. There was a plan for further tripartite collaborations—to complete the trilogy of Adams's contemporary issue operas with *Doctor Atomic*—but by then Alice had become a poet priestess (or poetess priest, or poet priest), and it didn't happen. Peter asked me to choreograph *Doctor Atomic*, but I chose not to, partly because Alice was no longer involved. Peter put together his own libretto, a pastiche of primary material and John Donne—he often adds other text from diverse sources. I suggested Lucinda Childs, who did a great job.

John used to ask me why I didn't choreograph more of his music. My reply: "I choreographed *Nixon in* Fucking *China* and *The Death of* Fucking *Klinghoffer*! What more can I do?" He later, in 2008, wrote a piece for me for the San Francisco Ballet and the new music group Alarm Will Sound, called *Son of Chamber Symphony*, for which the name of my dance was *Joyride*. Again I was on the receiving end of John's handwritten manuscript and those unlistenable MIDI recordings. I was in the Bay Area working on it—frankly, he was a little bit behind (shocking though it might be that a composer would be tardy)—and I'd call him up at his house in the Berkeley Hills, because I'd caught up choreographically, and ask, "Hey, John, do you have any more music? How do you get me out of this?" and he'd say, "I'll finish it this afternoon and get it right to you." The ink was wet on the page when it arrived. It was a close call, the closest yet, and somehow it worked out.

I don't work with directors anymore, but working with Peter did the opposite of putting me off opera. It only made me think, "If I'm going to choreograph it, I have to direct it. Otherwise, it's not worth it."

But perhaps one day we'll do *The Pajama Game*.

———

WE WEREN'T RIDDEN OUT of Belgium on a rail. We served out our contract, and when we finally left, Mortier, who'd been in my corner throughout, sold us sets and costumes and performance rights (that he could have denied us) on the cheap. We had to ship the sets home, which cost the earth, but it was a real kindness on his part.

If someone offered me the same opportunity again, I'd do it—but in a different way. I'd be like a traveling music director. I'd run a company in another city, but I wouldn't take my whole company. I'd recruit new dancers and direct them while we continued our work at home. Ironically, that may have been what Mortier was originally suggesting. He was probably right, as he generally was. I was stubborn.

I've never set foot in Belgium since. I've never even been through the Brussels airport, Zaventem. And I won't.

Julie Worden, June Omura, and Charlton Boyd in
"Polka" from *Grand Duo*, 2000. *(Marc Royce)*

Ten

Grand Duo

MDG started in 1980 but didn't take until 1984, and five years later—merely five years—I had that fabulous gig in Brussels. Now we'd been gone three and a half years, from 1988 to 1991, and though we'd kept the home pump primed with a little touring, it was hard to tell quite what we were returning to. Happily, we found we'd been missed.

People had read the newspapers and magazines reporting how deliciously awful everything was, how flamboyant, controversial, and American I was, and we found ourselves in demand, a bigger and better attraction. It was as if people loved me now not just as a choreographer but as an *American*. The group, however, was no longer simply a tightly knit group of friends. We'd become an institution. The stakes were higher and life needed appropriate recalibration. It was in Brussels that I learned to be more guarded. I worked out that if I said something bad, people got pissed at me. Without question, I developed more of a filter. But it was also just growing up. You stop doing the things you don't like or the things that don't work. One thing was certain: without an administration to answer to anymore, I could now make up and put on dances whenever.

We'd always known we were coming back, but on our return, having experienced all *that*, we wondered why we didn't have our own building. The answer was self-evident: "Because you're a Modern Dance company, the pathetic runt of the arts (mostly for pretty good reason), and you don't deserve it, because you're naughty and you haven't worked hard enough."

We had no choice but to get back into the old routine of rented studios with dirty floors and no hot water, heat, or AC (uncomfortable year-round) in warehouse studios where the elevators stopped at five p.m. That was every single available option: sixty dollars an hour for a shithole, dispiriting for dancers and choreographers alike. Back then, artists lived in lofts—SoHo, then Tribeca, before the exodus to Brooklyn—where they had a studio and a cramped bedroom in the back, which is what everybody did. But pretty soon money moves in and the artists move out. It's the natural order of events. We didn't have even the luxury of a loft (though we did occasionally rent Lar's studio, which was nice).

Our rehearsal schedule might be two to four-thirty somewhere in Midtown; the next day, ten a.m. to one p.m. in Chelsea, then six p.m. to eight p.m. on the Upper East Side. It was endlessly stressful. Eliot Feld wouldn't let us use his studios at 890 Broadway, because he thought bare feet would ruin his floor, though, in fact, it would only have damaged our feet—the tacky rosin rips your soles open. We weren't technically on the street, but it felt like it, living out of a bag, dirty because most of the places had no showers. And let's put this in perspective: I was a *successful* choreographer.

That's why residencies were so attractive and envy inducing. Jacob's Pillow for a few weeks in the off-season was an unbelievable luxury, and there were magical and valuable residencies at Boston, Champaign-Urbana, and Berkeley. It's also why the job at the University of Washington had been worthwhile: an excellent rehearsal space.

So we had the idea of our own building, a permanent home. And plenty of reasons to do it.

It just took ten years.

ONE WAY IN WHICH we'd kept America's interest piqued during our absence had its origin in another of those late-night conversations that take place in murky Belgian bars.

If it wasn't Le Cercueil, the Coffin, it was A la Mort Subite, the Sudden Death—you sense a theme—a famous old drinking hole where the ceiling, once Hapsburg yellow, was now tobacco brown. I always felt at home there, partly because the mean, fabulous barmaids somehow managed to treat you like family and like shit simultaneously, and partly because I'd choreographed a dance, long before, to some Poulenc for Boston Ballet (my first ever ballet commission) and called it *Mort Subite*. We'd generally go in a big mob, get smashed, and eat spaghetti Bolognese, the commonly acknowledged and ubiquitous hangover prevention, and my regular late-night snack until I found mouse turds in mine.

On this particular night, however, Misha and I were alone. He wasn't quite finished dancing yet; he wanted his career to *not* be over. He couldn't really do ballet anymore, but he could *really* dance. It's a letdown for the audience to see a forty-year-old dancer in slacks even if he's still dancing beautifully—you remember him as a ballet dancer, sexy in white tights—so it would have to be something else. His suggestion was "What would you think about a company of older people who are tired of dancing with other companies?" (He was maybe forty-two at the time, ancient for dance; I was a mere thirty-four.) It was that simple. We'd start a company together that did my work in the States while we were still in Brussels. I'd dance too. Great! Various dancers in the autumn of their careers sprang to mind: first and foremost Misha, but also Rob Besserer, for example, and Kate Johnson from Paul Taylor's company, Misha's suggestion. He'd already floated the idea with Rob, who'd encouraged him to talk to me: I was the choreographer with the dances, Misha had always liked my work, and the two of us were close.

He already had the backing of Howard Gilman (his benefactor for some while), the Gilman Foundation, and more generally Gilman Industries—*everything Gilman*—which had always supported both ballet and endangered species (by which I mean actual endangered wildlife species, not just dance, though the appeal of dance might have been its always imminent extinction). Gilman himself had fingers in a lot of pies, but his main thing was philanthropy in the shape of hospital wings, cardiology, not to mention a breeding center for those animals, insemination for cheetahs. All the money came from paper, mills, and forests. MMDG also had his very generous funding, and, as it happens, the dressing room at my building now is named for Howard. His picture is right by the showers, which is where he would have wanted to be. He wouldn't have objected to seeing the male dancers naked for all eternity. He and Misha were very close—an older brother/platonic lover relationship—and he was a wonderful friend to both of us.

And so it came to pass that we became the White Oak Dance Project, for which Howard built a studio on his seven-thousand-acre plantation White Oak, in Florida, north of Jacksonville: astonishing, a movie set, a James Bond villain's lair. You drove long, straight miles through forests until the road opened up onto a vast plantation, a corporate retreat for his company with a massive zoo area with its own staff who only looked after the animals.

When we first arrived, the studio wasn't quite finished. They cut down trees and laid a beautiful floor for us. Voilà! We all had our own little quarters—mine were right by the courts, a one-room residence with a kitchenette (fridge fully stocked with vodka and my favorite cheese balls, handy in case I happened to find myself stoned) and three walls of glass, with white rhinos loitering freely in beautiful nature nearby, and out-of-control deer abounding. I'd feed the giraffes, which were fenced in but just walking around, eight of them with their long black tongues. We'd get high and tool around in golf carts, not to mention the two-lane bowling alley and the giant fishing boat. It was very heaven.

But despite the temptations, we worked hard, stayed six weeks, and built a repertory. The agreement had been that it would be solely my choreography—some existing pieces, some new—but that after our return, White Oak would commission other work. The dancers—some of the great veterans— included Misha and Kate; Rob, Peggy Baker, and Nancy Colahan (who had all danced with me in Lar's company); William Pizzuto and Denise Pons from Boston Ballet; and Jamie Bishton, who'd danced with Twyla—just these few people, to whom we added dancers from my own company for the first tour, with Peter Wing Healey as my assistant and Linda Dowdell our musical director.

Portrait of Mikhail Baryshnikov and me by Annie Leibovitz, New York City, 1988.

Everybody was an adult, in their late thirties or early forties, and still dancing very well, though dance may officially have considered them over the hill—a fascinating group. Annie Leibovitz, who came for a month, commemorated the company's genesis in a handsome book.

Motorcade (a bold, brash dance to Saint-Saëns, from which there is a famous photo of Misha on Rob's shoulders on a beach) served as the announcement of White Oak, on a bill of my dances at a glamorous benefit at the Wang Center in Boston, on October 24, 1990 (just three months before *The Hard Nut* premiere in Brussels). This piece was made specifically to showcase Mr. Baryshnikov, and the various talents of the specific White Oak dancers, all of whom I knew very well, and whose skills were in the direction of either ballet (for example, Billy Pizzuto) or Modern Dance (Kate). I'd choreographed the dances on both White Oak and my company, as I did with *A Lake* and *Mosaic and United*, and the pieces often ended up with a mix of performers from both. The rest of that first program featured *Ten Suggestions* (Misha doing what had originally been my solo), *Pas de Poisson* (danced by me, Misha, and Kate), and *Going Away Party*.

I've always thought *Mosaic and United* one of my best, a dance to music nobody knows, in this case the moving primitive modernism of Henry Cowell's String Quartets nos. 3 and 4, for five dancers (partly because there are fives throughout the music). Dancers love *Mosaic and United*, and its particular quality is partly a result of my working with dancers I wasn't used to working with. When I make up a ballet on a ballet company, it happens in the room—I don't have it all in my head before I go in—and *Mosaic and United* was therefore a happy combination of the White Oak personnel in front of me and my own personal inspiration from the music right then. There's a wonderful openness in Cowell's music that doesn't lead the listener to a particularly foreseeable place, and the dance, which is very varied between movements, does the same thing. To this day, *Mosaic and United* surprises even me.

On tour, the company traveled in an old private propeller plane of Gilman's, together with all our musicians and the entire crew. We'd land in an airfield, where a van waited, engine idling; they'd have called ahead and kept a restaurant open for us, say a Benihana. Imagine the luxury: Benihana! On a day off in Nashville, we went to the Grand Ole Opry and got VIP seats right on the stage to see Porter Waggoner, then had to sprint on the tarmac to catch the plane, shopping bags full of newly purchased cowboy boots. Traveling with Misha offered a glimpse of a previously unexperienced level of fame. At the curtain call, women held up their babies so they could bask in Baryshnikov's glorious glow. He'd whisper as we bowed, "I hope none of them are mine." Perhaps these were the same women who, having paid someone off to find out on which secret runway our old plane was landing, waited to greet Misha in that obscure part of the airport with balloons and flowers.

White Oak lasted two seasons while we were in Brussels, but on our return it had become a repertory company commissioning work from many choreographers, and it didn't make as much sense to compete with another company doing my work, though it had been a good way to maintain visibility while we were abroad, which was Nancy and Barry's gift. In fact, White Oak lasted twelve years or more, until it no longer made sense.

I've since had retreats with my company at the White Oak plantation—we'd go on a day off in Florida—but it's very much diminished now. Gone are all the endangered species, including Misha and me. I have no idea what they did with the animals. Maybe killed them, ate them, skinned them, and made coats of the pelts. Unlikely. Gilman was always a class act.

As for Misha, he credits me with extending his performing career, which is kind, and also true. I accept that responsibility. And then, after I extended it, he kept going some more! He's *still* going. In fact, he's outlasted everyone because he's tireless, satisfied only when he gets to perform. That's very unusual since most ex-dancers become massage therapists. He always had a wide variety of very interesting, creative friends, among whom he can continue to act, dance, and perform.

He still likes me to make up dances for him. "I'll do a little dance," he might mention, "if you have something." Not long ago, I needed him as the Old Man character in the ensemble for my dance *A Wooden Tree* to some of Ivor Cutler's unusually beautiful songs.

ONE OF THE FIRST MMDG dances on our return to the USA reacquainted me with the music and genius of Lou Harrison.

We'd first worked together in Seattle on *Strict Songs* with the men's chorus, when my foot was broken, but we'd since become close friends, and I'd been visiting him and Bill in Aptos, California, for years. Whenever I played the Bay Area, he'd come to the show, and he was even at my mother's eightieth birthday, because he happened to be in Seattle. They were the same age, and they sat and chatted. Old people have that way of getting along.

While living and working in New York in the 1950s, Lou had a breakdown and subsequently moved back west to Aptos, then just a wooded hilltop above Santa Cruz, into a little shack without water or electricity, which he then expanded into a house he built himself, planting a beautiful garden along a mythological theme—acacia, acanthus, and laurel. There was a big patch of forest on a steep incline down to the ocean. Back then the two-mile walk to the Pacific was desolate; now it's completely filled in, basically a suburb, houses abutting one another. He painted the whole place himself too, and everything was decorated with weird details, like a museum, and far from fancy. With music too, he started from scratch, with new ears, looking west rather than east, writing music based on the Pacific Rim rather than Europe. *Strict Songs* had been one of the first pieces in his new style.

You could tell he'd been in that house for years. There were multiple carpets in the Middle Eastern way, a carpet and then a smaller carpet on top; you were ankle deep in beautiful kilims. The bathroom was called the Tchaikovsky Room, featuring a life-sized painting of the composer naked on the back of the door.

Lou was still teaching at Mills College and gave all the classes at his house, so the place was like a music shop, with instruments lying around, a gamelan room (of course), a harp (because Lou would become proficient enough on any instrument to be able to write for it), and a small living area, including a kitchen with a pot of soup perpetually simmering on the stove: he and Bill just kept adding to and eating from it for weeks. He even had Charles Ives's piano up there. Lou had more or less made Ives known, edited his music and championed him, though Ives subsequently didn't talk to him for years after finding out Lou was queer.

We'd pile into Lou's pickup and he'd drive us down the hill to this Mexican cafeteria, where he'd set the table, serve the food, and pay for everyone (maybe ten dollars). His boyfriend Bill was a little older and shorter than Lou, with a Rasputin beard, and he'd stand between Guillermo and me, posing for a photo, and grab our asses. You'd be talking to Lou (who naturally had a crush on Guillermo), and Bill would dart across the room naked behind him for the amusement of the guests. He had long been a guide for the Sierra Club, disappearing into the woods for a month at a time, and he carried with him the aroma of the forest. He died chopping wood on the path down to the ocean, a few years before Lou. Toward the end of his life, Lou stopped wearing shoes because his feet hurt, so he just wore galoshes with no shoes inside.

THE NEXT DANCE TO LOU'S MUSIC after *Strict Songs*, on our return from Belgium, was "Polka." I'd heard Lou's *Grand Duo for Violin and Piano*, and instantly decided to choreograph the fifth movement. The dance is four or five minutes, and can be done by any *even* number of people. Don't get me wrong. It wouldn't really be interesting with as few as two or as many as ten thousand. There's a sweet spot: about fourteen.

I told Lou that I was choreographing "Polka." He laughed and said, "Oh, that little *rumba!*" It's very hard to play, featuring among other complications an octave banger—a piece of wood, like the damper for the strings of a piano, padded and felted—which enables you to play a full octave cluster of notes on the black or white keys. Bill manufactured bangers; in fact he *invented* them. We used to order them directly from him, and he'd craft them by hand. (It turns out this was a courtesy. Now that Bill's dead, Johan makes them in about five minutes.)

"Polka" turned into something of a signature for us, and became the finale on every program we did for at least six months, a party piece resembling a five-minute scramble. (After some years' experience, we can actually manage polka tempo.) The costumes were a part of it. I'd seen a nightgown in the window of a Montreal department store, maybe Hudson's Bay, a woman's canary-yellow silk slip, and I bought it for a lot of money (maybe one hundred Canadian dollars, a foolish extravagance). These, more or less, were the costumes, the men's belted, the women's beltless. I don't like thongs on women (nor do they—thongs make dancing extremely uncomfortable), so the women wore briefs under their dresses while the men wore dance belts, ballet's version of an athletic supporter that makes the ass very distinct, even as the front package is "Ken dolled," reading only as a mound rather than a penis.

Buttocks were therefore glimpsed in the performance, and for some reason this was scandalous, but it was a scandal only because the asses were male. If it had been women's asses, no one would have said a thing.

We'd been offered a desirable off-season residency at Jacob's Pillow, early fall, two weeks in unwinterized cabins in the Berkshires. And that's where I retro-constructed "Polka," picking out the movement themes and developing them backward, with the idea that it would now be the last movement of the entirety of Lou's *Grand Duo*, from which it was excerpted: why not do the whole thing? I had the costume designer, Susan Ruddie, do the same. We retrofitted them from the last dance backward, adding longer pants and shirts to the earlier movements, so the dancers started off more or less fully clothed and those clothes disappeared as the dance went on, until they're scantily clad by "Polka." But I didn't have that in mind at all when I made up "Polka." *Grand Duo* was art from the end first, extrapolated backward.

People talk about *Grand Duo*'s tribalism, its commune-ism, its primitivity. What they want to say is its *Rite of Spring*ishness, whatever people think that means. It's all true; I'd just never describe my work that way. "Polka" is how I imagine cavemen used to dance for fun around the fire.

In fact, I didn't set Lou's entire score, only 80 percent. There's another movement, his favorite, a long, contemplative largo that would have ruined a dance that was already nearly half an hour without it. So I cut that out, which he didn't like, but allowed. There was to be payback for this.

AN INVITATION TO the Adelaide Festival of 1994 exposed me to an overwhelming amount of Eastern culture. My mind was thrown open to things I simply hadn't seen before, while the trip also affirmed some things I already knew but my dancers didn't, so it was valuable for everybody. It was also a breakthrough for my own work.

We were there three weeks, the only Western act aside from William Forsythe's great Frankfurt Ballet. Everything else was Asian or Australian, including aboriginal. Adelaide was Presbyterian and one might even say a little uptight, white glove, xenophobic, and a bit Belgian. The newspapers rejected this beautiful festival; one reviewer said it had too much "soy sauce." The genius behind it all, Christopher Hunt—the very same man who'd introduced me to Peter Sellars—invited us to do three different bills over thirteen performances in two different theaters: *Dido*, *L'Allegro*, and a repertory show featuring the newer *Grand Duo*, *Mosaic and United*, *A Spell*, and *Bedtime*.

There were all kinds of events—outside, inside—of which I went to two or three a day, whenever we weren't performing. I nearly lost my mind at my first Javanese *wayang kulit* puppet show all-nighter, dusk till dawn, those leather puppets rear-projected on a screen to the soundtrack of a big gamelan, all live. The narratives were all from the *Ramayana*, but the shows cited everything from local politics, sex, and current events right up to what had happened that day at the festival. There was an unbearably sublime Bunraku puppet show from Osaka, and some Vietnamese water puppets, for which the action happened on the surface, and the puppeteers operated the puppets from underwater. Sensational!

Christopher had had the brilliant idea of a performers-only lounge, so the festival participants had a place to go at night to congregate over drinks and food, and this made for a terrific sense of community among the performers. That's where we all became friends: drummers, dancing Cook Islanders, percussionists and singers from Sumatra, the Papuan theater company doing a show about being in a doctor's waiting room with a broken leg and VD. Everybody was selling crafts, sculptures, and puppets, wooden carvings from Papua New Guinea, like a flea market. It was twenty-four-hours-a-day fun, as though there was no language barrier. We put on talent shows in the theater, just for our fellow performers, sending up each other's work.

My big number was "Go Tell Aunt Rhody (the Old Grey Goose Is Dead)," which I played on water glasses with a spoon, with accompaniment from Linda Dowdell (who was my first ever music director) on the piano; everyone was flirting and who doesn't want that?

ANOTHER GREAT NEW COLLABORATOR of this period, and ever since—the most collaborative of all the collaborators—was Yo-Yo Erneste Ma (that's his middle name, born in France to Chinese parents). He was already a big star when I met him, though the exact time or day or season of that first meeting is lost to memory. He courted me professionally, suggesting the project that turned into the filmed dance *Falling Down Stairs*, our first collaboration, in 1995.

Completely out of the blue, he sent me a book titled *Baroque Dance Forms*, a rather awkward volume for a choreographer to receive, a little like me sending him *How to Play the Cello* by Mark Morris. The accompanying letter explained that he was involved in a project with the six cello suites of Bach, unaccompanied études, great pieces of music never intended to be performed for an audience, that had been introduced into the repertory by Pau Casals, the great Catalonian cellist. Yo-Yo, being Yo-Yo, wanted there to be a different collaborator for each suite: the ice skaters Torvill and Dean, the great kabuki actor Bandō Tamasaburō, the director Atom Egoyan, the dead architectural artist Piranesi, me, and . . . you name it. Yo-Yo was in cahoots with a Canadian film and television production company. Was I interested?

In the film of this collaboration, I wasn't lying when I told him that I hadn't initially wanted to do it, that I worried about committing a crime against the music. It seemed too obvious, a little like choreographing "Happy Birthday." But he explained the music's fundamental appeal to cellists. In short, he persuaded me.

The third suite in C major was the one I knew best (from Page in

Seattle), so I started on that. Yo-Yo mistakenly says that I had a dream about falling down stairs. This is how he remembers it, but in fact it was Ruth Davidson's dream. She dreamed that she fell downstairs at my mother's house, she took a horrible spill, and blood trickled from the side of her mouth, and I'd thought of it as the perfect visual for Bach's descending scale from C down to the C below it, and then an arpeggio to the C below that.

That was the theme. Yo-Yo began FedExing me cassette recordings of his performance the previous night on tour. I'd choreograph to these recordings in rehearsal studios all over town, and then we'd get together, for a couple of days every few months, because he wanted to be affected by the dancers around him as he played. Because of this, what I was doing started to subtly change too, and as I coached him, he played differently, which subsequently affected my choreography. It was genuinely collaborative.

With Yo-Yo Ma, during filming of *Falling Down Stairs*, circa 1994.
(Cylla von Tiedemann)

We filmed it at Jacob's Pillow. It was the first part of the series of six, and the camera's view was 360 degrees (there's no proscenium), so everything—monitors, cameras, and dancers—had to be fully choreographed. Not easy. Isaac Mizrahi designed the costumes beautifully, one of the first things he did for me. Everybody wore a different tone of silk velvet, loosely based on guild costumes from the Middle Ages, almost like costumes for *Die Meistersinger.*

The movie is good—and won an Emmy—despite committing the cardinal sin of making it seem like the dancing was Yo-Yo's vision, a bizarre faux hologram of his imagination as he played: "Here's the dance I see in my head!" The rosin you see flying off the cello strings is talcum powder, because he was finger-synching to a recording of himself. It was *stunt* rosin.

We had prerecorded the music in a quiet church with ideal acoustics in Lee, Massachusetts, near Jacob's Pillow. For this, Guillermo and I sat directly in front of Yo-Yo, miming the dance so he knew the right tempi and phrasing. It was an important recording, in that it would be commercially released (rather than one we'd simply use as playback for the film), so the vestry was teeming with Sony sound technicians surrounded by equipment. Barry, everybody's handler (a job he did very well for years), was there too and, crucially to the story, so was Johan, my technical director.

We'd just started the rehearsal when the cello—a Guarneri or a Stradivarius worth a billion dollars and a thousand years old—started making an awful buzzing sound. It couldn't possibly be played, let alone recorded. The nearest capable luthier was three hours away in Boston; it would have meant a helicopter, three days of blocking and gluing, and no recording at all. A disaster.

Johan picked the cello up, shook it, put his ear to it, tapped it, and diagnosed a crack at some precise point on the soundboard. He tore off a piece of duct tape and patched this priceless instrument, the varnish of which was probably the reason for its perfect sound. This silenced the buzz, Yo-Yo recorded, we mimed the dance, it sounded beautiful, and the duct tape stayed on there for years.

WE REARRANGED *Falling Down Stairs* for the stage—more straightforward than I'd imagined it would be, given the complexity of the TV version; we simply faced it to the front and Yo-Yo played in the downstage right corner—and premiered it in 1997, the same year as my not-quite-next collaboration with Lou, *Rhymes with Silver*, which he wrote for me. This was partly payback for my having cut that lengthy largo from *Grand Duo*. (There was also *Pacific* for the San Francisco Ballet in between, but we'll come back to that.)

On one of my trips to Aptos, Lou eyed me suspiciously and asked, "What do you want? You look like you *want* something."

He was right. I told him I wanted him to write a piece of music for me. I only later learned that he was done with the music industry, that he was only writing music for himself and his friends.

There had been two bad situations. The first bad situation was Keith Jarrett, the jazz pianist. Lou had heard Jarrett perform, improvising presumably, and told Keith that he should write a concerto for himself. Keith instead asked Lou to write one for him. One can only imagine the long-distance communication and labor involved in this, because Lou had a specific tuning in mind for the concerto, of course, and Keith was far away, in Germany or New Jersey, wherever. They both retuned their pianos, and Lou would send what he was writing to Keith to find out whether it was playable.

The result was a great piano concerto, which Jarrett premiered and then toured to acclaim—something of a comeback for Lou—but when Lou wrote to Jarrett's manager, asking if he'd be getting a check, the manager replied, according to Lou's biography, "There was no contract, was there?" In other words, the honor of composing for Jarrett should be payment enough. And that was that. Lou had been shafted—they didn't compensate him appropriately—and he was furious. He said it felt like a castration. Keith Jarrett: famously an asshole, and I suppose this is another instance.

Another debacle was the attempted Lincoln Center staging of Lou's opera *Young Caesar*, originally written as a puppet opera just as Haydn and Mozart had written for puppets, and an early example of Lou's new Eastern style. It's a presentation of the gay Young Caesar, his boyfriend, and fellow soldiers—Peking opera in style—and I was to stage it. I courteously mentioned that there wasn't quite enough music, and asked, "Could I get another couple of numbers?" He wrote three more arias at my request.

As things progressed, however, I decided to withdraw, very carefully, from the project. I didn't think it could be done well enough, and Lincoln Center wasn't much help. The new arias were great, but I wasn't sold on Robert Gordon's libretto, and I wanted to do more editing than I tactfully felt able to. In order to offend no one, particularly Lou, I blamed my departure on my schedule. No problem. My replacement was Bill T. Jones, a renowned choreographer, because that's how things go, but the problems with the libretto remained, so the libretto was revised without Lou's or Robert's permission, and presented to Lou as a fait accompli. I can only imagine his reaction. The project was dropped. Luckily, I was off the hook by then.

There's an excellent 2011 documentary, *Lou Harrison: A World of Music*, that contains a scene where Nigel Redden, who ran the Lincoln Center Festival, is at a meeting about *Young Caesar* with Dennis Russell Davies, the conductor, in which they're talking about my participation at the dawn of the project:

"Oh, we got Mark Morris! He's in!"

At that very moment, a framed picture crashes to the floor and the glass breaks.

Cut.

AS A RESULT of these and other disappointments, Lou, unbeknownst to me, had in effect stopped composing. I, in my innocence, was asking him to write again.

He started in immediately. "How long is it?"

I said, "I don't know; you haven't written it yet. I'm just asking if you'd consider it. However long you want, fifteen minutes, forty-five . . ."

"What's the orchestration?"

"Whatever you want. A boys' choir and five harps if you like. I'd like a piano part for Linda Dowdell and a cello part for Yo-Yo. Other than that . . ."

"Is there text? Is it sung?"

"It's up to you."

"How about cor anglais?"

"Great idea."

"Is it to go on tour?"

"Ideally, yes."

"So chamber music might be better. Do you want to make up the dance and I'll write the music to it? That's what I'm used to doing."

"Well, I guess I could . . . but I've never worked that way."

"Oh, you want the music first and then you make up the dance to it."

"Yes. If you want that."

After a long pause he said, "I'll write a piece of music for you. But never ask me about it again."

And that was it. We had lunch. I was dismissed.

As for when it would be ready, or what it was going to be: nothing.

TWO WEEKS LATER I received a big manila envelope marked "MM1," full of music. It was a kit, a compositional technique invented by Henry Cowell, used especially during the years he was imprisoned (for homo-sexuality, in San Quentin in 1936—Ives disavowed him, the composer Percy Grainger defended him), when he wrote parts for whoever could play an instrument, the point being that the parts could be played in any combination with any number of players.

This first music Lou sent me (and I had no idea how much more he'd be sending or what form it might take—for all I knew, this was all of it) was that kind of kit, including a piano part and a percussion part. The accompanying note gave some instructions:

Each line can be repeated any number of times or omitted.

The lines can be played in any sequence.

It can be played in any octave.

The tempo is basically fixed.

When you finish, hit the home key of G. That's the end.

Those were the Cageian parameters. The piece of music could ei-ther go on perpetually or not exist at all. My immediate thought was that this was punishment for my editing *Grand Duo*, that he was basi-cally dropping it in my lap. "Here's some music: you piece it together. Best wishes."

But that was just MM1!

Then I got MM2, MM3, and so on. These followed every week or so, some through-composed, some in kit form. There was a very difficult part for solo cello, some of which he'd already sent to Yo-Yo to ascertain its playability with an accompanying note:

> *I am sending off to you a piece which I have composed as a part of my commission from Mark Morris for a ballet. . . . In order to continue I would be very grateful if you would kindly look over the rhapsody to let me know how it fits. Please tell me "no no"s and "yes yes"es if you find them. You would do a great kindness to an old composer.*

Yo-Yo replied:

> *Yes, yes, I like it very much. I find it not only very expressive but eminently playable. . . . I am sure that the idea of a Kit will be a lot of fun to work with. You and I know that Mark will definitely have an opinion on that.*

No kidding.

THE COMPOSITION KEPT ARRIVING. There were some pieces he'd reworked from older music of his, a gigue from the 1940s written for clavichord rearranged for strings and percussion; and wonderful little dances including a Turkish-styled piece in eleven beat phrases. One of the pieces was a strange waltz for strings and piano. By the time of its arrival, I had the courage to send it back with the remark that it seemed incomplete, as though it didn't finish itself. I heard nothing; then a week later I got the slightly rewritten piece. Surprisingly, it wasn't longer but shorter by seven bars and it *was* complete—he'd heard it and reduced it to perfection. Then he decided to add a percussion part to

With Lou Harrison and Yo-Yo Ma backstage,
Berkeley, California, 1997. *(June Omura)*

Yo-Yo's cello kit, so he sent another. "Play it or not" was the idea, "repeat it or not."

Lou's letters were always typed in a beautiful, ornate medieval font
of his own design, often with the sign-off line "Have good health and a
rising bank account!" After I'd asked him (against his specific instructions) how everything was going, he wrote (on December 1, 1996):

> *I'm much working on music for you although I've no idea what*
> *may eventuate as to scenario. When we briefly met in Berkeley you*
> *recommended Slavitt's new* Metamorphoses, *which I've been reading*
> *with pleasure. Had some part of the work interested you as dance, and*
> *that you would like me to consider? If so, please tell me. . . . Please dear*
> *wonderful one, if you have any dance-desire that you might want me to*
> *try for, please let me know by letter, by fax, or by phone. Otherwise I'll*
> *just keep composing, composing, in the hope of pleasing you!!*

My reply:

> *I'm so happy and a little daunted to be working on this new piece*
> *of y/ours. It is beautiful & searing & varied & hard as hell. I've felt*
> *like I wanted more of the waltz. . . . I've pretty much set the Allegro kit*
> *(with 18 systems), the Gigue/Musette (which I'll slow down a little),*
> *the waltz (in its current form), the foxtrot—somewhat (which speeding*
> *up makes more of a rag—I'm treating it as a sort of Turkey Trot) &*
> *The Prince Kantemir's number (which looks 1,000 years old).*

And then that was it: for five players—violin, viola, cello, piano, and percussion. No cor anglais. No boys' choir. I even considered the possibility of two different dances that could be done either interleaved or separately, one for the solo cello section, and another for the other four instruments.

Linda and I, along with a percussionist, went through each of the pieces and played each kit at every octave or in multiple octaves. All the lines were the same rhythmic sequence, of course, in that they matched, so they could fit with any other part, and therefore we recorded all the parts on cassettes and from these I assembled the performance edition that I choreographed.

As a tribute to Lou, I called it *Rhymes with Silver* because his middle name, his mother's maiden name, was Silver (and because nothing rhymes with "silver"). It was the last big piece he wrote. It could have been almost any length, but the version I chose to choreograph was about forty-five minutes long, a big dance.

I commissioned the set from the great British painter Howard Hodgkin. It was our first collaboration. When I'd first met Howard, we hit it off immediately, though he was a rather stereotypical—to an American—cranky, harrumphing Englishman, whose look seemed designed to put people off. He wasn't dirty or scary, precisely, but he was rumpled, as though he'd fallen asleep on a park bench. This may have been partly self-protection. Later he was in a wheelchair, a bit of a sitting duck, and he neither wanted to make new friends nor have to explain his work to anyone. He seemed ancient at the time (fifteen years younger than Lou), but he was only the age I am now—funny how that happens!—and he'd just been to South India to receive Ayurvedic treatment for his arthritis, which is why I eventually started going. He became a darling, intimate friend. *Rhymes with Silver* brought his work together with Lou's, and with both of those older masters my attitude was the same: I love your work; do your work.

When he'd first allowed me access to his London studio, Howard might say, "Take a look at my new painting." He'd turn his back, and I'd go in, look at it for fifteen minutes, and then we'd go out to lunch. I wouldn't say anything except, "Howard, thank you for letting me look at your painting." I might go as far as "I love that red one." That would be it. Done. We'd talk about music. Neither of us needed an art analysis session about why I did or didn't like it.

Lou was much the same. That waltz didn't work, so I sent it back and he revised it, made it shorter. When someone like that says, "If you don't want this, send it back and I'll do something else," they mean it. When John Adams asked me of a piece of his music for me, "Is this danceable?" I told him, "Of course not: why would I be interested in music that was danceable?" Howard's attitude was "Take it or leave it. And if you don't like it, I'll throw it out and do something else."

I liken this to the friends I've made in India. They're my friends because I am not seeking enlightenment. I'm not going to India to bow at the feet of the great sages (and the yoga racket), thinking that every-thing an Indian says is a profound utterance of eternal importance. And I didn't want enlightenment from Howard or Lou either.

I wanted what they did.

In the case of *Rhymes with Silver*, the process was lovely. I simply told Howard, "Listen to this music; design a set for me, please." What Howard gave me—wavy lines in watermelon tones of green and red—was like one of his drawings or earlier paintings; some didn't like it because it wasn't the signature Hodgkin brushstroke, but I thought it was quite perfect.

That same year, I was asked to choreograph a piece for *Sesame Street*'s twentieth anniversary, for which I again picked Lou's music, along with a piece by Cowell himself. I was asked for only one minute's worth of choreography, so the pieces were very short: one an early pre–breakdown Lou piano piece, *Waltz in C*, and Henry Cowell's *Anger Dance*, written when he'd broken his leg. I could relate.

Cowell's doctor had told him that he'd have to have the leg amputated, and when he discovered this was a misdiagnosis (and I could relate to that too), Cowell was so furious—so relieved—that he played a phrase on the piano over and over, louder and louder, until he was worn out, which is how the piece is meant to be played, over and over until the pianist can't take it anymore because he's so angry and exhausted. Children should be allowed to feel anger too: that was my *Sesame Street*–appropriate idea, presented as a fight between me and some feathered puppets (each of which had two operators wearing black behind them, one moving the feet, the other the torso) that I choreographed on all of us.

I'D WANTED TO GO BACK to India ever since that magical time when Erin and I were falling in love. But I never had the money, and when I had the money, I didn't have the time. Eventually, Nancy applied for a large grant, of the research and development variety, that allowed Guillermo and me to go there for a month or more. All I had to do to justify this generosity was claim that it had somehow influenced a dance.

It was 1996, and I had some long-distance introductions. Sali Ann Kriegsman, the wonderful woman who was then running Jacob's Pillow told me about Nrityagram, both a dance ensemble and a community set up in the form of a village devoted to nothing but dance by Protima Gauri Bedi in 1990. I also wanted to seek out a famous dancer, Lakshmi Knight, daughter of the great bharatanatyam (South Indian classical) dancer T. Balasaraswati (though we didn't get along). Guy Trebay, a writer for the *New York Times*, had a photographer friend, Dayanita Singh, and she in turn recommended that I meet Lakshmi Viswanathan, a great dancer and scholar, both of whom are close friends to this day. That's the wonderful thing about my Indian friends. They never go away. They show up and there they are, forever.

We met up with Dayanita in Delhi, then went to Chennai (Madras) to meet the two Lakshmis, Knight and Viswanathan. We also met the influential music and dance critic S. Kalidas. He took us to our first house concert, which consisted of three musicians, a singer, a drummer, and someone on the veena (a plucked string instrument), playing for an inordinately long time, perhaps two or three hours (all Indian concerts are epic by Western standards), followed by a sumptuous buffet in the living room—as far from a potluck as you can possibly imagine—where not one grain of rice goes uneaten, like a three-day wedding where the host has to feed everyone who shows up, endlessly.

Guillermo and I also went to a public concert in a big ugly cement hall, a thousand degrees under a hundred ceiling fans. The moment the music began—heavily amplified as usual—the audience turned to each other, immediately acknowledging which mode the music was in, and then started to keep a strict rhythm, strong beats and weak beats, by clapping softly. Generally, at the climax, every single member of the audience arrives at the same resolution at the same moment as the musicians. If you don't know the music, it's quite amazing. But in this case, in the middle of the performance, the power went out: everything. The fans stopped so abruptly that there was immediately a cloud of mosquitoes, and though the deafening music suddenly disappeared— you could hardly hear it—everyone kept the beat with their clapping. The power finally came back on, you could hear the music again, but the show had never stopped.

On another trip, Kalidas joined a group of my friends at a fancy dinner. I overheard my painter friend David Deutsch, my best friend Shawn's husband, and Kalidas discussing classical music.

"It's like Monteverdi . . . ," David said.

"Monteverdi?" Kalidas was a little nonplussed. "Oh, you mean *Western* classical music."

They'd both been talking about "classical" music, but different classical musics with completely different rules. The truth is Western classical music simply isn't that interesting to many Indians. They might hear the opening chords of Beethoven's Fifth, and think, "When's the music going to start?" It's the reverse with Western chauvinists hearing Indian music for the first time; they have no idea what's happening.

OUR NEXT STOP WAS NRITYAGRAM, the dance community near Bangalore, to meet its founder, Protima. We immediately hit it off. Though she'd never set foot in the United States, I felt sure I'd met her at some SoHo party ten years previously, and she felt she knew me too. It was karmic. Protima was an unusual Indian woman, an outgoing adventuress who'd enjoyed London's swinging sixties and returned to her own country a cosmopolitan feminist. She wore her hair short— rare—and looked like a model (which she'd been), spoke elegant English, and had a glamorous and notorious history, including having been India's first streaker at some Mumbai beach party, not to mention her marriage to the famous actor Kabir Bedi (more universally known as the villain in *Octopussy*). She was, as far as India was concerned, unusually feminist, unusually Western, and, if you like, a loudmouth; I loved her instantly.

At the age of twenty-six, having seen a life-changing Odissi dance recital, Protima offered herself as a disciple of the guru Kelucharan Mohapatra. She showed up on his doorstep, knowing hardly anything about dancing, and devoted herself to his instruction. Despite not really getting going until she was thirty—and traditionally if you don't start by the age of nine, you'll never become a dancer, which is more or less true anywhere in the world—she became as great a dancer as she had been a celebrity. She stayed with the guru for years and founded this *gurukul*, a residential school or commune, on farmland in Nowheresville that she'd finagled through her Bollywood connections.

I was there with her for only a few days. We went for a walk to the local village, Hessaraghatta, she in a long skirt rather than a sari. The farmers, dressed in loincloths with their oxen, prostrated themselves before her, lying down to touch her feet. "Please don't," she'd say as she blessed them.

We sat together in the ruins of a tiny old temple, and she quizzed me on the rudiments of how a dance company tours, how one raises money. She was so worldly seeming and yet completely naive. It turned out she didn't know anything except the one thing she did know. She was as wonderful as she sounds.

Two years later, when I was about to go back to India, partly to spend time with Protima, a writer, Dr. Sunil Kothari, interviewing me for the *Hindu* newspaper, showed up with a copy of that day's *New York Times* open to Protima's obituary. She had died dramatically in a mudslide in the Himalayas on a pilgrimage to a particular sacred site to pay tribute to her son, Siddharth Bedi, who had committed suicide a year or two previously. I only had that one chance to meet her. The Nrityagram dancers refer to her as Gaudiji, an honorific. She's the guiding spirit behind everything they do.

Surupa Sen, the great dancer and choreographer, runs Nrityagram now. There wasn't a resident choreographer before her. Their shows are always great. The music is live, a compilation of various pieces, some of it especially composed, and the lineup generally comprises a singer who plays harmonium, a drummer playing a two-headed drum, a flautist, a violinist, and someone who plays bells or cymbals. The dances vary in personnel from solos to five or six women, but Nrityagram is best known for the duets between Surupa and Bijayini Satpathy.

For the shows, the dancers iron their own saris, cut fresh flowers for garlands, and put on gorgeous makeup. Before the dance, they place an oil lamp in front of the figure of the god Jagannatha that stands like a scarecrow in the corner, and then the dancers thank in turn the floor, the musicians, and the gods. They thank *everything*. Even before their own rehearsals, which take place undercover but basically in open air, in ninety-nine-degree heat, they thank me, they thank my feet, and they thank the floor; then they touch each instrument, thanking the wood that made the flute. It's so beautiful. The shows are always narrative, because there's no other kind of dance, and the stories are generally mythological (if you consider the Mahabharata mythological—some people take it literarily, like the Bible). I brought the company to New York for Sounds of India, a mini-festival within the White Light Festival at Lincoln Center in 2016. They were six dancers (all female) in total and six musicians (all male) stage right. (Nrityagram, the place, is like that too. The gardeners and security guards may be male, but that's it.)

A while ago, they performed at the Joyce in Manhattan. I found their performance so moving that when I went backstage afterward, I wanted to touch Surupa's feet in reverence, as you might give someone a garland. When I arrive at Nrityagram, they line up to greet me that way, a little embarrassing to a westerner but a great compliment: the dancers first, then their manager, Lynne Fernandez, who embraces me, and then Surupa and Bijayini (the greatest dancers of all time, by the way—and if I happen to have said that about more than one person in this book, it's all true). They take their shoes off, kneel, touch my feet, and give *pranam*. Then I'll invite them to stand up, embrace them, and thank them. And that's it. Once each trip each way—hello and goodbye. So I thought I'd repay the honor.

Surupa is normally rather composed, but she completely freaked out. "No! You can't! You can't do that! Please don't!" It almost brought her to tears. I had only wanted to say, "I loved that performance so much," but the gesture was in total violation of a position I didn't realize I held.

Sometime later, we did a talk together at which we took questions. I brought this awkwardness up, and she explained, "Well, you are our guru." I was, whether I wanted to be or not, because of my age and my experience, and because I'd been a peer of Protima's. In Surupa's eyes, it belittled me to touch her feet, and it was therefore embarrassing in front of other Indians. Then of course she was also upset that she might have hurt *my* feelings. She wasn't offended, just gobsmacked. I could lay a garland upon her, but I couldn't touch her feet.

INDIA-WISE, I hit pay dirt (lifelong friends and immediate major discoveries) on my first real visit. A few visits later, I went again for five weeks, to the Chennai music festival and to Kerala for Ayurvedic treatment.

There I had one of the most surprising experiences of my life. I had a full sexual awakening at fifty. I didn't even know that was possible, but you don't know what it's like to ride a bike unless you *can* ride a bike, and sexually speaking, I was born again. It had something to do with the Ayurvedic treatments.

During a massage in the second week of these two-massage days, when I was worn down and accustomed to the schedule, I had a spontaneous ejaculation. The massages were in no way "feel-good" erotic (or likely to have a happy ending)—there was no specific genital contact—but they were intense. I was outside, covered in hot oil, wearing a little loincloth, which was removed when I was facedown. Sometimes two men would be working on me, chatting away in Malayalam, and if my dick got in the way, they'd just slap it away—it was of no importance, causing no offense. But the orgasm had nothing to do with sex. There was friction, of course—there's no other kind of massage—but I suddenly had this full-body tantric orgasm experience within three seconds, from nothing to full erection, to ejaculation, and then de-erection. As you can imagine, I was shocked, and I apologized, then I went back to my room and wept.

The Ayurvedic doctor, to whom I later mentioned my embarrassment, said, "Please don't worry, it happens all the time. It's just like a sneeze."

THE INCREDIBLE ANNUAL winter music festival in Chennai has been going on for about seventy-five years, runs for about six weeks, and takes place in the Tamil month of Mārkazhi (mid-December to mid-January). It's much like the Edinburgh Festival or Adelaide but even more intense—hundreds of concerts all the time in hundreds of venues, from stars who play thousand-seat halls to duets of teenagers playing saxes for their families. I would sometimes squeeze in three shows a day.

Chennai itself is a city of perhaps five million people, a somewhat conservative Boston-like city, the headquarters of the Classical Music Police. The festival occasionally presents a Western concert or a jazz-fusion concert, some Hindustani (North Indian) music, or guest artists from Singapore, but the focus is almost exclusively on Carnatic (South Indian) music, including ragas for that particular time of day— the eight a.m. or eleven p.m. raga—or music devoted to that particular day's deity or the phase of the moon. The music is generally two hundred or three hundred years old (for example, that of Sri Tyagaraja, the saint who wrote the music I choreographed for *O Rangasayee*, sung by M. S. Subbalakshmi) and incredibly sophisticated. To think it's from the same time as Beethoven!

The concerts themselves are fabulous and free (though you wouldn't go if you didn't belong). The seats toward the front look empty from behind, but only because they're occupied by tiny old women with iron-colored plaits in their hair, wearing saris, cashmere cardigans, and running shoes. And they're all experts on the music, every single one. The VIPs are ushered right to the front row, no matter what (it's acceptable to walk in in the middle, and in fact it's considered a little chic to arrive late and leave early), and the musicians greet you even while they're playing. Politicians and other celebrities walk across the front row even in the middle of the show, shaking hands as they go, giving out their business cards. It's shocking, perhaps even a little vulgar, but much less precious than the Western equivalent. When the drum solos begin (toward the end of every concert), the older men (and their enlarged prostates) all leave to pee, then bring the car around, ready for their getaway. In 2018, I had the honor of being the Chief Guest—an actual title—to open the dance festival portion at the Music Academy, the headquarters, and to present an award to my friend Lakshmi Viswanathan.

There is no better music in the world. It's the most rocking, syncopated, thrillingly exquisite music, more interesting (in my opinion) than ravishing Hindustani music, which is Persian influenced, where Carnatic music is not. I've been going to the festival every two years for twenty years now. I love it, though it's a pain in the ass to get there. I always swear I'll never go again, and then I go right back.

On a trip in 2004, I found out on my arrival in Chennai that the beloved M. S. Subbalakshmi had died: a national treasure had "dropped her body." On the front page of every newspaper in the country were photos of her corpse lying on a pallet, heaped with marigolds, prepared for cremation, surrounded by music pandits and government notables. Appropriate adoration, respect, love, and honor for a revered, cherished artist.

We can still hear her voice, and her spirit, in the inheritors of her art, the profound Carnatic vocal artistes of today.

With Paul Simon in rehearsal for *The Capeman*, Westbeth, New York, 1997.
*(Sara Krulwich/*The New York Times*/Redux)*

Eleven

The Capeman

We were everywhere. I was traveling all over the world, all at once, as an individual and with the company.

Some shows went perfectly; some didn't. But then not many people have risked collaborations with Christopher Hogwood and Paul Simon within eighteen months of each other. When you consider that those two productions bookended the stage version of *Falling Down Stairs*, the production of *Rhymes with Silver*, *Sesame Street*, and the direction of a Rameau opera at the Royal Opera House in London, you'll understand the insanity of my schedule.

It's hard even to remember the order of events from *Orfeo*, which premiered in April 1996, to *The Capeman*, which premiered in January 1998.

MY NEXT OPERA brought me back to Orpheus, *Orphée*, or in this case *Orfeo*, the original Vienna version (which lacks a couple of the bring-the-house-down arias, written for the Paris Opera production twelve years later) on tour with the Handel and Haydn Society of Boston.

I was very eager to work with Christopher Hogwood, its musical director, the earliest of the early music geniuses and a great musical mind. Barry, a baseball queen, was friends with the baseball fan who worked at Handel and Haydn, and the production was made specifically for our two companies to tour together. It didn't work out as well as we'd hoped.

In Arlene Croce's brilliant volume *The Fred Astaire & Ginger Rogers Book* (which has a two-directional flip-book in the margins and contains many marvelous details, like the fact that the water in the Venetian canals in the classic movie *Top Hat* was dyed black so it read better on black-and-white film), she talks about what they called the Big White Set. We too went for that, with S-curved stairs, high-gloss black floors, and white draperies on curved tracks, in front of a huge suspended decorative lyre with leaves and laurels: very 1930s, everything in black and white, with gold features. Orpheus, Eurydice, and the dancers wore ancient costumes, while the chorus was resplendent in black tie, tuxedos, and gorgeous evening gowns—it was breathtaking. There were small problems. For instance, the drapes we used didn't turn out to be as translucent as we wanted. I'd wanted ghosts behind the white drapes, like the photographs of George Platt Lynes, the sensational 1930s and '40s fashion and dance photographer, famous for his beautifully composed and inventively lit portraits.

The main problem, however, was Hogwood himself, who, despite his great musical mind, was impossible, and I learned firsthand that his recordings were far better than his live performances. (Not to mention the fact that when we started the tour, half the players in the orchestra were different from the ones we'd used in rehearsal. You can imagine how I feel about that. Why bother to rehearse?) Though he and I got along fine, he didn't overly like Americans (the whole company), or women (half the cast), or gay men (which is not unusual with gay men), or people of color (my Eurydice, the African American singer Dana Hanchard).

Perhaps it was just us he didn't like.

I HAVE, as you may imagine, many rules about what you should and should not do when putting on a show, of which only one is "If you want to perform in the show, make sure you're at rehearsals."

Firm as these rules are, however, I break them as often as I obey them. "Never use a chair in a dance"—that's a solid NO because it's the oldest cliché in the world. (I used a chair most enthusiastically in *Ten Suggestions*, which consists of everything one can possibly do with a chair. One reviewer described it as a "duet with a chair.") Another rule is "Never bring a live animal onstage, or a countertenor." Of these many strictures, none is more serious than "Never start the show before the music starts."

We disregarded that one most blatantly for my version of Rameau's *Platée* that year, for the Royal Opera, which started with a dumb show prologue that began nearly twenty minutes before the overture began. We opened the house at the half hour, and the performers slowly meandered onstage to set up the story. In French baroque times, the conductor would hit his staff on the floor three times to signal the start of the music. My version was set in a bar, so a drunk Mercury, sung by tenor Mark Padmore, head slumped, slammed his bottle three times on the bar to get another round. And the overture began.

Platée—une comédie lyrique, or some such designation—featured Jean-Paul Fouchécourt, a singer who had the precise and very unusual vocal type required for the lead role, an *haute-contre*, a tenor who can sing very high in full voice without a countertenor's falsetto. This was with Nicholas McGegan conducting, décor by Adrianne, costumes by Isaac, lighting by James F. Ingalls, and it was a beautiful show.

The idea is that Platée is a hideously ugly toad who lives in a swamp. She's grand, delusional, and in love with Jupiter. Jean-Paul was a great comedian and singer, and we depicted Platée, more or less, as Margaret Dumont in the Marx Brothers movies—a frog with huge green rubber digits, not to mention great big flipper feet that went *smack-smack-smack* as she walked, wearing a glamorous 1920s dress (frog colored with a pinkish-white belly), a lorgnette, and a little handbag. It was magically beautiful, slightly hideous, and apparently disquieting to some. Like many of those Lully and Rameau pieces, *Platée* is a grandiose spectacle with dancing, singing, and exquisitely beautiful music, featuring wonderful imitations of nature: frog calls, birdsong, crickets chirping, a thunderstorm, all beautifully painted musically. The characters are the various denizens of the swamp and assorted gods.

Platée, Festival Theatre, Edinburgh, 1997. *(Bill Cooper/Arena PAL)*

I could set it in any swamp I chose, and I set it in two. Adrianne and I placed the prologue in an exact model of the McManus bar on Eighteenth Street and Seventh Avenue in Manhattan, specifically because it has an aquarium behind the bar, which we changed into a terrarium in which a lizard, or more pertinently a frog, might live. The show opens in this insalubrious bar, with the appropriate characters: a nightstick-wielding cop, a drunken bum (Bacchus), an old rich lady, a bartender serving drinks at a perfect replica of the actual McManus bar (with the racks of potato chips and the fairy lights), a showgirl after work in feathers and fan, and an SM satyr with leather chaps. At the end of the prologue, the bar split in half, and the terrarium (which contained only a stick, some gravel, a fake plant, and a water dish) opened up to become the entire stage, with a huge stick, a big fake plant, a massive orange water dish, a floor painted to look like sand, and a back wall that looked like glass.

Half of the dancers were birds and half were reptiles, everyone in their appropriate skintight unitard, with special-effects costumes for a snake dance with the dancers' tails stretching back into the wings. The text also specifies a "dance for philosophers and babies": a couple of people in big fake beards with togas and books, *thinking*, and two people dressed in diapers and bonnets with rattles. Mercury arrived in tennis whites in the basket of a balloon (deus *fully* ex machina). Juno was dressed like the queen in Snow White, while the King had a big golden crown, red velvet, ermine. Just before the intermission there was a huge thunderstorm, signaling the arrival of Jupiter. The dancers, birds and personifications of wind, ended up splashing water from the onstage fountain (the water dish) all over the stage (which we then spent the entire intermission cleaning up). Quite a hallucinogenic extravaganza and very beautiful musically.

The production was designed for the Barbican—it was a commission from the Royal Opera when Covent Garden was closed for renovation—but they failed to tell us that there were also three other operas hanging in the theater. So every pipe was full with lighting equipment and drops, and we had to fly in sideways pieces of scenery that should have come straight down. It was dangerous.

The Barbican itself has very long rows, a door at the end of each, and no middle aisle. You're shut in and it's claustrophobic. At the dress rehearsal with a full audience, they hadn't left a space for me, so I found myself watching from the middle of one of these long rows. Everything was progressing quite smoothly until this great plywood cotton ball cloud flew in. (A singer was sneaking in behind it, to be revealed when it was flown out.) The cloud came bumping in, and I realized to my horror that it was about to do some real damage to someone, which no one onstage had realized, and nobody in the house who had the same view as I did was doing anything about it. And I had no way to get to the stage quickly and quietly, since we were aisle-less, so I had no choice but to yell from the middle of the hall, "STOP!"

The singers and dancers were used to my bellowing, so they stopped dead, but the band played on as I got to my feet. "Maestro! Nick! Stop! STOP!" I took the most direct route to the stage over the seats, clambering over people's heads, walking down the armrests, apologizing as I went, while shouting, "STOP! This is dangerous!"

The stage manager (with whom I'd gotten along famously and whose job would have been on the line if someone had been seriously injured) emerged from the wings, where he'd been following along in his score, and brought everything to a standstill. I finally made it down to the front, then onto the stage, from where I was able to reassure the audience, "Ladies and gentlemen, we have a technical problem that we're going to stop and fix. And then we'll continue. We apologize. You understand it's a dress rehearsal. We'll be right back."

Backstage, the stage manager said, "I'm sorry, Mr. Morris, but you can't stop the show."

"I just did."

He went back onstage and announced, "Maestro, we'll start at measure 188. *Thank you very much.*"

Sometimes when people say "Thank you very much" in England, it means "Go fuck yourself."

There was another occasion where somebody was barefoot and bleeding. I stopped the show then too. These are real people performing; it's not just moving scenery.

HOWEVER, ALL SUCH production problems pale into insignificance before the overall disaster of the next project. I'm proud to say that I ended up the director of one of the biggest disasters in Broadway history.

At Joe Allen's, there's a side room with posters of the greatest Broadway flops. Finding myself there recently, I asked the waiter if *The Capeman* was still on the wall.

"Oh yeah!" he said. "It's there. Pride of place!"

Rightly so.

Paul Simon's *The Capeman*—his musical about the life of Puerto Rican gang member Salvador Agron—had its premiere at the Marquis Theater in 1998 but ran for only sixty-eight performances. Thus far, it's my only brush with Broadway.

In a sense, that's strange (unless the reason is that I wound up on some kind of blacklist), because there are certain places where I can happily intersect with that world. I like *Peter Pan* as much as anyone in the world; I wish *The Pajama Game* had come to pass. We talked for years about doing *The Hard Nut* there.

It's true that I basically couldn't care less about Broadway—I want it to be great; it almost never is—but I used to see a lot of shows, often at the invitation of either Allen Moyer (who designed the sets for many of my productions) or my costumier friend Marty Pakledinaz, who spent much of his career there. I loved Marty. His chief joy was to bring together all his friends from the various worlds of opera, dance, and Broadway in which he worked, to insist they meet—not particularly with a view to future collaboration, just for the pleasure of their meeting, so that we might all appreciate each other as he had appreciated us. Before he died in 2012, Marty himself asked me to speak at his forthcoming memorial service. On that sad afternoon, as I took stock of the variety of the gathered throng, I was able to proclaim his victory: "Marty, you won! We're all here!"

With Marty Pakledinaz, 2000. *(Courtesy of Maureen Morris)*

Working in that neighborhood for months, as I did on *Capeman*, going to the divey after-hours bar where everyone went to fix their shows, I learned one thing: there is an actual Broadway community and I loved it. They're killing themselves slowly with eight shows a week, and they don't make enough money, but it's a real community, so different from any other. Even if I hated a show, I'd still love everybody who worked on it.

Let me be clear: if I could make a lot of money for not doing much work, particularly work that is already created, I'd do anything, as would we all. I'd love to choreograph another Broadway show. *The Lion King*? Absolutely. I envy Garth Fagan. To choreograph one single Disney cartoon for five minutes, I'd fuck a mouse. Only one of us would survive, and it would be interesting to find out who.

BARRY SCHEDULED ME for a meeting with Paul Simon, whom he worshipped.

I'd always thought Paul was fabulous too (and if anything I liked him more *after Capeman* than I had before). I hadn't listened to all his music as it came out—that's not quite my way—but I liked his approach. He was smart, interesting, and kind, and he'd already devoted years of research to this project. The meeting went along these lines: "Here are a thousand copies of contemporary newspaper articles with pictures of Agron, here's a huge amount of text written by the Nobel Prize–winning Saint Lucian poet Derek Walcott, and here's some music I've been working on." We listened together in his gorgeous apartment—that's how he likes to do it.

Agron, "the Capeman," born in 1943, was a small-time petty criminal (for which the period term was "juvenile delinquent," like the kids my father used to teach) with no great criminal record, on the West Side of *West Side Story*, almost precisely where Lincoln Center is. He ended up murdering two students, and wearing a cape like a superhero because it was chic and it was the sixties. He therefore became known as the Capeman, which gave the musical its name, though it was a bad title from the start—whenever you told anyone, they thought it was *The Caveman*. "Capeman," simply the word itself, is hard to say. Agron was imprisoned, had a long-distance love affair, cleaned up his act, got a degree, was released, and then died. There was a subplot involving Santeria, that esoteric Afro-Catholic ceremonial religion; hence our visit to that secret rum-spitting Santeria ceremony in the Bronx.

Paul had always been very interested in and involved with doo-wop, a cappella street corner music, as many of his generation were—that's what they sang—which of course tied in with his well-known affinity for musics of the world, his South African *Graceland* record, and *The Rhythm of the Saints*, the Brazilian candomblé-infused follow-up. Now he'd flipped for Cuban, Dominican, and Puerto Rican music, and his own songs in those styles were to be the music for *The Capeman*. Did I want to choreograph it? They were never supposed to be big Broadway dance numbers, rather the vernacular social dances that occurred naturally in the narrative, so I was a good pick. And the soundtrack would be lovely Paul Simon's excellent new songs, his first musical. How could it go wrong?

Here's how.

Paul was always aiming for Broadway, but it was never going to be a feel-good show, where everybody stands up at the end and sings the reprise of the big theme song from act 2, and my initial impression (which I voiced) was that it would be a great BAM show. I wondered, apart from anything else, whether there was any real reason to dance in the show. The singing made sense, but jubilant dancing seemed potentially jarring in a show about racism and gang warfare, imprisonment, and born-again Christianity. The subject matter was *grim*. Half the show was set in prison. What were we going to do with that? "Jailhouse Rock"? Have the inmates do a number with shivs? Paul would say, "We need a dance here," and I'd present this point of view: two women are having a big fight, pretending to forgive each other in church, because one of them killed the other's son, and . . . *mambo?*

Despite these minor and seemingly surmountable misgivings, I was genuinely excited and I agreed. There were definite difficulties in putting the show together—and here we get to the crux of the matter—because Paul was very much under the influence of his librettist, the famous poet Derek Walcott. Paul's friend, the literary critic Michiko Kakutani, had introduced them, and Paul had fallen in love with Walcott's work. He worshipped Walcott as a mentor, artist, and Svengali. Derek had written the book for *The Capeman* (everything—dialogue, stage directions, he had even co-written Paul's lyrics) and would continue to write throughout rehearsals. Paul was my boss; he'd let me know the dances that were required, which numbers he was working on, but whatever happened, Derek was apparently on top of the pyramid, because all the text came from him.

This was not a good situation.

Almost immediately, the first director was fired. Paul and the producer were rightly scared of it being a flop, and perhaps they didn't like what they were seeing, but directors were ditched throughout with alarming regularity.

PAUL HAD FOUND all the singers, some from the street, some from the airwaves and screen.

The main trio was astonishing: Marc Anthony, a radio star not yet known to English-speaking audiences (although Paul knew all about him), who has since become the multi–Grammy Award–winning best-selling tropical salsa artist ever; the wonderful Puerto Rican singer Ednita Nazario; and Rubén Blades, already famous, who had recently mounted an unsuccessful campaign to become president of Panama (though he did become minister of tourism). Rubén was a strong-willed, complicated, perhaps impossible individual, and I loved him. When we finally got to Broadway, he had his dressing room, the least nice of the three, decorated as a prison cell, with great ostentation, walls painted black, a cot. It was a good joke. Imagine Marc Anthony, on the other hand, as the young Frank Sinatra, skinny, gawky, and shy. He wouldn't take his shirt off, because he was self-conscious about his scrawniness, but he was very sexy and sweet; we bonded over cigarettes. Ednita, only really known to a Puerto Rican audience, was kind, maternal, and protective—the glue of the show, the center of the family both onstage and backstage, and a great singer. That trio was genius, every second of every rehearsal and every single performance.

We were still auditioning constantly—Paul and I, a couple of the producers, sometimes Barry—in a studio. Paul was too sweet to hurt anybody's feelings, so he sat out of view, where no one could read his expression, and we'd pass handwritten notes to each other: "Horribly flat!" "I'm going to kill myself!" or "This is the greatest thing ever!"

Paul communicates music by singing to, then along with, somebody. He taught the vocal parts by standing right next to that singer and singing it to her, sometimes just by sitting and playing the guitar quietly. Not all of the singers could read music, so that's how people learned their parts. Everyone he hired had to be able to sing really well—not one person was along for the ride—but very few of them were dancers. This was another problem. Aside from a few Broadway gypsies (as they were once known), there were a lot of people who not only had never performed on Broadway, but who'd never been in any kind of show. Many of these great singers had sung in studios, backup vocals, but had no previous stage experience and therefore no basic stagecraft. Everyone could *dance*, in the sense that they knew the local vernacular, but it was harder for them to actually learn fixed choreography and do it the same way twice.

One of the reasons the show burned through so much money—as it famously did: you don't get your poster on that Joe Allen wall for nothing—was because it was the most fun ever. For example, when we rehearsed at Westbeth, everybody, and I mean *everybody*, came to every rehearsal, thirty people at a time, some (Rubén) ferried there in limos. The band, these big, sweet pencil-mustached guys, were there too, all eight of them, all day, including a conga player, a trap set player, bass, keyboard, someone on tres, and another on cuatro. It was insane luxury. In fact, it wasn't even just everybody in the show but friends and family too. The first half hour was spent hugging and kissing. People brought food as though it were a potluck and shared pictures of their new babies, always with the ribbon in a big bow. Then everyone would start jamming, and that would be another half hour up in smoke, but who'd want to stop that? Not Paul! Not me! Incredible fun.

Amid all this, a rehearsal would slowly break out. A whole day might be spent micro-fixing the music, say, two hours for two minutes of music. Paul would stop everything—the band would finally peter out—and, as everyone stood around, he'd go over to a young woman in the chorus, singing with twenty-five other people, and say, "Let me hear what you're doing." She'd show him; he'd hum along with her and say, "Yes, that's it!" and patiently encourage her for fifteen minutes. Oscar Hernández, Paul's bandleader, whom we all loved, the pianist and director of the Spanish Harlem Orchestra, would be trying to hear what was changing as they sang it, and suddenly there'd be a new part added in the chorus that no one had managed to notate. You simply couldn't keep up with it all. It was very hard. I did at least have the assistance of my longtime dancers Guillermo and Megan Williams. But to say that the time could have been better budgeted is putting it mildly. We could have been working on scenework elsewhere.

This routine took over my entire life for months and months, nine to five, followed by lengthy production meetings every evening.

WHEN WE FINALLY moved to Broadway, I suddenly found myself the director, perhaps the fourth. I was simply the last man standing, the person in the room with the most institutional memory. At this point, with all the comings and goings, mostly goings, I knew more about the show than anybody else; no one else *could* have taken over by then. So I did because they asked me to; and that's how you become the director of the biggest flop in Broadway history. It's assumed that the show failed because no one involved knew anything about Broadway, and though there's an element of truth in that, it's not the whole story. Certainly, however, it wasn't the way things were normally done on the Great White Way.

The show had always been too long, and in my new role as director, I could at least finally try to make some of the cuts I'd been hoping for. I wanted to get rid of one long stand-alone ballad, "Trailways Bus," a description of what the singer sees out of the bus window. It was a great Paul Simon song, but it didn't work as part of the show. I fought to shorten *Capeman*, to lose some of the more nonsensical elements of Derek's book. But the moment we'd cut a scene, he'd come up with something new, arguably worse, often longer, to replace it. I remember trying to get the word "manhood" taken out of the libretto. He meant "cock."

Walcott was perhaps the most difficult person I've ever worked with, and I had to deal with him every single day. He was ham-fisted, bigoted, lecherous (he came on to every single single woman), dismissive, patronizing, and belligerent. There was almost nothing on the plus side, except that he was a great poet. At every meeting he'd interrupt you, just to say, "Let me finish," though he had nothing more to say, merely to put you in your place.

Paul is not a braggart. He's very modest about his intelligence; for example, he thinks that he should be able to read music better than he does. Derek played on his insecurities, a dynamic that was in action long before I appeared, and steamrolled him. Paul was powerless in his sway. A director should take over a production, a librettist shouldn't— he should be done—but Derek's attitude was consistently "This goes in or I walk." I wish he'd walked six months previously, because nobody could work with him. Derek was the dictator, Paul was trapped, and I was trying to deliver what I could. Derek started as a jerk, ended as a monster, and finally disowned the whole thing. There may be many reasons why *The Capeman* failed, but I am convinced that Derek was the main one.

The situation got quite crazy in previews, not that it hadn't been before. Normally, you might lock a scene down *before* the first preview, but during our previews, we were working all day long, adding another number, taking something out, changing the staging. Bob Crowley's spectacular set was supremely complicated—thousands of set moves and light cues—and it took an hour of rehearsal time (in a theater with a union crew at huge expense) to fix one minute onstage. I was up until the middle of the night, every night, working, not to mention attending the emergency meetings to replace a cast member. Paul was with me every moment for the entire process, and we kept working on it until the very night it was shut down.

It was too long, too complicated, too sad and overwritten, and there was too much music. At the eleventh hour, I was fired too, and in came Jerry Zaks, the legendary director and show doctor, empowered to walk in and do things I'd been trying to do for months. Zaks brought with him a new choreographer. We got along fine, and I kept going to rehearsals, but working those last few weeks after I was dismissed as director was among the hardest things I've ever done, both emotionally and physically. I wasn't there to play the martyr; I was there because it was the right thing to do, and because I wanted to help and support my colleagues in any way I could. *The Capeman* had been my entire life. (I don't storm out—sometimes it would be better if I did.) The show was lightened; the dances were weakened, made to look more like every other show. It became poppier and perkier. I went to every single performance until it closed.

It was famously, and somewhat racistly, decided that the audience for the show, Latinos, didn't buy tickets in advance. They wait until the last minute, see if they have enough money, walk up, and pay cash. The irony is that the theater was always packed. People came to see the show again and again. The night we shut down for good was chocka-block with Puerto Rican flags, people crying, waiting for autographs. All very moving.

It was simultaneously a huge hit, for sixty or so performances, and an even huger catastrophe. So in Broadway terms it was a piece of shit because of Paul's hubris. Paul, who (it's true) had said probably inadvisable things about Broadway in his interviews—"It sucks, it's a dead genre, we're going to fix it," or words to that effect. There's a long and acceptable history of saying "Ballet is dead! Here's a ballet!"—I say it all the time—but Broadway doesn't like its hand bitten. The show might have stood a better chance if he hadn't gotten Broadway all riled up. But it probably wouldn't have changed much. It just means they'd have said, "He did his best, that kind *world music* guy," and the show wouldn't have received such immediate vitriol, reviews written before the show was even seen. I read every single one.

Paul was fleeced. He felt terribly sad about the whole thing, and he had every right to. He was betrayed. It started out dicey and then got worse. He and I still have very pleasant, though rare, contact, and a few years later we had a visit at my building. He'd just heard about Harry Partch's instruments—I might even have told him about them—and he wanted to use some of them on his next record. I was thrilled.

It's the kind of mutual interest that was the reason he came looking for me in the first place, all that time ago.

The Capeman would have been great running for a few weeks, then touring, a staged concert like a Laurie Anderson show. Hindsight is all, but there was a way to do it that didn't involve full immersion in Broadway's bells and whistles. It didn't belong there. The music was out-of-this-world great, the band and cast were fabulous, and it was a family-friendly vibe. The culture of *The Capeman* was beautiful.

On the site of the future Mark Morris Dance Center, 1999.

Twelve

Home

Our building was finally becoming a reality.

We'd started fully exploring the idea on our return from Brussels in 1991, and the gala opening was in 2001. So that's how long *that* takes.

MMDG *needed* a home. In fact, it was far more important for the company to have a home than it was for its founder. I've always thought of mine as a peripatetic existence, out of a suitcase on the road, and for much of my life, I haven't even owned my own place, happily serving time in other people's apartments. Besides the fact of touring, I've loved to wander around the world in my spare time, and very rarely felt the need to nest in the way that people do.

More generally, I like to live modestly. I now have an office at Mark Morris that's nearly as big as my actual apartment. (It's funny having a building named after oneself, but that's the way we refer to it: I haven't made the move to talking about myself in the third person quite yet. Things happen *at* or *in* Mark Morris. It's weird when they happen "in" you.) And that office has a genuine stand-up porcelain urinal in its adjoining bathroom. That's a little immodest perhaps, but what gentleman hasn't always secretly wanted his own porcelain urinal?

Nancy is always asking me if I want to move somewhere bigger, a cute brownstone in Brooklyn, but I don't want more than I've got, which is all I need. I always wanted a balcony (though no one in New York uses his balcony anyway), and I don't need an extra room for someone to stay over. You'll note, as we quickly walk through my apartment (it doesn't take long), that the sofa is very shallow and doesn't fold out. My theory is: if you want to stay with me, you have to sleep with me. You actually have to have sex with me, then leave before breakfast. I really don't want people to stay over.

Twyla Tharp has an apartment on Central Park West with a studio; Paul Taylor had a house on Long Island; Lar has a nice apartment here, one in Chicago, and a house upstate that he shares with Rob. What's my problem? I've never been ambitious in either a real estate way or a competitive way. We never even got that Hoboken loft fixed up enough to make it into a magazine! When the company went to Brussels, I suddenly found myself in a glorious apartment with three bedrooms, and friends as housemates. When I returned here on tour from Brussels, Mr. Baryshnikov offered me his beautiful four-thousand-square-foot loft, complete with housekeeper and a big white piano, whenever I came to town. When that finally sold, Nancy found me this apartment, in the Murray Hill area of Manhattan, of which Bobby Bordo said, "Nobody lives there but flight attendants," and I've been here ever since, nearly thirty years. Things are wearing out a little, as is its occupant. I should throw a lot of things away and fix some others. Or Guillermo should. He comes over and helps with the odd jobs.

I'm lucky. I could go away to a number of my friends' beautiful houses. So I stay here, with this one orchid that'll be dead by the time you read this.

———

I'm not worried therefore about myself, but the company needed somewhere to work.

Originally we had been looking in Manhattan rather than in Brooklyn, and at one point we were close to sharing a large hangar (where they made the floats for the Macy's Thanksgiving Day Parade) with Annie Leibovitz. The idea was we'd fit up a couple of studios, one for her, one for us, and she'd use it as a home base—a wonderful idea that never quite got going. Then we were asked to come in on the ground floor—project-wise rather than physically—of the New 42, the studios on Forty-Second Street (before the area became all Disneyfied). The project was a smart idea, and the offer was generous, but there was a problem that turned out to be a deal breaker—the layout of the studios meant we'd have to share dressing rooms. We needed greater independence. Besides, can you imagine an entire company going to work every day at Forty-Second Street and Times Square, dodging life-sized Elmos and Woodys as they try to get you to pose for a photo with them? That would result in frustration or tragedy.

Then a piece of land turned up in Brooklyn, distant, unpopular Brooklyn, back when a Manhattan taxi wouldn't take you there. The first possibility was a little triangle of dead space around BAM that had a gas station on it. That space, a block away from where we ended up, now boasts a skyscraper, like every square foot of Fort Greene.

When we first saw the building we're now in, it was vacant (next to a parking lot), having originally been built as a bank in the 1840s, and most recently used as a state-run mental health outpatient clinic. Anyone who had ever been to a show at BAM had tried not to step in it. We mounted a capital campaign, for which there's a nice little ten-minute promotional film of me in the shell of this building, standing in inches of pigeon shit, tiptoeing through the condoms and hypodermics. I could hardly breathe. Many of our best friends and supporters contributed to the movie. Yo-Yo called the building "not a luxury, but a necessity." The New York state senator Velmanette Montgomery said, "The community is waiting for this to happen." Misha simply said it was "a really sensational idea." And it was. The film ended with the following statements:

> Renovation of the existing structure at 3 Lafayette Ave in Fort Greene, Brooklyn, will begin January 1999.
> Once completed, the Dance Center will provide three studios and support space for the creative and educational activities of the Mark Morris Dance Group.
> These facilities will also offer much-needed rehearsal space to local arts organizations.
> The Campaign goal: $6 million ($5 million—renovation and construction, $1 million endowment).
> Completion of the Dance Center is scheduled for Summer 2000.

We acquired the ruin and, full of funding, approached the architectural firm Beyer Blinder Belle, which had just completed the renovation of Grand Central Terminal. (I'd always loved it because, when we did *The Hard Nut* for the first time away from Brussels, Anna Wintour and *Vogue* threw us a big party there. A blizzard meant that half the people couldn't get to the show, though they did miraculously manage to make it to the *Vogue* party, for which a special subway train, called the Pirlipat, was arranged to ferry us from the Atlantic Terminal to Grand Central.) The architect was Fred Bland—it was his look—but Nancy and I had very firm ideas about *everything*, from the materials onward, a vision that had emerged from our thorough analysis and appraisal of the shortcomings of every studio we'd been forced to work in over the last few years.

For example, we thought it a good idea that, when you came in to work, you had to walk past people and therefore greet them, whether you wanted to or not. The dancers walk through the office to get to the dressing rooms, and everyone passes me, so if my door's open, say hi! There were a hundred little ideas like that. Experience told us that where a dancer dropped his bag on the first day of rehearsal would be precisely where it went every day for the rest of time; you make that a habit. We knew, for example, that nobody ever uses those little cubbyholes by the dance barre, so why have them?

Barry's particular contribution was the dressing rooms, which is why they're so great. Being a baseball nut, he'd based them on the Yankees' locker room, on which they may even be an upgrade. Dancing is a serious vocation, a full-time job, yet any gym in the world has a nicer dressing room than the average dance studio. American Ballet Theatre is home to perhaps seventy-five dancers, gorgeous, beautiful professional dancers who are there every day, yet the men's dressing room has torn carpet and a broken urinal hanging from the wall, half the sinks don't work, there are rat traps in the corners, the metal gym lockers are broken like in an underfunded high school, it smells horrible, and there are uncomfortable skinny benches. We wanted someplace where you'd feel at home, or at least not like an unwelcome visitor, where you didn't feel you had to live out of your dance bag, where you had somewhere to eat lunch, charge your phone, work on stuff, or watch a video. We wanted to make it easier for dancers, even launder their towels for them. That's not too much to ask of a dance company's headquarters.

It had always been my intention for our building, when we finally had one (if we ever got one), to be a dancing *school* of some sort, a version of Verla Flowers Dance Arts. George Balanchine famously said,

"But first, a school!" by which he meant that before you can have a dance company, you have to teach people how to dance, and that was back when nobody was doing classical ballet in New York. New York City Ballet still gets all its dancers from its school, the same School of American Ballet that Balanchine and Lincoln Kirstein founded. Nowadays, our ground floor, with its classes and studios, has become a defining and vibrant part of the community aspect of the building.

Given the mass move to Brooklyn, I'd envisioned adult and advanced professional classes, but it became immediately evident that the adults wanted classes for their children. I shouldn't have been surprised—Brooklyn is so fecund. The dream did come true, and in the most Verla way possible: kids everywhere!

ANOTHER DEVELOPMENT, not very long after we opened, involved the Brooklyn Parkinson Group, which contacted us to ask whether we'd send someone over to teach a movement class. Nancy said, "Why don't they come here? We've got studios!" John Heginbotham and David Leventhal (an excellent dancer with me for ten or so years) taught the class, ten people once a month. They figured out a syllabus based on my work, and ideas developed organically, into a curriculum designed in coordination with the Brooklyn Parkinson Group.

The idea is to improve the well-being of people with Parkinson's. The class makes them feel better. It's precisely the same techniques and point of view I use to teach class for my own dancers—holding hands, looking someone in the face, people simply singing and dancing to music. That's my esthetic. They've put on some very joyful shows, sometimes performing excerpts of my dances. I jokingly compare it to a carwash—they come in looking one way and then leave shiny and sparkling. It's therapeutic but it's not therapy per se. They sing and dance. If you want to watch the class, you have to take the class. You're not allowed to study it; none of the participants wants to be scrutinized.

Over the last seventeen years, this has become a worldwide phenomenon: for example, it's now sixty to seventy people in class at the dance center, and that's just one of ten locations in New York City. David, who goes all over the world to give workshops to train potential teachers, is head of the program, and the board of advisors is full of neuroscientists. Frankly, it's nearly a bigger deal than my company.

BUT NOW, if you'll follow me, let me take you past the school, and past the offices on the third floor, all the way upstairs, because the fifth floor is the glory: a giant column-free sixty-foot square studio, doubling as a theater. There were plenty of creative ideas for this, but I didn't want anything clever or original, just a square studio with high ceilings and a sprung deck. I wanted neutrality, a blank space, as much natural light as possible, a certain height of ceiling. I didn't want barres attached to the wall (though dancers prefer the stability), because it had always been my desire to have performances in the studio space, and I wanted it to convert easily into a theater (which it does, but it doesn't, because you have to put in lights, 150 seats, and risers, and it's a lot of work). It works almost perfectly and hemorrhages money.

We're subsidized, so we can rent the studios for cheap. And we don't, for example, charge for auditions, which unbelievably some people are cynical enough to do; I'm not sure who started that trend. Oh, right . . . Twyla Tharp. Young hopefuls, having traded their work shifts, had to pay ten or fifteen dollars to hear immediately after one move, "Thank you! You're not what we're looking for." To me, that was insulting to all dancers, particularly hard-up dancers (which is all of them).

The irony of Mark Morris, by which I mean the building rather than myself, is that even people who aren't my greatest fans—and I say that diplomatically—are dying to rent the best studios in town for ten dollars an hour.

THE SOFT OPENING of the dazzling new building—a gala dinner for the fine and the fabulous, the donors who'd given most generously—was on the night of September 10, 2001. You know the end of *this* story. But that evening was truly celebratory, drinks among the concrete and tarps on the ground floor, still completely raw, and then upstairs for a delicious dinner in the finished studio, a before-and-after of the work in progress for those who'd helped us make the dream come true. We were to start classes right away.

Very early the next morning I had a Pilates session at my friend and teacher Clarice Marshall's studio on Forty-Fifth Street and Tenth Avenue, and I was already there when the two planes hit at 8:46 and 9:03 a.m. Barry called me to let me know what was going on, and Clarice and I listened on the radio. From there, not knowing quite what else to do, I went to a scheduled meeting with Adrianne Lobel about the sets for the forthcoming production of Purcell's *King Arthur* at her place right by the Joyce Theater on Twenty-First. We looked down Eighth Avenue at the burning buildings. It was a beautiful day, and the large Greek columns in her designs seemed eerily appropriate. Over in Brooklyn, Nancy and Johan christened the new building by handing out bottled water to people fleeing over the Manhattan Bridge to safety.

The next day, the *New York Times* chose, for some reason, to put the World Trade Center, as opposed to the opening of our dance center, on their front page. But there was an article on the front page of the Arts section, MARK MORRIS DANCE CENTER ADDS LUSTER TO BROOKLYN.

Not a mention of the terrorism and tragedy of the previous day, of course, since it had all been written on the tenth: "'It is beautiful, it's great,' an exuberant Mr. Morris said, as he paused for a cup of coffee in a blindingly green office that still looks half lived in. 'It is sort of perfect.'" All true, despite the bad timing.

Finally, a place to call home.

Mark Morris Dance Center, 2008.

EVEN AS WE CELEBRATED the majesty of the new building, things started going downhill with Barry.

Barry had made good money for years as the face of the Mark Morris Dance Group. He'd always wanted to be an entrepreneur—*Sol Hurok Presents*—and that is what he'd worked toward. He was connected, and we'd been very successful, but his vision had started to diverge too much from mine. I felt he was leading us up undesirable garden paths and I couldn't allow that; plus they just weren't very good ideas.

Other difficulties were more practical. Barry, as a Deadhead with impaired hearing, liked music louder than I, and he'd say the shows were boring unless the music was blaring. So we'd have a tech rehearsal at which, among many other things, I'd set the sound levels. By this time, I was watching shows more than I was performing in them, and when I'd go into the house for the second half, the music would be much louder. I'd have it turned down. In the middle of the show, Barry would charge up the aisle, hissing, "Turn it up!" And I'd leave the auditorium because I couldn't stand the volume. We were going through soundmen like *The Capeman* went through directors. Barry was also giving advice where it wasn't required, telling dancers, for example, to go for bigger laughs. I want no one to do that *ever*.

Nancy was in denial about the deterioration of the relationship. I'd never say "I told you so" to Nancy about *anything*, but she was late realizing that it was an insurmountable problem, the healing of which could never happen. Nancy and Barry had been not only a team but close friends, closer than I was with either of *them*—I was the talent allowed to get on with his work—and though Barry and I had started as very good friends, I was done with him a couple of years before she was. For the last year, we communicated only through her. Nancy's attitude was "If you'd just stop arguing and realize that you're after the same thing, everything would be fine." But it was irreparable. In the end, he went too far with me and I couldn't work with him.

Suddenly, he was obsolete; his charm was fading, and though he was good friends with producers around the world, with people who hired us, Nancy was having to do all the heavy lifting. He traveled with the company still, ate the buffet (as usual), did the schmoozing, and greeted people in the lobby, while Nancy ran the business end. But he was only there to attend the reception, drink the drinks, then leave.

Barry felt emasculated in more ways than one, but the root of the problem was less metaphorical. As the company got bigger and he got older, Barry didn't retain the same sexual magnetism he'd previously enjoyed, and he never came to terms with that loss. He regularly borrowed money for drugs from the dancers, and he took advantage of some of them in the worst way (and he was married to more than one of them). He fucked a Don Giovanni list of women. The company, sadly, was enabling this and it had to stop, though he wasn't going to like us wresting power from him.

By the time we moved into the new building, he was basically finished, but still it went on. He'd be gone for months at a time, his office door locked; no one ever saw him. If he was there, he was on the phone, smoking cigars, jerking off, whatever. By the end, it was tragic. He had nothing to do with the company. He'd come to a show purely to hate it, then walk out, which he did every time. The music wasn't loud enough, or he didn't like somebody's dancing, or he disagreed with some other aspect.

Then things totally fell apart; his parents died in close succession. The big change finally came in January 2005 when he returned from Susan Sontag's funeral in Paris, and we wondered whether some new addiction had kicked in there. He was never quite the same. It got to the point where we were forced to cancel his credit cards and change the locks on the doors, by which I mean we didn't just "change the locks on the doors," we *literally* changed the locks. Barry disappeared into the arms of a millionaire.

The separation agreement was signed in May of that year, and a poker-faced press release went out in June: "General Director Barry Alterman has resigned for personal reasons. . . . 'Barry will be missed by all of us, but we know that he will be a success in his next chosen pursuit,' said MMDG Board Vice-President Mark Selinger. Alterman's vacated position will be consolidated with MMDG Executive Director position now held by Nancy Umanoff."

There was a concern that Nancy might not have the wherewithal to take over, but the truth is she'd been doing Barry's job for years, covering for him to an extent even I had underestimated. She's now one of the most revered people in her job, the dance company executive director that everybody either knows or knows about. People call her when they have a problem, because she'll have the answer. She's beyond anything you can imagine.

Outside the toilets with Nancy, Ventura, California,
Ojai Music Festival, 2013. (*Johan Henckens*)

Misha and Barry had been close friends, hanging out, enjoying high times in Vegas. (Misha has for a long time been a wonderful parent, producer, and friend, but he was a bit of a playboy when I first met him, a little spoiled and, coming from Russia, fully capitalist.) So

Misha, feeling sorry for Barry, mercy-hired him to work for the newly founded Baryshnikov Arts Center, because Barry needed the money. There was some trouble. Now if you mention him, Misha only hisses, "Fuck him!"

Barry did come to the twenty-fifth-anniversary performances at BAM in 2006. He remarked to Nancy that *Cargo* was a piece of garbage, but that *Candleflowerdance*, to Stravinsky's Serenade in A, was really something. It didn't go unnoticed that this dance was dedicated to Susan Sontag.

THINGS HAD BEEN changing for me too.

All dancers must finally stop. For many years, I could warm up for ten minutes to dance for two hours. Then, at a certain age, let's say forty, I realized I was warming up for two hours to dance for ten minutes. The payoff was wrong. After a while, I didn't want to warm up *at all* anymore; I'd done it enough. And I was never one of those people who worshipped that ritual. I was still dancing well, but it was getting harder, and I didn't want to spend all the time I *wasn't* dancing recovering from dancing.

I remember asking Nancy if I was too old, fat, and ugly to dance, but not smart enough to realize it. I feared that, next to my younger dancers, I might be beginning to look like the creepy uncle, hanging around in my van near the playground trying to lure them in with a puppy. Peter Sellars once asked me bluntly, "Why are you even *in* that dance? You're so much older than everybody else!" I didn't want to be, in English terms, mutton dressed as lamb.

So I stopped.

I felt an immediate and terrific sense of release. I could have extended my dancing career if I'd wanted to, without doubt, but I have no regrets about it, because I'd have had to put myself through the agony of endless gym, which I'd hated ever since school. I never wanted to stay in that kind of shape, and I gained weight. I don't miss dancing for a second, and I love watching other people do my parts. I'm not looking for a comeback. *The Hard Nut*—there's always room for one at *that* party (and it's good for box office)—and *From Old Seville* are the ideal exceptions, though when I recently did that little sevillana, I had to pull myself together and my knee hurt terribly.

But it wasn't the case that I decided to give up because my body couldn't do it, though it now can't. It was more that my body could only do it if I worked at it and killed myself working at it and that there were other, better ways to spend my time.

I'd rather make up dances for other people.

They can do the dancing instead.

LOU'S SERENADE FOR GUITAR, a tender and finely webbed late piece for guitar and percussion, was the last dance I made up for myself: a solo, in 2003. I called it *Serenade*.

Lou's music was in five movements—a round (the only piece with no percussion part), an air, an infinite canon, an *usul* (a system of rhythmic modes used in Turkish traditional classical music), and a Scarlatti-flavored sonata. The theme was metal and wood: a guitar and a gong played by the two musicians, and the "props" that I used— castanets, a hand fan, finger cymbals, and a metal pipe (in tribute to an old boyfriend of Lou's, the wonderful choreographer and illustrator Remy Charlip, who in his sixties did a beautiful dance with a shiny copper pipe that caught the light perfectly). The finger cymbal part was notated, so it was fair enough for me to play that, but I thought the sonata could perhaps use some castanets, even though Lou hadn't written any in. I meant to call him to ask his permission to play those castanets, since it essentially added another rhythm element to his score, but I didn't get around to it. A day or two later, Lou died on his way to a festival celebrating his own music in Columbus, Ohio.

I took his silence as tacit approval. I'd imagined him giving me a long-distance eye roll, accompanied by a sigh: "Go ahead if you must; you'll do it anyway." So I strapped on my castanets and danced to his memory and to his unequaled influence on the Great Big World of Music.

I probably knew this was the last piece I'd do for myself, one dancer alone on the stage in a very private conversation with the two players. I viewed it as a set of five separate vignettes, stories to be told around a campfire: here's the story with the fan, and now the one with the copper pipe. It was appropriate that Lou wrote the music for my last dance. I don't do the dance anymore, but for whoever dances it, I play the castanets. I've had luck bringing various pieces back from the tomb (though I never look for a trip down memory lane, as I'd rather just make up a new one), and Lesley Garrison danced *Serenade* gorgeously.

After he died, I got one of Lou's bolo ties.

Hail Lou! Hail Terpsichore!

AROUND HER EIGHTIETH BIRTHDAY, in 1997, Maxine, my mom, had started showing signs of confusion.

She'd come to a *Vanity Fair* party with my sisters. She'd lost a little bit of weight by then, and it happened that her stockings fell down her thighs without her noticing. Guillermo was there, with a couple of other dancers; they immediately covered her as he got down to his knees and pulled her stockings up. Maxine just stood there. She hadn't noticed. That wasn't necessarily a sign of dementia, but she wasn't getting any younger.

My sister Maureen and her partner, V'kee, took care of her in the house where we'd always lived. What they did was heavy and amazing.

I made a mix tape of her favorite tunes, including the ones we'd sung on those summer drives to Montana. Though she was eventually beyond speech, she'd get up every morning to "Seventy-Six Trombones" and, later in the day, dance to "The Beautiful Blue Danube."

Ten years later, when she was about to turn ninety, I was at work on Prokofiev's *Romeo and Juliet*, which poses some interesting questions about death. Leon Botstein, a terrific fund-raiser and the conductor of the American Symphony Orchestra (famous for premiering various lost works of music), had asked if I'd be interested in choreographing it, with the caveat that he conduct the opening night at Bard, a condition to which I should never have agreed.

The ballet had a fraught history. Prokofiev had disowned the score, which had been Stalinized beyond recognition. Simon Morrison, the great Russian music and ballet scholar, found the sketches for the original production in the Russian State Archive of Literature and Art in Moscow—a considerable scoop—which revealed that the Soviet committees had reordered, edited, and orchestrated the music (originally in the scale of his classical symphony, a small orchestra, Mozart-sized), turning it into epic cinematic sweeping romantic bullshit it was never intended to be . . . and this on top of the changes Prokofiev himself had already wrought on the plot.

He was required to adhere to Shakespeare's original tragic ending to get the ballet approved, but his Christian Scientist faith dictated that he also reimagine it. Everything goes along quite as one might expect until act 4 when, after Juliet has taken the sleeping potion, things get weird. From my synopsis: "Romeo returns. He goes to Juliet, sees that she must be dead, and makes to kill himself. Friar Laurence intercedes. Juliet gradually revives. Friar Laurence summons the townspeople while the lovers slip away. Everyone rushes into the empty room. Friar Laurence indicates the direction in which the couple have fled. Montagues and Capulets rescind their old vendetta.

ELSEWHERE.—Love triumphs. Juliet and Romeo live in love forever." Romeo and Juliet themselves are missing, but not dead. They're in Eternal Love Land, dancing. It's a tricky ending.

In order to figure out how on earth (as it were) to present this, I had a long session with Peter Sellars, a lifelong Christian Scientist—all religion is suspect, and Christian Science is no weirder than all the others—to discuss what it meant, in a Christian Science sense, to be *not dead.* Christian Scientists don't believe in death, which is why they don't believe in medicine. The point is that you don't die; you're transformed. I wanted somehow to capture all this. There was some original Prokofiev music that hadn't been heard before, including that of this climactic apotheosis featuring some of the familiar themes, but higher and higher, with bells, simpler, quieter. Celestial. Infinite.

I went to Botstein's first orchestral read-through of the new score, which had been painstakingly realized by Gregory Spears, at Riverside Church in New York City. The streamlined orchestra was meant to be only thirty musicians, but there must have been seventy-five at rehearsal. The maestro assured us that this was just for the read-through, that in performance we'd use a smaller band (though in the end we used seventy-three at the premiere and fifty-five on tour). But then what was the point? I wanted to hear the music. It was immediately obvious to me that Botstein, who seemed to be sight-reading, beating it half speed like the old version, hadn't done his homework, perhaps hadn't even opened the score. My dance didn't stand a chance.

It was all about Botstein. He conducted the first night at Bard on July 4, 2008, having barely watched rehearsal, and never quite knowing the tempi. But there were other things on my mind.

It was getting time for Maxine. I'd spoken with her on the phone before the show, though she could only listen, and afterward I found out from Maureen that she'd died during the performance. The show ends with the lovers alive, dancing a duet in heaven on earth, in infinity. Straight after the premiere, Leon Botstein insisted that I honor a commitment to talk at the big gala fund-raising party right then. Nancy advised him that though I would attend, I wouldn't, for obvious reasons, be making any speeches. So we went. But after his own comments, Botstein ambushed me, more or less forcing the microphone upon me.

I said: "I hope everyone has a good time, and here's to Maxine."

It was horrible.

MERCE CUNNINGHAM SENT me a postcard that I keep next to my desk in Brooklyn: "Dear Mark, I am sorry to hear about your mother. She asked me to dance with her one time. I was forced to say 'no,' and have regretted it since, all the best, Merce."

Maureen wrote, "She didn't have to die to go to heaven. Because she could hold a cat and she would be in heaven. She could see Mark dance

With my mother, Maxine, on the porch. *(Harley Soltes/*The Seattle Times*)*

and be in heaven. She could watch her grandkids build a fort or put on a show. . . . Her life was Heaven on Earth."

Maxine is the reason I had any possible contact with or interest in dancing. For years, I always thanked her on the back of every program for every performance: "Thanks to Maxine Morris and god," in that order and those cases.

Pepperland, Royal Court Theatre, Liverpool, 2017. *(Robbie Jack)*

Thirteen

Pepperland

My principal job and interest has always been choreographing for the Mark Morris Dance Group; after that, choreographing for a classical ballet company; then directing and choreographing operas. Actually, the priorities may have changed somewhat. Choreographing for ballet companies has become a problem. I don't really do ballet commissions anymore. Times have changed; the dancers can't do what I want.

In 1995, I choreographed *Pacific* for San Francisco Ballet to some wonderful music of Lou's. I picked chamber music on purpose, just as I'd picked solo piano for *Drink to Me Only with Thine Eyes* at ABT with Misha way back when, because I didn't trust ballet orchestras. The fewer the players, the more you'll be able to rehearse with them. A single pianist? Ideal. He learns the dance when the dancers do.

A lot of serious music people can't bear to go to the ballet, not because it's going to be recorded music and it's going to be *bad*, but because it's going to be live music and it's going to be *even worse*. For decades New York City Ballet was known to have the worst band in town. It's not necessarily the musicians' fault. They have a huge repertory, scant rehearsal time, and a new combination of pieces every night. Often they don't rehearse with the dancers, so they don't know how the dances work. It's a perpetual emergency trauma situation. Things have improved somewhat, but the music director for a ballet company remains something of an object of pity. If he could be conducting a symphony orchestra or an opera, he would be.

It turned out that the San Francisco Ballet orchestra was very good, though I hadn't trusted that they would be, so when I finally did use them for *Sandpaper Ballet* in 1999, my apology and joke was to use the music of Leroy Anderson, a composer famous for writing novelty numbers, pieces of three or four minutes destined to be played as encores for the Boston Pops: for example, "Sandpaper Ballet," where the percussionist plays a soft shoe with sandpaper blocks. (I didn't use that particular piece, though I did like it for a title.) A lot of these pieces highlight one section of the orchestra: "The Typewriter," for example, features a percussionist "playing the typewriter" with the keys and the return bell. An orchestra generally gets to play only one of these fun numbers right at the end, rather than a whole evening's worth, so this was a complete gift, with not only "Sleigh Ride" as the overture, but "Syncopated Clock" as the finale.

But believe me when I say that my general distrust of ballet orchestras is entirely reasonable, which is why the first thing I'd choreographed for San Francisco Ballet, *Pacific*, was set to two movements of Lou's piano trio, for nine dancers: a quartet of women, a trio of men, and then a male-female duet. They did this modest, romantic dance beautifully, though it was very much in the style of my own company rather than theirs.

Recently, however, I watched a performance of *Pacific* by a ballet company that Tina, whom I send as my representative to set my pieces, had taught them. It was not good: flirtatious, faux seductive, *ballet naughty*. My moves are meant to be performed without irony, and this was the antithesis of what I'd intended. It wasn't a bit off, it was *oppositional*. My personal chamber-sized dance had become a cheap, crappy come-on, a parody of itself. Twenty-five years previously I'd had at my disposal five San Francisco ballerinas, powerful dancers with women's personalities, skills, and intuition. Here I had flirtatious post-Balanchine coquettishness, the Coppertone girl with the dog pulling down her bikini bottom; the men, shirtless, pumped, and dominant—styles of sexuality I find repulsive.

I was mortified and couldn't go backstage. It freaked me out. And not only me. My friends hated it too and left. I don't want to see my work turn to shit while I'm alive and can still do something about it, so I decided to cancel my commission with that particular company; they'd done two pieces and they wanted a new piece from me. Nancy talked me out of it, so I made up a lovely new dance for them, the simplest dance in the world (though it looked complicated), and it nearly killed me.

At first I suspected it was all Tina's fault. I'd trusted her to set it. I knew the dancers themselves weren't to blame; they weren't doing anything wrong. They were simply dancing in today's ballet style. I felt, however, that I'd seen the glimmer of perhaps one of them doing it right, so as an experiment, I had Tina teach *Pacific* to my dancers, who don't dance on pointe, aren't classical ballet dancers, and are in many cases older. They were nervous, because though they all speak ballet, it's not what we regularly perform (and in soft shoes we never use), but they learned it in a second and danced it perfectly. It looks a little different, since it isn't on pointe, but it's the precise same text. That was when I realized that I don't need to work with ballet companies. My own company can do this now.

The fact is: I don't want my work to live on after me if it's going to look like that version of *Pacific*. I'd rather no one saw it at all. I'd rather it died. I'd basically—and this would be ideal—like to be paid a huge amount of money for my dances not to be done. But failing that, I would donate to a commission to prevent them being done badly. I would give you money to stop it all right now. Forever.

THE BACKGROUND IS THAT BALLET has reconservatized. It's reverted to that post–World War II, 1950s, uptight Eisenhower sexuality, pre-feminist, pre-queer. Everyone gets along fine, but either the women are once again powerless while the men are charming and dashing or conversely there's a unisex anodyne mediocrity. That's not enough for me, and it never was. I see new ballet choreography and sometimes even *like* it, but it doesn't mean much to me. It's reverted and I haven't.

Those legendary 1970s ballerinas were big stars, wonderful dancers, and fabulous feminists. Now the women are presented as demure, made up and hair sprayed, superfemme, like it used to be. Outside the studio they seem to be normal: they drive cars, have boyfriends, and talk on the phone like modern people, but when they come into the studio, they're pastel kittens. The men, on the other hand, are big and butch. The concept of the Hotshot Male Dancer started with Nijinsky, then Nureyev, and Misha; men hadn't been great dancers before. In early ballet, up through Balanchine, men carried the women around, did a single pirouette, and exited stage right. You needed a core of thirty-two identical women to do *Swan Lake*, *Sleeping Beauty*, *Giselle*, *La Sylphide*—the classic nineteenth-century "white ballets," as they're called—and a couple of men who betray the ethereal, virginal women. Nowadays, most choreographers want an equal number of men and women in their work. The men are rewarded for having personalities: they want to dance a lot or they'll leave. The women on the other hand are once again rewarded for having no personalities: they're in purdah.

So it's back to what it used to be, infantilizing for women and aggrandizing for men. Women aren't allowed to dance alone anymore because of the way partnering has developed. Once upon a time, they were the whole story. It's why those classic ballets now seem obsolete.

This harsh gender divide is a symptom of the work itself. In that intervening quarter century, the requirements (as they should and must) have changed. Choreography has become more robotic, demanding a flexibility and virtuosity that leaves me cold. It's ugly. I'd rather see *Giselle*. The tone of my work is less Balanchine and more Ashton or Bournonville, gentler and more feminine, and it feels out of place on a program full of pieces featuring impossible pyrotechnics: men tying women in knots and carrying them off.

When Misha was running ABT, this wasn't the case. There was a nine-year moment of really interesting dances, some of which I didn't like, but all of which were new and interesting, and some of which (I'm happy to say) were by me. Then there was a backlash, though it wasn't necessarily against the work. It had to do with the economics and the distribution of money.

What has since developed I call the "International Style." The marketplace is now global, and none of the choreographers have their own companies anymore. Once upon a time ballet companies were all run by women, like Ninette de Valois and Lucia Chase, who founded what became the Royal Ballet and ABT, respectively. Now everyone hires the same itinerant choreographers who apply a similar wash. Much like the chain store–filled downtowns of the world, there's no difference between the Royal Ballet, New York City Ballet, the Mariinsky, and the Paris Opera. Why do we even have to travel anymore? Perhaps we can do away with that too.

One advantage to this is that there are now international dancers fluent in the International Style all over the world. They no longer have to learn how they do it in Paris or London. However, they don't get to learn how to dance anymore, and there isn't time to rehearse. That doesn't mean it's bad work, and it doesn't mean they're bad dancers, though some is and some are. But some of the work is beautiful. Alexei Ratmansky, who ran the Bolshoi for a number of years, is a choreographer with whom I identify. He's done many pieces for New York City Ballet, is currently choreographer-in-residence at ABT, and works exclusively in the medium of classical ballet. He's a strange cat, prolific, reticent but great; his work looks like ballet, it's on pointe, it's all girls and boys—all the assumptions of classical ballet I've sought to subvert—but it's brilliantly historically informed. He's a conservative in the good sense. He knows dance history.

I love classical ballet, and I speak the language fluently, but I'm somewhat out of fashion in the contemporary ballet world. I'm more trouble than I'm worth. The kick people get from my work (because it's not like the other pieces on the program) isn't perhaps a big enough payoff when balanced against my demands, financial, musical, and otherwise. I may be pricing myself out of the market. And there are stipulations: you can only buy a new dance if you've previously done two other pieces by me, so you're pre-vetted. What you then get is my new dance. It'll be me (an old, mean, curmudgeonly perfectionist) doing my best work, but there's no actual guarantee that people, your audience or your critics, will like it. It may not fit as they wish. That's what makes it so interesting. Put simply, it's easier for that company to buy a dance that they saw another company do at that festival, that seven other companies are also doing. It's a guaranteed success, the easiest way to participate in a prevailing esthetic with which I disagree. And that's how it's swung.

City Ballet has more money than any dance company in America. The dancers are great, but my taste doesn't run in that direction; the audience is little girls dressed in pink and their dads waiting in the car. It's precisely what my work—and far from *only* mine—has been pro-

testing all these years. This has reestablished the old-time schism between downtown (Modern Dance: intellectual and artistic) and uptown
(ballet: dainties for the bourgeoisie). So the very situation out of which
my dance emerged is re-creating itself right now for someone else exactly like me. But much younger.

I'm not sure Big Ballet and I are on speaking terms.

SOMETIMES I'M NOT on speaking terms with anybody.

Recently, I had a late-arriving realization—an extremely important
one—that my behavior toward my dancers in MMDG had to change,
a conclusion I didn't come to alone. Discourse that had been appropriate two generations previously when we began didn't fit anymore; what
made sense in the 1980s had ceased to, in the same way that my dancers were no longer comfortable with the naughty ass-swatting gesture
in *The Hard Nut*. It was past its sell-by date.

It all came to a head in 2016, when I went a little crazy for a couple
of months in the summer, a confluence of many things, but partly
political. Everyone was so mortified after the election. I was desperately trying to be optimistic, at least professionally, with regard to my
dancers—"We'll get through this like we always do"—but it affected
me far more than I knew. Although I genuinely believed that it was the
perfect time, if only by way of antidote, for us to be making the most
beautiful art we could, I found myself sinking too.

I tend not to diagnose myself as "depressed"—I prefer country and
western terminology, "sad" or "blue"—but I was depressed. I'd arrive
at work each morning feeling I had nothing to offer, not even ideas
(which is often true, though generally I manage to come up with something anyway). I was in a weakened state, both physically and emotionally, and suddenly things seemed bleak, though I was trying to keep
things going against all odds. (Not long before, I'd experienced my

first panic attack on a plane. "Join the club," said Isaac, only somewhat sympathetically. "I've been on Xanax all my life and I've outlived seven therapists." Everybody said it was nothing, but it was *something*. I became a little bit claustrophobic as a result.)

This malaise dovetailed with other pursuant postelection worries of a professional nature: for example, the certainty that the NEA was going to be shut down, and that, more generally, the basic tenets of our art and our lives were under attack. Art is no longer greatly valued in our culture, an anti-intellectualism that's been setting in for some time, as criticism slowly disappears from the newspapers. It isn't part of everyone's life anymore. It's not merely that I'm a dinosaur (which I may be; there aren't many one-person Modern Dance companies left in the States) but that this way of working is endangered and the whole thing may be over. Money is an issue at the *best* of times. And that's when the political becomes personal. Though I'm lucky to be—to have been—successful, everything was going south at the same time.

The long and the short of it: I was freaked out with mortal thoughts, and I began selfishly taking it out on my dancers, like when I'd been on crutches in Seattle. In a particular rehearsal, while trying to work something out, I vented my frustration by announcing, "We're all working on the same problem! Let's use one big mind instead of fifteen tiny little minds!" In another context, that would have blown over immediately, but given the general froideur, a dancer challenged me: "Excuse me! That's really insulting. Can we take a break?"

In this instance, I hadn't seen the remark as a particular violation or personal insult of any kind. Although I said it in entirely the wrong tone, I'd meant, "Let's get together and think through this as one." I was thinking of my own as one of the tiny minds that we should pool into one great consciousness. Be that as it may, the group was proud of that person for standing up to me.

Another example, and this one is bad: I have regularly and blithely used the phrase "Exit now and don't forget to take your ass with you!" It's a dumb joke, a turn of phrase, never aimed at anyone in particular more than anyone else. More recently, I said out loud of someone I didn't know, who happened to be doing a turn at that moment, "Your ass looks like when a dog puts its face out of the back window of the car and the lips flop around." That's what popped out, something so *wrong*, so *inappropriate*, about the wrong person at precisely the wrong time. Jaws dropped, like the audience watching *Springtime for Hitler*. What I consider "humor" (in that case) or "frankness" (in others) is sometimes a cruelty. I feel terrible about that, while simultaneously recognizing another failing: that I'm not very good at going back and saying, "Remember when I said you were an asshole? You weren't."

When I was a young functioning adult with dances to make and a new company of friends, I told my dancers straight and they told me back. I once tried to throw Tina out of a rehearsal. Her reaction was "Fuck you, Mark, I'm staying!" And she did. The mutual relationship was more or less equal, and the repartee was, to put it mildly, lively. There was a "frank exchange of views." That made it much easier for me. "Let's take a break, Mark," Winkie would say, "you're getting a little bit *crazy*," whereas Guillermo would simply yell, "Simmer down! Fuck you!" and demand we stop for the day. And we would stop. But today, I no longer have a company of friends and I am no longer my dancers' contemporary. Their immediate artistic life is temporarily in my hands, and this relationship is potentially dangerous. This revelation caused a major recalibration of everything.

In fact, as time has gone by, I've generally become more straitlaced, more guarded in the way I talk—I wouldn't boo Twyla anymore or open with "*Je déteste Béjart*"; it's more trouble than it's worth—but I've always been *vulgar*. The word "irreverent" doesn't quite cover it. There's always been a coarseness about me; it's true that I like dirty, naughty, and profane. I've never liked the churchification of anything.

I can be nice, but I can certainly be mean, and this could become abusive. In the old days, when Guillermo wanted a solo, I'd say, "Give me a hand job and I'll see what I can do for you." It was absolutely a joke, and he was the perfect demographic for that horrible joke, but that joke has ceased to be funny. Imagine "Give me a kiss and I'll give you a big solo" nowadays, with me, forty years their senior, and their boss. Times have changed, and my role in the dance world has too. No one needs to have the workplace so sexualized.

When I was in high school, my friends were of all different stripes, sexualities, and races. It was a little rough-and-tumble for me personally, but I survived, and I learned to be tough, because I was a sissy. I loved queer culture; the secret part was the fun of it. Now everything's been revealed, we've come out, we're the people next door with no need of our own private language, and we can get married if we like (though as you know I don't recommend even straight people should get married). The race thing went the opposite way. Back in those black power days, I imagined everybody would become everybody else's best friend and look beautiful with similarly neutral toning. I thought it would be the same with religion; it would all be washed out. I believed in all that pie-in-the-sky utopian fantasy.

At early auditions in New York, I was thrilled to find coeducational dressing rooms in the Modern Dance world. There were no proper facilities—we were in somebody's loft—and everybody changed, danced, and re-changed together. In the early days of MMDG, you got used to nakedness. It wasn't a sex thing. We did have sex, occasionally with each other, but that wasn't what it was about. Back then, the word for this would have been "liberated." Now the word is "threatening."

Of course, "young people today" aren't the way our earlier generations were. No member of any succeeding generation ever has been (except a has-been). I'm now dealing with people *two* generations younger than I. I'm sixty-two—that's a grandparent's age, not even a parent's—and they're in their twenties. At its dawn, and for some time, my company was me and my friends, some of whom were older than I. Twenty years on, it was people twenty years younger, though our mutual relationship was still perfectly viable inasmuch as they weren't offended if I mentioned that I'd had sex. You can believe your parents had sex—you exist!—but your grandparents? Gross.

Nowadays, the prevailing atmosphere reminds me of the genius of Sidney Lumet's movie *Network*: "I'm mad as hell and I'm not going to take this anymore!" It has much to do with the president we elected in 2016. Not only do I fully applaud the new activism, I also feel part of it. I've always felt that way. I don't feel, and have never felt, like the statue of Lenin being torn down in the square. I feel like the person tearing it down, even if most of my demolition work was done some time ago. But having to monitor everything one says and does is a little *eggshelly* for me. I'm less good under scrutiny. Interviewers often say sarcastically, referring to some supposedly outrageous opinion of mine, "Tell us what you *really* think!" (I don't then point out that that was already the watered-down version in order to keep things civil.) I'm from a long line of nihilists and Seattle Noir humorists. I tend to the dark joke, the Charles Burns and Charles Addams aspect. Later on the very night that my mother died, Guillermo asked, "Is your mother still dead?"

But this has led to some pretty bad recent situations in class and rehearsal. I've recognized the potential problems. For the last few years, I've always started rehearsals with a ballet company with the opening remarks "I will touch you as needed, in the interests of teaching you. I use adult language and I am likely to say 'goddammit,' so if you're uncomfortable, cover your ears. Anybody who doesn't want to be in this dance for any reason—the music, my methods, you're tired, I've asked you to dance with someone you just broke up with—please take this opportunity to withdraw yourself."

I found myself coming into class at MMDG in the morning, telling whatever ghastly story I had to tell, to find them rolling their eyes, leaving me to wonder why everyone was so lifeless. I persisted, because that's what I do, and they stopped responding. Around this time, some of the dancers approached Nancy to tell her I was freaking them out, that I'd said something terrible, and that they were scared to talk to me directly, fearing my response would be a chilly "And?" Occasionally, dancers have asked me why I'm mean or impatient with them: I can be both. If they threatened to walk out, my response might be "Okay!" And nobody wants to hear that. Nancy confronted me: "Mark, everyone's scared to talk to you. You've got to do something." I'd occasionally tried to argue my corner, but not in this instance. Life will throw many hurdles and obstacles at these dancers, all of which they'll have to jump and avoid, or they won't get anywhere—they'll need to be tough, and I will *always* demand perfection—but I mustn't myself be an impediment.

The dancers staged a power coup, an organized boycott, presented to us by the company. The message was that I was mean and insulting, that they didn't want to hear my shit anymore. They were annoyed not that I was treating them like slaves, which I wasn't, but that I'd gone too far, assuming a different familiarity, an overfamiliarity, with them. I know I can be a bully, but I was honestly surprised to hear how much it upset them. I'd like to think that it's not constant, but rather part of a broader repertoire of behaviors that makes up a more attractive whole. (Of course, I'd like to think that!) The boards of companies all across America have drawn up new policies to deal with such things, policies that have already been in play at universities for years, and so MMDG did too. Nancy wisely suggested, among other outlets for expression, an anonymous suggestion box so people could comfortably submit their grievances, knowing they'd be heard. That thing filled up quickly.

I've generally had good personal relationships with my dancers: some very close, others not so much—I've worked with people for fifteen years yet never eaten in a restaurant with them—but I finally realized, with Nancy's help, that it's okay, even desirable, to become less personally invested, to be someone who doesn't talk to everyone freely and openly all the time. Though I like to gossip, to know about things, boyfriends and families, I would no longer intrude on my dancers' private stories; that in itself is inappropriate.

In collaboration with my company, I've somewhat let go. It turns out that this hasn't had a negative effect on the teaching. The dancers haven't lost their confidence either in my capacity to make up great dances or in my fundamental kindness, even if it's sometimes obscured beneath a pile of horror. They love my work, and they want to work with me or they wouldn't. They know I love them.

Or do they?

Nancy has been telling me for years, generally in reply to some random remark of mine that a particular dancer is fabulous, "Have you told *him*?" To which my response used to be "No need. He knows."

Finally I understand that he didn't necessarily know, because he doesn't attend the question-and-answer sessions I do after the shows, when I say just that. Nancy has always said I'm not complimentary or praiseful enough of my dancers and musicians. She's right. I don't overpraise; I don't feel that way. I don't really do group hugs. It doesn't mean I don't love the people I work with. I'm not physically affectionate; I'm physical in my actions.

If I say "Good show," that means it was *fabulous*. But a fabulous show is our job. That's the level at which we work. You may or may not like the shows themselves, but there isn't a wrinkle in the backdrop: Johan wouldn't allow it. The floor is clean. The sound is perfect. The dancers must meet the surrounding perfection. We work at a high level of expectation and competence.

If you're not a good dancer or a good musician, what are you doing here?

BUT SITUATIONS SOMETIMES combine to prevent your doing the best show possible. That is a prime source of frustration. And it's *never* my dancers who are to blame.

Whenever I saw Yo-Yo in the intervening years, he'd say, "I'm waiting for you to have a dream like you did for *Falling Down Stairs*" (see above: I'd corrected him a few times). His next big idea was Silkroad, a humanitarian umbrella organization under which wonderful artists could do whatever their hearts desired, inspired by the ideas and traditions along the historical Silk Road from China to Italy, all with the idea of the advancement of global understanding through the arts. Yo-Yo is quite sincere when he says he wants to heal the world through music. It's deeply admirable, but I'm here to say you can't, but that clean water would help. That, and a blanket.

Yo-Yo was being Marco Polo, collecting artists he loved and adding others from obscurer cultures—Chinese noodles meet New World tomatoes and let's make spaghetti marinara! Of course I was a shoo-in with my love of the world of music. It was a beautiful idea, the only caveat being that it might turn into airport gift shop "world music," where everyone and everything is of equal value. (In fact, everyone is of equal value as a citizen, but everyone isn't of equal value as an artist.) His stated intent was to model Silkroad on MMDG, his concept of which was that everyone contributed. (That may be true, but I'm the boss, and that's how I like it. Otherwise I'd join a commune.) He asked Nancy's and my advice, but the truth is that the "rules" of MMDG can't really be applied elsewhere. It's not, nor can it be, a model for anything.

One of his suggestions was Uzeyir Hajibeyli's 1908 music for the first Muslim opera, *Layla and Majnun*, the seventh-century Arabian love story of Qais ibn Al-Mulawwah and Layla, whom Byron inaccurately called the "Romeo and Juliet of the East." I thought about it for a long time, ten years, in fact, because, though I loved it, I feared it wasn't necessarily good for a show, a little bit too sad, too slow, and not quite *enough*. So I rejected it more than once, and every time I saw Yo-Yo, he'd remind me about it. Meanwhile, Johnny Gandelsman and Colin Jacobsen (both violinists with the Silkroad Ensemble), in collaboration with Azerbaijani singer Alim Qasimov, had rearranged and reworked the music further. There was a lot of anti-Muslim feeling around at the time, which has only worsened, and I finally decided to do it, which led to its premiere at Cal Performances in Berkeley in 2016, after a further year making the dance up. Yo-Yo was fully behind the project, but the moment I agreed was the precise end of our collaboration.

I basically hired the Silkroad Ensemble as a band of eight musicians (two violins, viola, cello, bass, pipa, percussion, shakuhachi). I'd said from the very beginning, as I always do, "If you can't play all the rehearsals and the performances, I don't want you in the band." That's the way I work with my own musicians, and it's a firm rule. (And that's why *Falling Down Stairs* had worked so well with Yo-Yo in the first place, because we rehearsed it together.) They said, "Well, the bass player can't make it to the first week of rehearsal, but he'll be there the rest of the time and for the whole tour." I made that one exception, because I knew him to be reliable. Then another of the musicians needed to teach for seven days in the middle of the run; suddenly only *these* players could do this city and *those* could do that.

"Okay," I said, backpedaling slightly after my first failed ultimatum, "but I won't work with people who haven't rehearsed with me." If it's a big Broadway show, you might agree to do it for a lot of money, then phone it in or, as often happens with orchestras, send your students to play. Such cavalier behavior is quite common, but I don't work that way. We were compelled to pay for fourteen musicians for the rehearsal week (and two more were added once we were on tour), and I felt duped. Johnny Gandelsman, who did most of the arrangement, played the first gig and departed; so Colin Fowler, my music director, the singers, and I found ourselves in charge of the music. What was consistent at every performance was the six Azerbaijani artists. It was the eight musicians of the Silkroad Ensemble who changed at almost every stop, except for the bass player, who never missed a show. The musicians themselves were innocent, but you can't just drop in as a guest artist when you're playing second violin. How is that going to be good? It felt as if the musicians were the only people on that stage who didn't know the music. And the truth is that the music for *Layla* wasn't even that difficult. I might as well have used the MMDG Music Ensemble. And I would have. I was furious.

When we were just about to open in Berkeley, I complained seriously and intensely to Yo-Yo. His argument was that the musicians were young players, there wasn't much work, and they had families. All perfectly true. But of course my dancers were paid much less than the musicians, and they're also young and there's even *less* work.

This was right when Howard Hodgkin, the show's designer, and I shared our only tense moment. There had been slight miscommunication from the beginning.

Come to think of it, Howard had also taken us back to the drawing board when he designed the sets for *Mozart Dances*, a big project that premiered in 2006. We visited London, told him the music we were going to use—he was accidentally listening to the wrong concerto for a while; didn't matter!—and gave him a basic outline. In return, he gave us five very interesting, colorful, and complicated sketches to take home, to use however we liked, assuring us he could do them again if necessary. We left with them, Nancy carrying this priceless art around under her arm.

After we'd brought them back to the States, he unexpectedly contacted us: "Send those back, they're *wrong*; I've been thinking more about it and I don't like them." So we returned them and received a different five. Again, he didn't specify precisely how to use them beyond "use only these ones, not the first ones." I could change sets fifteen times if I wanted, like we had with the drops and scrims in *L'Allegro*, or use just one, rather as Lou had let me do what I wanted with the music for *Rhymes with Silver*. In the end, I used three to go with the three pieces of music and the three dances. Howard had wanted to do the costumes too, but I didn't let him (which is why he got to do them for *Layla*), though he insisted that Marty's costumes be monotone—black, white, gray, exclusively—in front of his beautiful painted backdrops in black, white, and red.

For *Layla*, from the very beginning, I'd wanted his central painting, the magnificent backdrop, to be a letterbox rectangle shape, because of the Muslim association, the horizontality of old Islamic architecture. I was particularly thinking of the bilateral symmetry of the university in Samarkand, where everything is low and wide, and only the minaret rises above it all. I wanted that look, so we'd already decided the dimensions and position of the drop.

I first saw Howard's painting *Love and Death*, just after he'd finished it, in his condo in Mumbai.

"I think this is it, Mark," he said. "You look at it and tell me if it's not."

He sat in his wheelchair as I went into the studio alone, the painting wet on the wall in front of me. It was very profound. And quite the wrong dimensions.

Antony Peattie, Howard's husband and manager, and Andy Barker, Howard's close friend and studio assistant, explained, "Howard, you know Mark wants this to be a slice of that."

Andy made a frame that he'd hold over different parts of the painting. So the finished backdrop, in all its beauty, is actually a detail of that original painting.

That all turned out fine, but the point of tension in Berkeley was that Howard wanted the risers (as opposed to the tread) of the stairs painted a painfully bright acid green, so that if you were looking from the front at that precise level, you wouldn't see the black treads, just the green block. It was not pretty. It ruined the whole look.

Howard arrived at the theater, having seen nothing of the set previously except perhaps the most rudimentary mock-up. And there was this hideous green. He looked at it.

"Howard," I said, "we have to decide today, because the paint has to dry before we can dance on it, and I have a real problem with this green."

James Ingalls demonstrated the effect of lights on it. If you threw green light on it, it disappeared into gray; if you put red on it, it turned brown. It was beyond his help. We were all being semi-diplomatic, waiting on Howard's word as he scrutinized it.

"I can't tell under these lights!" he barked. "It looks fine to me."

"Hey, Johan," I said. "Will you tell Howard what you told me?"

"Howard," said Johan firmly. "I hate this green."

"Well, it's decided then," said Howard. "Get rid of it."

He couldn't have been more English. We painted it black and everything was fine, but it was tense. He'd never seen his idea full scale under the right lights, and that's a different consideration entirely.

The fact is *Layla* was a beautiful show that improved night by night, though it would have been consistently better if the same band had played in each venue.

Silkroad is itself a wonderful organization. It has developed and changed meaning over the years, but it's hung around doing good

With Yo-Yo Ma and Howard Hodgkin on opening night of *Layla and Majnun*, Graduate Hotel, Berkeley, 2016. *(Nancy Umanoff)*

work like White Oak did. Yo-Yo is more an eminent representative now, and Silkroad is to *world music* what TED is to talks and Aspen is to ideas.

EVEN MORE RECENTLY, we premiered a show in Liverpool called *Pepperland*.

I don't worship the Beatles. It's not like I never loved them, but put it this way: I choreographed Yoko Ono's music over thirty years before I got around to her husband's band. They were certainly important to me in many ways: the foldout poster with the *White Album* had that photograph of Paul McCartney holding a towel. It implied dick. I, too young to masturbate, simply didn't know how to handle the feelings engendered within me. Paul, being so cute, had been my favorite, but I soon grew to prefer John intellectually, not only his music but also the drawings and the writing. In fact, Paul's cuter songs—"Michelle,"

"Yesterday"—were the first to cloy, and I felt a little swindled as my musical taste developed.

I listened to *Sgt. Pepper* straight through for the first time in thirty years and I loved it. Not only that, but I knew everything about it, even the precise length of the gaps between the tracks, indelibly imprinted on me since I was twelve. I'm re-appreciating it now partly because the music and melodies are wonderful, and partly because, for *Pepperland*, they have been rearranged and recomplicated for me by the composer Ethan Iverson, my immediate choice for the project. I wouldn't do it if I didn't *like* it, of course, but I also wouldn't do it if it were just the Beatles. There'd be no reason.

The ambitious commission came from Seán Doran, who throws a good festival. This one was specifically to celebrate "Sgt. Pepper at 50." Apparently, the original idea had been to commission different artists to do treatments of different songs, but I'd either misheard or misthought, and I presumed I was supposed to do the whole album. So we went ahead with a treatment of six of the *Pepper* songs, interspersed with original music by Ethan that linked them in fascinating and suggestive ways.

Once that was all straightened out, I started work at the beginning of February 2017 for a May premiere. That may seem a long time, but with all the company's other commitments—touring, teaching, out-of-town workshops, and so on—it was a very fast turnaround, perhaps the quickest ever for a long piece. I shoehorned the *Pepperland* work in as I could, but I found myself increasingly haunted by visions of the relentless sands of time in a completely imaginary hourglass as the deadline approached. This was complicated by the fact that Ethan was writing the music as I was making up the dance, even as Nancy was obtaining the global performance rights from a thousand different organizations.

Making up the dance itself was sometimes a nightmare. For weeks

I worked on a piece Ethan wrote called *Magna Carta*, his thesis being that "the Beatles are sacred; everyone worships them; we should do that as a proclamation." So he wrote a Gregorian fanfare that starts with the end of the first song, "Sgt. Pepper's Lonely Hearts Club Band," as they introduce "the one and only Billy Shears." Ethan's idea was to then introduce various characters pictured on the iconic album cover. It was to be an introduction to the cast, the concept, and the cover.

I worked on this for weeks, driving the dancers hard during that period of strife, hating everything I came with up and everything they did, which is what I'd told them to do. We'd come back to it every few days, but I couldn't find a way for it to make sense; we'd start from scratch, but it was all so complicated and stupid, and none of it worked. And then a few days later we'd get back to it: "Oh shit! *This again!*" Finally, I found something usable: the dancer came on as herself—"we'd like to introduce to you . . ."—acknowledged the audience as if she were in a fashion show, turned around, put on reflective shades, then turned around again as . . . "Marlene Dietrich!" Ta-da! So we went with that, each celebrity with the appropriate gesture: Albert Einstein sticks his tongue out; Fred Astaire does a suave dance move. We'd picked the celebrities whom an English and an American audience would recognize by name and gesture. I'd solved the *Magna Carta*. And then it was time to introduce "the Beatles."

As we were working, Johan heard some of Ethan's music. In short, he hated it. Under no circumstances would Johan let such feelings affect the quality of his work, but it meant something to me to know his opinion, because Ethan and I weren't overly happy with the music either. Our subsequent decision was to change the instrumentation. The mezzo voice was too close in timbre to the theremin—the overall effect was too "haunted house"—so we listened to four singers, three women and Colin's suggestion, a man with whom I'd just worked in Britten's *Curlew River*. We hadn't been planning to use a male singer, but Clinton

Curtis's baritone was the unanimous choice. Instrumentally, what we'd had originally—trombone, soprano sax, theremin—was too washy rhythmically (it was hard to find a beat: there was nothing aside from the keyboards that had much inherent rhythmic vitality). We needed a little kick to give us a stronger dance rhythm, so we added drums, and suddenly the music began swinging in much more interesting ways. The harpsichord also helped. Pop music of that period had so much harpsichord.

This was all decided just a few weeks before we opened, and we didn't rehearse with the band until about the week before we left. As for the set, Johan had opened the conversation with "There's no budget, either for a set or for freight."

"Okay. Thanks."

A few weeks later, he added, "Well, I've been thinking about it . . ."

That's how he works. I'd said I wanted something very reflective and shiny. Partly this was because of that druggy phrase "kaleidoscope eyes" from "Lucy in the Sky with Diamonds," but also I knew I wanted to keep psychedelic cliché—for example, oil and water overhead projection—at arm's length. I also remembered the first off-Broadway production of *A Chorus Line* at the Public Theater. I'd joined Eliot Feld's company just after that play had moved to Broadway; we rehearsed at the Public, and the original mirrors (nothing more than frames covered in Mylar) from that relatively cheap production were still in the studio. They weighed nothing, the reflections were distorted, and nothing could have looked cheaper, and I liked them.

Johan ordered some possible material to replicate that effect—once he starts on something, he's going to see it through—and hung some panels in the studio. They looked irredeemably terrible, not even *good* bad. Then he had the great idea to bring in some of those hypothermic survival blankets for marathon runners who are about to die venting off too much heat after a race—"Heatsheets" is the trademarked name

(Mylar coated in a thin veneer of aluminum)—which come in a tiny package and unfold to human proportions. Johan built a mountain range out of cardboard and covered them in this material. It looked like titanium, picking up the light in scintillating ways. He called the set Pepperhorn, because of its resemblance to a Toblerone package.

Then came the mirrored reflective sunglasses, the "kaleidoscope eyes," because I wanted something even scarier, something a little North Korean. The saturated mod colors of Liz Kurtzman's costumes were textbook and looked sensational in front of Pepperhorn, but despite its origins in *Sgt. Pepper*, the dance doesn't necessarily take place in 1968.

Opening night was drawing ever closer. There were so many moving parts, and we didn't get to do an out-of-town tryout of the show (not that these are common anymore), so the attitude was very much: "Here we go, Liverpool! Hope you like it!"

WE BOARDED THE PLANE to the United Kingdom hours after the terrorist bombing at the Ariana Grande concert in Manchester Arena on May 22. Colin flew the next day, his plane packed with every available American TV news team.

Pepperland was to kick off the City of Liverpool festival. The venue was the Royal Court, set up like a casino—tables, drinks, cabaret seating in tiers—with a small, square stage. Ethan was revising the music right up to the day of the show, and even into the very last rehearsal, I was asking the keyboards to move up and down an octave, or the drummer to leave out a fill here or there; we were still balancing not just the sound but the entire composition.

Nor was the music—a beautiful, weird adaptation, loud and quite extreme—particularly easy to play; there was plenty to worry about. We'd been working so hard, so last minute, that even Nancy hadn't seen the show until opening night, which is almost unheard of in the history of the company. There was just no time. It was a gamble, but we were going into the premiere secure in the knowledge that if we could just drag ourselves over this particular hurdle, we wouldn't perform it again for six months afterward and that, if it didn't pan out, we had that interval in which to fix it.

The first-night audience was fascinating. Of course, all the festival people themselves were there, the producers, the lord mayor with his big necklace, and the lordress mayoress too, not to mention all the co-commissioners. (Just as my work finishes, at the first performance, Nancy goes into overdrive. She'll greet every single person from Boston, Seattle, and Toronto, where we'll later be doing the show, even as she's hoping that someone comes from Japan who'll take it there.) However, the most interesting aspect of that audience was a group of semi-unaccompanied kids upstairs, the kind of group that start laughing and wolf whistling as soon as the lights go out. From the downbeat the entire upstairs was clapping along like crazy, singing and shouting the lyrics as though it were three in the morning. I was in the front row, exchanging glances with Colin and the cats in the band, who were thinking, "What the fuck is going on?" It was noisy, and the atmosphere was fantastic. It boded well. Plus, with the cabaret seating, you could drink during the show, and there's nothing better than that. *Pepperland*, one hour with no intermission, was a two-glasses-of-wine show. I started the second glass halfway through. Perfect.

I'd made up some of the dance almost in real time. *When I'm Sixty-Four* danced is a kick line, a vaudeville number. At first it's one person, then three, then nine, so it multiplies and the line gets longer. The dance is simple, but then there's a three-part canon with twelve people, which looks like total chaos, and the music—although it's always the same beat and someone's always playing the tune—is in 4, then 6, then in 5, but the dancers stay in 4. Everyone upstairs was clapping along, and then, suddenly, because of the new time signature, they couldn't anymore. The music perhaps sounds wrong and broken, but it's meticulously *right*, just a wonderfully weird idea. It breaks down and then comes back together. (My friend Nora saw the show and thought this movement was the perfect metaphor for aging. We're all about sixty-four now.) The teenagers were screaming and clapping, but it was very hard to keep the rhythm, so it turned into rolling applause.

There is, however, one poignant and musically uncomplicated moment, an original piece that Ethan wrote for organ, theremin, and interjections by soprano sax and trombone, an adagio, part soap opera, part church. I was going to do it as a romantic pas de deux with three couples, all doing the exact same material, at different rhythms, slow and circling. The dancers were completely exhausted at the end of a particular rehearsal, so I asked them to slow dance, nothing more. While the other couples are dancing, one couple comes in late, slow dances for a little while, and then leaves. It's nothing more than that, unchoreographed and natural.

Pepperland ends with one phrase repeating, improvising, getting louder and faster—what Ethan calls the "disco coda"—under the words "sorry but it's time to go," which loops in an exhilarating groove, a sequential canon leading to incredible chaos, that ends as you never should (as Doris Humphrey warned many times), *exactly as you began*: another rule made to be broken. Perhaps there are no rules. The music starts with a chord that lasts thirty seconds, and the dance starts in a spiral and then unspirals, and the very end is the identical chord, like a time lapse of a rose blooming. It's the most obvious device in the world, and here it felt perfect.

I'd wondered whether *Pepperland* might be shot down, particularly in Liverpool. Some of the beats are in the wrong place, shockingly wrong sounding, and I thought people might not like it, given their investment in the songs, but the final note was met only with pure, beautiful enthusiasm in a screaming standing ovation.

One afternoon I was walking back from the theater to my hotel after the matinee. It was hot and sunny, perfectly lovely, and everybody was drinking in the middle of the afternoon. Three sunburned middle-aged women sitting at an outside table yelled, "Hey, Mark Morris! We love you!" They beckoned me over, just as they'd stopped every single dancer who'd come by. They remembered every detail of the matinee they'd just seen. They were Liverpudlians, they thought Clinton sounded like John Lennon, and they were so truly touched by the show that they asked me to autograph their arms. That made me so happy. My favorite review said *Pepperland* "wasn't nostalgic."

The Ariana Grande concert was one bookend to the trip; the Tower Bridge incident in London on June 3 was the other, the day we got back to America.

THE LIVERPOOL TRIP was only a few weeks after Howard Hodgkin's death.

Antony Peattie, Howard's husband, came to the *Pepperland* opening but was too moved by the whole situation to join us backstage. We'd spent a lot of time together during *Layla and Majnun*, Howard's last big project. After the *Pepperland* premiere, I made a sojourn to London to visit Antony and Andy Barker in the house near the British Museum where Antony and Howard had lived together for many years. They'd never hired anybody to help out, even as Howard became more fragile and less ambulatory—he'd had health problems for years, a whole bunch of conditions and their resultant surgeries. He didn't want strangers around. My theory is that he was incorporeal. He lived in his brain—painted from his eyes, his brain, and his hand—and that therefore the rest of his body wasn't important.

We sat for a while in Howard's brightly sunlit all-white studio, the floor splattered with the accumulation of all his paintings. I'd known him for years before I was ever allowed in there. In fact, I hadn't even known there was a studio in the place. Unfinished paintings faced the wall; he'd then turn them around and work on them, either finish them or turn them around again. So he had all these projects going on simultaneously in his home in London, his house in Normandy near Rouen, and also in Mumbai, India, where he wintered every year for many years (and a wheelchair in India is tricky).

It was very hot in the studio, and the last dozen paintings Howard had finished were hung on the walls around us, facing out. Different pictures would draw attention to themselves as their palettes were activated by the changing light of day. It was a very serene and enviable place to be, as we remembered Howard. I asked about his last days, when he'd stopped painting, and I finally got to the inevitable question: "What do you do with the paintings he didn't finish or didn't want released?" The answer was that Howard had wanted them all destroyed without trace, burned, to avoid any future misuse. He'd felt very strongly about it.

Antony, in tears for the first time that day, showed me a video on his phone of the bonfire that they had built in France. They'd piled up all the unfinished paintings on the lawn, doused them in kerosene, lit a match, and watched them burn, no sound but the crackling fire. Howard had always painted in oils on the backs or fronts of old frames, so the thick smoke billowed black as they incinerated at least a hundred paintings, if not more. My first thought was of the cremation fires of Varanasi or Dido's funeral pyre. It was karmic: those paintings would no longer exist in the same form; now they existed as smoke and carbon, wherever that went.

The same place my dances will go.

Rehearsing *Grand Duo*, Mark Morris Dance Center, Brooklyn, 2015. *(Amber Merkens)*

Fourteen

Above and Beyond

ow close am I to being done, either with this book or making up dances?

Well, I have amazing news: this is the last chapter, but even after my death, there will still be new Mark Morris dances.

There is currently much attention given to the fact that choreographers are dying. Apparently, everyone was surprised when Pina Bausch died. No one seemed to see it coming, despite the fact that she looked like she'd already died once previously. Merce Cunningham died in 2007, Trisha Brown in 2017, Paul Taylor even more recently. The industry is decimated. How did these choreographers do it, and how will the dances be preserved? It's a particularly pressing problem that those increasingly rare companies led by a single choreographer—for example, my company—are having to deal with.

We started a capital campaign called Above and Beyond to deal with, among other things, the preservation of my dances and, more vaguely, my legacy. The grant-giving bodies won't give money just to put on a show anymore, but will give money for *education* or *legacy*, which is how we've been able to hire people full-time to digitize the archives over three years. My old dancers go down there, sift through the past, and sob.

But I don't just want to preserve the dances I've done, say *L'Allegro* and *The Hard Nut*, and then have them danced forever (or until they've bored people) as museum pieces. And I certainly don't want people to mess them up like *Pacific*. I've always said that the school will be my legacy, and of course I want to keep my company working, and the building full and fully operational, and it therefore occurred to me that I should keep making up dances while I'm alive and alert enough to do so. So rather than just filming my existing dances and notating them, the new plan is to keep on making up dances just as I've always made up dances: one a year that no one will see until I'm dead.

Specifically, the idea came from Nancy, her inspiration being an article concerning the author Margaret Atwood, the first contributor to a public artwork called *Future Library*: a story of hers would be stored away and remain unseen for a century. The project, conceived by artist Katie Paterson, began with the planting of a forest's worth of trees in 2014, trees that will be cut down in 2114 to make the pulp for the paper on which the one hundred new pieces of fiction (one a year by different writers) will be printed, and then read. A future library for a future society!

Nancy, sensing a scheme, asked if I'd be interested in a similar arrangement, and I said, "That's the grisliest, most horrible, morbid thing I've ever heard of in my life. Yes!"

Atwood said that wild horses couldn't drag any details of the story from her, but we announced the idea in the *New York Times* in April of 2018 and revealed that the first of the series (and as I write, the only one finished) would be to the keyboard music of Scarlatti. And by "finished," I mean *fully* finished: the order of the music known, fully choreographed, documented at every stage of its development, and notated, designed, and lit. The dance, for twelve people, is half an hour long, and quite as arduous as every other dance of mine. But these ten dancers won't dance forever, so at some point they'll have to teach it to someone else. We'll put the dance in its casket and revisit it whenever a dancer leaves and we hire new people, who'll then learn this piece as we would just as if we were going to perform it next week. And one day, it *will* be about to be performed next week, but I won't be around to see it. I'll be dead. What will I care?

I hope to develop a posthumous repertoire of fifteen or twenty dances. If someone gave me a million bucks toward the project, I *might* let him watch a rehearsal. But that eventuality aside, it's locked away. It's a perfect situation for a workaholic like me (can you really be addicted to *workahol?*), because it means I can keep making up dances, even beyond the capacity of the world to digest them. I'm keeping *myself* busy just as Verla kept me busy fifty years ago.

AND THERE ARE so many ways. To celebrate our twenty-fifth anniversary, back in 2006, we did a series of programs of dances new and old, old being *Gloria*. My first reaction was, I admit, "Do we have to do that again?" Nancy said, "You should conduct it." It was all her idea.

At first, I demurred, thinking it presumptuous. People who have a lot of *book-larnin'* see me as an autodidact and think that because I didn't go to school, I must have wacky ideas. I may or I may not, but I do know a lot about music, and finally I thought: why not? I've always worked closely with my conductors and I always coach the musicians. Years before, James Levine, for forty years the musical director at the Met, had told me I should conduct when he found out that I'd coached a show he'd seen at Tanglewood that included Brahms's *Love Song*

Waltzes. (I thanked him for the compliment and told him I'd been conducting for years . . . *electricity*.) So I studied with Craig Smith, learned the Vivaldi Gloria, how to beat it, how to run a rehearsal, and then I practiced on the musicians on the road with me. It went well. At least, we all hit the Amen at the same time.

I still only conduct a few pieces. I know my strengths. I'm communicative and I'm physical, I know the music, I have a good time, and the singers and players are supportive, including Stephanie Blythe, who's too great a star to have to humor me. At some point, I felt brave enough to do *Dido*. Then I wondered whether I might conduct *The Hard Nut*, so at Tanglewood (where my company had been every summer as the only dance company on the program for the last fifteen years, and where everybody's time is very precious) we assembled a string quartet and a pianist in order to allow me to conduct *The Nutcracker* from the score from beginning to end, both acts, ninety minutes. It was an extremely intense experience, and . . . I wasn't ready. Colin took it on. And when I conduct, he gives me notes. It's a perpetual learning situation.

I don't do it merely to satisfy my ego, and I'm no Danny Kaye, guest-conducting symphonies for the Pops evening. At first I was terrified; it still makes me nervous. And I didn't realize I had a bald spot until I started conducting, but I saw pictures of me in action, from behind, and, lo! There it is!

Conducting is not a slow exit from dancing. It's a new viewpoint. It involves me with the music and the production in a different way. Plus, and don't think these things aren't important, I'm cheaper than everybody else.

I even recently sang with my company (in public) for the first time—a medley of songs from the 1920s and '30s first sung by Gertrude Lawrence and Jack Buchanan—because I couldn't find a singer to sing them just right. Nancy insisted I audition for her, then gave me the job under one very reasonable condition: "You can do it if you practice."

I still love watching people dance, and though dancing itself became tiresome for me, I admit that I *am* still intrigued by the idea of making a film of just my face and hands dancing. My last dance *Serenade* to Lou's music was already heading in that direction.

I'M SIXTY-TWO and I feel guilty if I'm not working, so I work all the time: I love it. (Apparently, I even want it to look like I'm still working after I die.) It's a Protestant work ethic as opposed to Judeo-Catholic guilt. I want to be involved, active rather than busy, which seems to me like filler. I'm also an expert procrastinator.

I am a working-class boy, skeptical and distrustful of danciness, and I agree with people who find ballet to be effete and elitist. The dances I choreographed for ballet companies in the 1980s addressed the things that I didn't like about ballet: the hierarchy, the star system, the gender politics. My critique of ballet is in those ballets, but they weren't anti-ballet, they were fully based in the world of ballet.

Nobody talked about being gay then, so I said it a lot. That was a battle that I wanted. Now ballet is back to being just as uptight and esoteric as it was before. We don't need to play the gay card anymore, so I don't do it because I no longer care. I was strong willed, and I still am, but there are certain battles that either I have won or no longer concern me. I got my way. I don't have to get it again. I don't expect people to agree with me, or care if they do, but if they don't, they should at least have an argument.

Part of the reason that people dance to better music and live music a lot more nowadays is because of me, part of the reason that a lot of choreographers and dancers are out as queer is because of me, and part of the reason that dancers nowadays look like real people is because of me. It wasn't me *single-handed*; it was a movement of the time. Bill T. Jones always used dancers who didn't look like dancers, and Yvonne Rainer before us.

People have often said of my company, "They don't look like dancers"—well, they're *dancing*, aren't they? What do *dancers* look like? They look like people! As though it was wrong, as though it could have been any dog from the kennel, any stranger off the Greyhound. It's not true, but it *is* true that I didn't want identical duplicates of people. It wasn't the *Boys from Brazil* dance company; I didn't need a long line of identical swans for *Swan Lake*. But I didn't pick people with big asses or glasses, African Americans or homosexuals or balding people or Christians or short people, to make it a circus, or "a girls' basketball team," as someone once called them. I did it because they were great dancers. It's somewhat contrarian, sure. But the combination of contrarianism and conservatism is precisely why I am, or was, called an enfant terrible (what?!): it's also very American. I'm gay; I'm a little "fuck you," but I'm also very polite; I try to be kind, but I know I'm terribly demanding of my dancers; I have good manners; and I'm impatient. I've been rude. I'm interested in a lot of things, and it bothers me when people aren't. I have a fully blessed life.

I DO ENDINGS well in my dances, partly because I don't make up the ending first. Another thing Doris Humphrey advised, "Don't leave the end to the end," but I do. I also don't end dances until it's time to. I see what happens. I make up way too much stuff, and when I've satisfied myself? Done. Dancers, I love you.

Time to get back to work.

ACKNOWLEDGMENTS

There are many people, projects, and stories that didn't, for whatever reason, end up in this book. I apologize for leaving you out (or leaving you in). Maybe the sequel.

Many thanks to Christopher Richards, our editor, for his initial enthusiasm and subsequent support, good words, and hard work; to Claudia Ballard at William Morris Endeavor for agenting *Out Loud* into existence; and to everyone at Penguin Press, particularly those involved in the book's production. Thanks also to those, including MMDG staff and friends, who worked on the book's preparation: collation, detection, verification, perusal, and advice.

Thanks to Mr. Wesley Stace, without whom . . . And to his family, Abbey, Tilda, and Wyn, for their warm welcome.

Thanks also to the many presenters and producers, at the many venues and organizations, for their past and current invaluable trust in my work: Jane Moss of Lincoln Center; Robert Cole and Matias Tarnopolsky of Cal Performances; Harvey Lichtenstein and Joseph V. Melillo of BAM; Mike

Ross of the Krannert Center for the Performing Arts; Ellen Highstein of Tanglewood Music Center; Rick Davis and Tom Reynolds of George Mason University Center for the Arts; Josh LaBelle of Seattle Theatre Group; Janice Price of the Luminato Festival and Banff Centre for Arts and Creativity; Liz Thompson, Sam Miller, Sali Ann Kriegsman, and Ella Baff of Jacob's Pillow Dance Festival; David White of Dance Theater Workshop; Mark Murphy of On the Boards; Matt Krashan and Michelle Witt of Meany Hall for the Performing Arts; Val Bourne and Toby Beazley of Dance Umbrella London; Jeremy Alliger of Dance Umbrella Boston; Martha Jones of Celebrity Series; Alistair Spalding of Sadler's Wells; Brian McMaster of the Edinburgh International Festival; Graham Sheffield of Barbican Centre; John Berry of the English National Opera; Nicholas Payne of the Royal Opera Covent Garden; Michael Mushalla of Double M Arts and Events; Helgi Tomasson of San Francisco Ballet; and Mikko Nissinen of Boston Ballet.

Particular thanks to the smart, generous, and levelheaded members of our board of directors: Judith R Fishman, David Resnicow, Mark Selinger, Jane Stine, Sarabeth Berman, Margaret Conklin, Fred Bland, Suzy Kellems Dominik, Shelby Gans, Sandy Hill, Timothy McClimon, Helen Meyer, Ellen Offner, York-Chi Harder, Nicholas Ma, Kathleen Howard, Allan Bufferd, Linda Rawlings, Harold Snedcof, and Cathryn Collins. Many thanks also to these great friends of MMDG: Ellen Poss, Antony Peattie, David Deutsch, Liz Liebman, Howard Hodgkin, Ellsworth Kelly, and Howard Gilman.

Regarding the Mark Morris Dance Group, I am humbly thankful for the enormous amount of work by so many dedicated people in so many ways to present what we create to the public. The planning, the training, the rehearsing, the designing, the advertising, the fund-raising, the travel, the payroll, the laundry. The magic part where everything comes together for a couple of hours in the theater for a new audience every night in every city. The enthusiastic belief in this very particular and inclusive culture. The priceless engagement with the neighborhoods and communities everywhere we go. The perseverance and unlimited imagination involved in perpetuating a band of artists as fine as this one. All in the service of the dance and the music—the core of who we are and what we have to give.

I am deeply grateful to the dancers and musicians with whom I've had the opportunity to work over all these many years. You know who you are. I appreciate every one of you for your diligence, devotion, and good humor; your variety and your depth of talent.

My humble gratitude to every old friend, every teacher, every partner, from every branch of music and dance, all over the world, who have variously stimulated, challenged, and inspired me for so long.

With my deepest love to my dear sisters, Marianne and Maureen, and their spouses and all of their progeny through all the generations. For my mother, Maxine.

—MM

INDEX

INDEX